STORIES FROM THE BARRIO

A HISTORY OF MEXICAN FORT WORTH

Carlos E. Cuéllar

STORIES
FROM THE
BARRIO
A HISTORY OF MEXICAN FORT WORTH

Carlos E. Cuéllar

TCU PRESS • FORT WORTH

Library of Congress Cataloging-in-Publication Data

Cuéllar, Carlos Eliseo, 1950-
  Stories from the barrio : a history of Mexican Fort Worth / Carlos
Eliseo Cuéllar.
      p. cm.
  Includes bibliographical references (p.   ) and index.
  ISBN 0-87565-275-1 (hardcover : alk. paper)
  ISBN 0-87565-290-5 (softcover : alk. paper)
  1. Mexican Americans—Texas—Fort Worth—History. 2. Mexican
Americans—Texas—Fort Worth—Social conditions. 3. Mexican
Americans—Texas—Fort Worth—Interviews. 4. Fort Worth
(Tex.)—History. 5. Fort Worth (Tex.)—Ethnic relations. 6. Fort Worth
(Tex.)—Biography. I. Title.
  F394.F7 C84 2003
  976.4′53150046872—dc21
                                                2003001146

TO MY WIFE

ANGELA GUERRA CUÉLLAR

CONTENTS

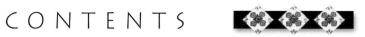

Preface ix

Acknowledgments xi

Introduction xiii

1. Mexicanos Arrive in Fort Worth 1

2. Stories from the Barrios 19

3. Making a Living 35

4. Family Life 77

5. Religion and Education 99

6. Community Life and Organizations 129

7. Arts and Culture 155

8. Challenges 177

Appendix A *Fort Worth City Directory*, 1920
   Street Listings of Inhabitants 199

Appendix B
   Wesley Community House Daily Schedule, 1932-1933 201

Appendix C
   Wesley Community Center Report, circa 1953 203

Appendix D
   Medicinal Herbs and Their Use 205

Notes 207

Bibliography 231

Index 235

PREFACE

This is one of the first attempts to tell the story of Fort Worth's Mexican population. It is impossible to know who were the first Mexicanos to arrive in Fort Worth, the circumstances that led to their emigration, when they arrived, or where they first settled. The reason for such obscurity lies in the scarcity of information concerning Mexicanos in that period: There are few personal records, memoirs, or diaries. Despite the paucity of official documentation, we know through stories of later immigrants, that—sharing similar backgrounds, experiences, and aspirations—the Mexicanos who made Fort Worth their permanent home quickly developed a sense of community.

Most came from the populous south-central Mexican states of Jalisco, Michoacán, Guanajuato, and San Luis Potosí. The majority of these families had been forced out of their *patria* because of the violence and dislocation of the Mexican Revolution. In many cases, the males arrived first in search of employment. Once work was secured, a line of communication opened between the jobholder and his family. His *parientes* (relatives) and friends from the same village in Mexico soon made their way to Fort Worth, one by one or in small groups. The stories of these immigrants are full of celebrated American virtues of perseverance, hard work, willingness to risk, love of country and family, and the entrepreneurial spirit. However noble their stories are, they are also disturbing in the revelations of the very real physical hardships these people faced in emigrating. The hardships they encountered in their new country were less tangible—racism, discriminatory laws and unofficial practices, and a predatory economic climate that had still not yet pulled itself out from under the twin legacies of slavery and Reconstruction.

Hard-pressed to find employment in order to survive, this immigrant generation was forced to accept work that few others cared to do. Although they were generally proud people who valued their employment, to the larger culture there seemed to be nothing extraordinary about their situation or circumstances. And this very lack of notice precluded the amassing of materials documenting the history and lives of those people occupying the lowest rungs of Fort Worth society. In other words, they were not considered worth writing about by people outside their ethnic group or, sadly, even among themselves. And so, for years, Mexicanos, especially in their role as minority immigrants in a strange land and in an alien culture, seem to have been largely invisible and ahistorical—that is, having no story and no worthwhile contribution.

Throughout much of American history, emphasis has been on the western-European aspects of its history and culture. The contributions of other races and ethnic groups have often been slighted, even ignored. But, over the last six decades, this focus has gradually given way to the recognition that history is not complete without an account of all society's classes. Earlier books on Fort Worth's history scarcely mention "Mexicans," much less give any indication of their contributions to the city's history and culture. J'Nell Pate's *North of the River*, published in 1994, was the first book to acknowledge the life and contributions of a few area Hispanic families.

To reconstruct the history of an ahistorical people, one must rely on discovering what documentation is available from local official records, while depending heavily on "unofficial" sources of information—informal interviews with older residents of the community and the reminiscences of younger members of the culture, remembering what they can of the stories told by their parents, grandparents, and great-grandparents. Unfortunately, once the elders are gone, an important piece of history has been lost forever. Younger Hispanics find that, in the attempt to discover their family's history, they are led to the larger saga of their shared culture, which often helps them to establish their identity, bind the family closer together, teach them valuable lessons based on past experiences, provide guidance for the future, and promote an appreciation for history and the historical process. It is in this spirit that I began the first history of Mexican Fort Worth—an attempt to discover family and cultural stories—in hopes that more and more written documentation will emerge in the process of looking at this important part of the culture at large.

CARLOS E. CUÉLLAR

ACKNOWLEDGMENTS

The enormous task of writing this book could not have been accomplished without the generous spirit and assistance of many fine individuals to whom I am eternally grateful.

My thanks go out to Chris Bonilla and Delsa Bonilla for initially pointing out the overwhelming need for a Mexican history of Fort Worth. They planted the seed that led me to pursue this subject.

Michael and Hope Ayala, lifetime residents of the North Side, were instrumental in opening many doors for personal interviews with families who could contribute valuable information for this project. Without the Ayalas' help, and the help of their entire extended family, this book would have foundered.

A special thanks goes out to Pauline Willis Estrada, whom I met quite by accident at the TCU Library. She afforded me one of the most pleasant surprises of the project as she revealed her interesting past. Pauline and her husband, Sam Estrada, graciously treated me as family, while explaining Fort Worth's valuable and unforgettable musical past.

In addition to a volume of information regarding the North Side and *La Yarda,* Benito Soto Mercado gave me several tours of the different barrios and accompanied me on a trip to Oklahoma City, to meet several former North Side residents. Soto Mercado went the extra mile, and he represents all that is good, friendly, and hospitable about Fort Worth.

A warm thank you goes out to Bennie Cardona, who initially agreed to see me for a "brief" interview that ended up lasting from 11:00 AM to 7:00 PM. I have often wondered what the long interview would have been like.

North Side realtor, J. Pete Zepeda, helped me locate Fort Worth's Hispanic movie star, Pilar Bouzas, who has resided quietly in North Hollywood for many decades. When I commented that he and other Mexican Americans no longer live within the confines of the North Side (and other Fort Worth barrios), having expanded out into previously all-Anglo neighborhoods, Zepeda sat back on his office chair, smiled with satisfaction, and said, "We are taking back the Southwest one lot at a time!"

My gratitude also goes out to community leaders such as Herlinda Balderas García, Sam García, Jacinta Juárez, Mary Lou López, Rufino Mendoza, Jr., Carlos Puente, Cecilia Reyes, Ciquio Vásquez, and Louis J. Zapata for their valuable insights into the political and social life of Mexican Fort Worth.

A delicious thanks to all the wonderful restaurateurs—Mary García Christian and Hope García Lancarte, Yvonne ("Kiki") Martínez Cisneros and Mary Martínez Garza, Alfred and Alex Gallegos, Jr., Joe Holton, Sammy Pantoja, Robert Pulido, Sr., Rudy Rodríguez, and Lou Caro Whitten—not only did they grant tasteful and fascinating interviews, but they helped me become a more well-rounded individual, *gracias a* their delicious cuisine.

I am tremendously grateful to professor William H. Beezley for his steady encouragement and valuable assistance. TCU's legendary gentleman of history, Donald E. Worcester, graciously read all chapters and gave reasoned observations. D. Clayton Brown and Kenneth R. Stephens both took keen interest in my research and provided wise guidance throughout the process.

Mexican American historian, Arnoldo De León, of Angelo State University, read the manuscript and made helpful suggestions. I am greatly indebted to him for taking me under his wing and teaching me more about the history and experiences of Mexican Americans and Chicanos in communities throughout the United States.

Judy Alter and Susan Petty at TCU Press believed in this project from the beginning and supported it all the way through developing the final manuscript. They were extremely patient with me; I am deeply indebted to these talented people.

I wish to thank my lovely wife, Angela, my son, Carlos Eliseo, Jr., his wife, Jennifer, and my daughter, Anna Crista, for their love, patience, and encouragement. Without their steadfast support, none of this would have been possible. And, lastly, I never cease thanking God for my family and for His guidance in my life and work.

The history of Mexican Fort Worth does not begin at a specific point, say 1883, the year the first Mexicanos are mentioned in the *Fort Worth City Directory*, but rather takes into account the sum total of their collective past. This complex history must include the story of their original circumstances in Mexico; their sources of livelihood; the social, economic, and political conditions with which they had to cope; the reasons for leaving their country; the exodus to the United States; the choices they made as to where to go and what to do; and the obstacles they faced.

Since the time of the *conquista*, when Cortez and his men subdued the mighty Aztec empire, Spaniards and native Indians intermarried to create *mestizaje*—a new mixed-blood nation with unique characteristics, institutions, and culture. The conquest of the New World, with its annihilation and subjugation of native peoples and culture, together with the terrors associated with the Inquisition, engendered a stereotypical view of Spaniards as a brutal and flawed race. The Alamo, Goliad, the Mexican War, sporadic border banditry, and Pancho Villa's exploits all reinforced negative Texan attitudes regarding their neighbors to the south. This mentality affected Anglo-Mexicano relations for generations.

MEXICANOS IN EXILE

From 1876 to 1880 and then again from 1884 to 1911, under the dictatorship of Porfirio Díaz (1830-1915), Mexico enjoyed political peace and prosperity unknown since colonial times.[1] But the peace came at a price—generating prosperity that was enjoyed by only a few. During this time, called the *Porfiriato*, Díaz ruled with an iron hand, and the living standards of the very poorest of Mexico's population fell to unthinkable levels. Simmering resentments of the obdurate policies of Díaz, which alienated his former supporters, coupled with the disparity in wealth, came to a head in 1910 and sparked the Mexican Revolution.[2] The decade from 1910-1920 is characterized as one of the most turbulent periods in Mexican history. An outgrowth of the *Porfiriato* and its repressive policies, the revolution united Mexicans of all classes to overthrow the despised dictator. While upper class Mexicanos fought to regain political power and protect their wealth, the peasants of the lower classes were caught in a war they didn't really understand and were unable to protect themselves from. If they chose to bear arms, they were invariably the population most likely to be killed. Their only other alternatives were to hide or to flee to America.[3]

The construction of railroads in Mexico and the dislocations associated with the *Porfiriato* and the Mexican Revolution contributed to a mass exodus of Mexicanos from their beloved *patria* into the United States. Many sought refuge in Texas, finding employment as agricultural and livestock workers, coal miners, railroad crewmen, construction workers, packinghouse workers, steelworkers, cooks, dishwashers, and domestics. Fort Worth and surrounding areas, experiencing a steadily expanding population and burgeoning economy, provided many opportunities for immigrants.

Before 1910, Mexican migration north had been light, and most of those who came intended to return once they had earned enough money to satisfy their needs. The instability and violence of the Mexican Revolution caused hundreds of thousands of refugees to flee north to the safety of the United States. By the end of the 1920s, a number of barrios had developed around the major industries in different areas of Fort Worth. And the barrios soon expanded with immigrant Mexicanos, eager to begin a new life in a new world.

Many worked as migrant agricultural laborers—cotton pickers who followed the annual "Big Swing" harvest cycle that began in South and Central Texas and ended in the northern and western parts of the state.[4] Fort Worth's railroads, stockyards, packing houses, steel plants, hotels, restaurants, and coffee shops offered the migrants and refugees opportunities for steady employment in one locale.

Thrust into an alien world, Mexicanos did their best to adjust and adapt to a new environment and culture. Some came with the intention of returning as soon as Mexico's crisis abated, but in spite of initial obstacles, most Mexicanos stayed, made "*Fore Wes*" their home, and demonstrated a resiliency that helped them overcome the social, economic, and political challenges of subsequent decades. For most Mexicanos it was a positive change; some even succeeded in a big way. The "American Dream" became not only their dream but also their reality.

Their children's identity underwent a significant transformation. They attended American schools, spoke mostly English, and embraced many aspects of the new culture. This was the Mexican-American generation—children born in America who were bilingual, bicultural, and, for the most part, unfamiliar with their parents' homeland. To avoid pronunciation difficulty teachers gave many school children Anglo names, while others readily adopted them for assimilation purposes. With few exceptions, the tendency to assimilate increased with each succeeding generation; conversely, Spanish literacy gradually decreased.

World War II brought additional challenges and unprecedented opportunities. Fort Worth's Mexican Americans enlisted, trained, and fought on many fronts. While some paid the ultimate price, many veterans returned determined to forge changes. The ensuing civil rights movement focused attention on opening up greater opportunities in jobs, housing, and education. Barrios exploded beyond their previously fixed boundaries, greater numbers of Mexican Americans went on to college, and career opportunities broadened dramatically.

From the mid-1960s to the mid-1970s, the Chicano movement called attention to the social, political, economic, and cultural realities of a growing ethnic population. As a result, Mexicanos and Mexican Americans were no longer viewed as a passive, invisible, or ahistorical people. Chicano historians such as Ricardo Romo, Albert Camarillo, Richard Griswold del Castillo, Mario T. García, Arnoldo De León, George J. Sánchez, and F. Arturo Rosales depicted their subjects as people who adapted to changing realities and who created a world and culture all their own.

The stories from the barrios are fascinating and reveal much about the social and cultural nature of the people. Residents from most of the barrios—North Side, South Side, Rock Island, *La Corte*, and *El TP*—share where they came from, how they happened to arrive in Fort Worth, and what life was like in their barrios. A housewife, a mailman, a Hollywood actor, a street urchin, a railroad worker, a restaurateur, and a mystic engage in discussions on home remedies, natural medicines, border and Mexican cuisine, success in business, wakes and funerals, racism, pilgrimages, and mysticism. Each has added immeasurably to the character of Fort Worth and without them and their stories, our city would be a poorer place to live.

Fort Worth has indeed never been the same. The contributions by Mexicanos have been incalculable: Their labor transformed the skyline and allowed the economy to grow and prosper. Their cuisine forever changed the city's eating habits, and their music, dances, and customs added diversity to Cowtown's already rich cultural legacy. They are an integral part of Fort Worth's history.

Chapter 1

MEXICANOS ARRIVE IN FORT WORTH

The history of Mexicanos in Fort Worth goes back almost as far as the history of the city itself. Early Mexican residents arrived in the 1880s, finding a settlement that had been established less than forty years earlier.

EARLY YEARS

In 1849 Major Ripley S. Arnold set up an army camp on the bluff overlooking the Trinity River at the confluence of the Clear Fork and the West Fork. The camp occupied part of the land now graced by the Tarrant County Courthouse. In those days, the threat of marauding Indians was ever-present, and the outpost was part of General Williams Jenkins Worth's plan to build ten forts to mark the Texas frontier. As always, where the army went, so went entrepreneurs eager to make a living providing services to the military population. The 1850 census count for the fort was 111 total—two commanding officers, one doctor, ninety-two soldiers, four adult women, six adult men, and six children. The army occupied the bluff site until its evacuation in 1853. After that, settlers came in to take possession of the buildings and facilities the army had left behind.[1] The area was now poised on the brink of settlement and expansion. Schools were established, retail stores flourished, and both the Butterfield Overland Mail and Southern Pacific stage lines set up Fort Worth stagecoach stops on their routes to California.

During that same year, 1849, Tarrant County was officially established by the Texas legislature. It took its name from General Edward H. Tarrant, who was instrumental in driving the Indians from the area. The county seat was Birdville, a town in an area now encompassed by Haltom City; the first county election was held in 1850. Prominent Fort Worth citizens soon began lobbying to move the county seat to that city. Grievances began to build and came to a head in 1856 in a vote to select the county seat. Both counties were in the habit of bringing in whiskey to encourage men to vote in their favor, but Tarrant County partisans took the tradition a step further: On the eve of the election, they stole the influential barrel of whiskey right out of the Birdville courthouse (really nothing more grand or substantial than a log cabin). The whiskey was apparently the deciding factor, because Tarrant County won the election by six votes. The county seat was transferred, after a long and bitter struggle, from Birdville to Fort Worth, and construction of the new courthouse began in 1860. The courthouse might have become the symbol of a new era of prosperity for the city had it not been for the outbreak of the Civil War. That conflict and the ensuing Reconstruction period, wreaked havoc on the Fort Worth economy. The population shrank to about 175. Those few remaining faced many hardships, lacking food, money, and other vital supplies.

After the Civil War, South Texas ranchers began driving their cattle north to the Kansas markets and created "trails" the cowboys followed through the brush. As cowboys became accustomed to stopping off in Fort Worth on their way to Kansas, the economy revived.

During this time Fort Worth became known as "Cowtown"—it was the last stop on the Chisholm Trail, which led to markets in the North. Of course, along with the cowboys came the need for recreation and for letting off steam. The area known as Hell's Half Acre sprang up, providing all the amenities for steam-letting—saloons, dance halls, gambling establishments, and houses of prostitution. The Acre occupied about two-and-a-half acres in downtown Fort Worth, an area bounded by Main Street on the west, Jones on the east, Seventh Street on the north, and Fifteenth Street on the south. This area is now home to the Fort Worth Convention Center and the Water Gardens. In the 1870s however, Hell's Half Acre was notorious around the state for its lawlessness. While this appealed to the cowboys, the local citizenry took a dim view of the rise in crime and the salacious reputation. Desiring to make their city a safer place, they elected "Longhair" Jim Courtright as city marshal in 1876 with the mandate to clamp down on crime. Predictably, the stricter environment resulted in an economic slump, as the cowboys saw no reason to tarry in a place that no longer offered their accustomed amusements.

In 1875, the population of Fort Worth numbered about 800.[2] The city earned another nickname, "Panther City," for being so empty and uneventful that panthers slept in the streets. But the arrival of the Texas & Pacific Railroad in 1876 put an end to that supposed quietude, and by 1880 the population of Fort Worth had grown to 6,663. The railroad quickly took its place as one of the main economic forces in the city in the late nineteenth century. People took advantage of the new, more convenient means of transportation and the possibilities of jobs working on the miles of track to be laid, leading to phenomenal growth between 1880 and 1890. During that decade, the population swelled from 6,663 to 23,076—an increase of 246 percent.[3]

THE EARLIEST MEXICANOS

The tenth United States census for Tarrant County, taken in June 1880, reveals the first evidence of Mexicanos in the city of Fort Worth—fourteen men ranging in age from fifty-five to twenty-one. In addition to the first and last names of the informants, the census data also included age, marital status, current status, occupation, country of origin, as well as the origins of their parents.[4] The "current status" category apparently was reserved for those who were prisoners in one of the local jails. (See Figure 1-1.)

Most of these Mexicanos were single, with the exception of D. Gómez, and most were young, in their twenties or thirties. Mexico was the country of origin for most of the informants, as well as for their parents, indicating that the men had recently emigrated to find work in the United States. Four of these—De Bare, Gonzallas [sic], Slaughter, and Sánchez—migrated from other parts of Texas. All worked in low-paying, bottom-tier occupations, such as "laborer," which probably meant that they worked for one of the railroads. Keeping in mind that the first railroad, the Texas & Pacific, arrived in 1876 and the first Hispanics show up on the 1880 census, it is safe to surmise that the railroads were instrumental in bringing the first Mexicanos to the Fort Worth area.

The other categories give sketchy but tantalizing glimpses into the lives of these men, raising more questions than they answer. Both Lorenzo and Carión

FIGURE 1-1   THE TENTH U.S. CENSUS, 1880

Name	Age	Marital Status	Current Status	Occupation	Father	Mother	Self
Lorenzo, Francis	35		prisoner	laborer	Mex	Mex	Mex
Carión, Juan	30		prisoner	cook	Mex	Mex	Mex
De Bare, Peter	21			barkeep	Tex	Fr	Mex
García, Andrew	23	Single		dishwasher	Mex	Mex	Mex
Gómez, D.	33	Married		laborer	Mex	Mex	Mex
Gonzallas [sic] Joe	25	Single		herder	Tex	Mex	Mex
Pas, Narciso	55	Single		laborer	Mex	Mex	Mex
Torris[sic] Gorgona	50	Single		laborer	Mex	Mex	Mex
López, Manuel	31	Single		laborer	Mex	Mex	Mex
Martenas[sic] Arhill	30	Single		laborer	Mex	Mex	Mex
Slaughter, John	27	Single		laborer	Tex	Mex	Mex
Sánchez, John	22	Single		laborer	Tex	Mex	Mex
García, Angel	25	Single		harvesting	Mex	Mex	Mex
González, Clemente	40	Single		harvesting	Mex	Mex	Mex

SOURCE: Taken from the Tenth Census of the United States. Population schedules of the tenth census of the United States, 1880: Texas. National Archives microcopy no. T9. Roll 1328: Tarrant, Taylor, Throckmorton, Titus, and Tom Green counties.

were incarcerated in the city jail. What had they done? What were their stories? A product of a mixed marriage, De Bare noted his country of origin as Texas, whereas his father's was France and his mother's, Mexico. How did he come to Fort Worth? What drew him? Joe Gonzallas' occupation is listed as herder, and, although he is shown as Mexican, he is the son of a Texan. We can only guess at possible scenarios: Had his family previously emigrated to another part of Texas and then returned to Mexico, perhaps to be confronted with difficult economic times that drove them back to Texas? Did Joe come to Fort Worth hoping to bring his family later, as so many immigrants did? It is unfortunate that this census data does not reflect addresses: A specific numbered address would have been invaluable in helping to resolve precisely where Mexicanos first congregated.

The annual *Fort Worth City Directory* (the first was published in 1877) provides another source of information about Mexicanos' first appearance on the scene. [5] Although heavily sponsored by ads touting local businesses, city directories functioned as more than commercial directories. Listings included residential address, head of household, occupation, and sometimes place of employment. As telephones became more common, telephone numbers were also included. Another significant function of the earlier directories was promotion of the city to outsiders, usually with bright promises of commercial opportunities to be found in Fort Worth. No Hispanic surnames appear in the city directories from 1877 to 1882, even though the 1880 U.S. Census lists fourteen such surnames. The 1883-1884 *Fort Worth City Directory* is the first edition in which Hispanic surnames were found—and there were only two: Riley Gonzales and Antonio Peña.

A comparison of the 1885-1886 and 1886-1887 city directories (Figures 1-2 and 1-3, respectively) reveals a pattern of transience in the immigration of Mexicanos to Fort Worth. Residents listed in the 1885-1886 directory do not appear in the subsequent edition, suggesting that, for some reason, most of the earliest Mexicanos arriving in Fort Worth did not stay long. The transient nature of the Hispanic population could be attributed to a number of factors such as ill treatment, lack of satisfying jobs, search for better employment situations elsewhere, or the longing to return home. Nevertheless, the information contained in these city directories also shows the beginnings of the neighborhoods. Sanborn maps for 1885 and 1889 show mixed commercial and residential use in those blocks where the directories indicate the Mexicanos lived. Although the intersection of South Rusk and East Twelfth was dominated by residences (some labeled "Negro Shanties") in 1885, the businesses included two saloons—one with a dance hall. A female boardinghouse was immediately next door.

Calhoun Street, between Seventh and Eighth, is the business address given for Mr. Balcazo, but no residence information is provided. The 1885 Sanborn

FIGURE 1-2   FORT WORTH CITY DIRECTORY, 1885-1886

Name	Occupation	Residence
Aguilar, Hijínio	tamales peddler	bds J. G. Carper
Canapa, Manuel	groceries	nw cor Twelfth/Rusk r. same
Delagarcía, José	tamales peddler	Bds J. G. Carper
García, Miguel	tailor Dahlman Bros	bds Mrs. S. H. Price
Gonzáles, Félix		r. ns T&P Ry nr Pine
Gonzáles, Riley	lab	r.es Arizona Ave bt Elizabeth and Henrietta
Leal, José	tailor Dahlman Bros	bds Mrs. S. H. Price
Mendoza, Millie Miss	actress	Theatre Comique
Treviño, Frank	tamales peddler	bds J. G. Carper

FIGURE 1-3   FORT WORTH CITY DIRECTORY, 1886-1887

Name	Nationality	Occupation/Business Address or Location	Residence Address or Location
Balcazo, Hilerio		Calhoun bt 7th & 8th	
Baloayo, Hilario		wks John S. Andrews & Co Stockyards	
Estrada, Antonio		saddle girth maker	r. 312 Bluff
García, Pedro		wks stock pens	rms near same
Garza, Antonio		wks coal chute	r. 417 Louisiana Ave
Gonzales, A.		performer Fashion Theatre	r. E. Tenth
Gonzales, Henry		Comique Theatre	r. cor Twelfth & Rusk
Gonzales, Riley	Mex	wks stock pens	r. cor Elizabeth/Arizona
Leal, Joseph		tailor Dahlman Bros	r. 300 Grove cor Second
Treviño, Frank		lab T&P Stockyards	bds stockyards

map does not include that half of the block (the northeast side of Calhoun), but the block just north (between Sixth and Seventh) was designated mixed use. In the 1889 Sanborn map, the block on the northeast side of Calhoun between Seventh and Eighth was occupied by the Kentucky Stables and Stock Yard. It is quite possible that the listings of Balcazo and Baloayo could refer to the same person. Records confirm the occurrence of the surname Balcazo, but not the name Baloayo. To complicate matters even more, the surname Valoayo also occurs. It would not be unreasonable to find the name written with a "B," given the similarity in the Spanish pronunciations of "b" and "v"—most English speakers would transcribe "Valoayo" as "Baloayo."

Only three Mexicanos seem to have lived in Fort Worth when both the 1885-1886 and the 1886-1887 city directories were published: Riley Gonzales, José Leal, and Frank Treviño. Although they are listed in the 1885-1886 directory, Hijínio Aguilar, Manuel Canapa, José Delagarcía, Miguel García, Félix Gonzales, and Millie Mendoza do not appear in subsequent editions. Hilerio [sic?] Balcazo, Hilario Baloayo, Pedro García, Antonio Garza, A. Gonzales, Henry Gonzales, and Frank Treviño—listed in the 1886-1887 directory—do not reappear in the directory for the following year. As so many individuals were transient, it is difficult to find materials documenting their lives, and so stories must be pieced together and surmised from the available data.

THE NEIGHBORHOODS EMERGE

In Fort Worth, as in most places, economic opportunities dictated settlement patterns. The earliest Latino enclaves or barrios included *La Diecisiete, La Corte, El Papalote*, North Side, *La Yarda, La Loma, El TP*, and *La Fundición* (South Side). (See Figure 1-4 for the locations of the earliest barrios.)

LA DIECISIETE

The initial concentration of Mexicans was at the intersection of Thirteenth and Rusk (now Commerce) streets and the 1300 to 1500 block of Calhoun Street. Early Fort Worth city directories point to an area bounded by Twelfth and Seventeenth streets and Commerce and Calhoun streets (the southern part of Hell's Half Acre) as being the first barrio where Mexicanos tended to live. [6] This first geographic core eventually spread north, south, east, and west to other barrios as more industries were established. Gradually the core neighborhood shifted a few blocks south and became popularly referred to as *La Diecisiete* (seventeen).

Riley Gonzales, one of the two early Mexicano residents of *La Diecisiete* found in the 1883-1884 *Fort Worth City Directory*, was a laborer who lived on the south side of Seventeenth Street between Brewer and Elm streets, about five blocks north of the Union Depot and Fort Worth's original stockyards (the present-day intersection of Interstate 30 and Interstate 35). Mr. Gonzales settled in Fort Worth early and lived in the city until his death. He worked at the stock pens until about 1925, but the directories show that he moved almost every year to addresses either north or south of the stock pens and always within easy walking distance of that facility.[7]

It is easy to track Riley Gonzales in the various city directories, but the trail of Antonio Peña, the second Mexicano in the 1883-1884 directory, is much more difficult to follow. The address listed for him ("r. ss 19th bt Adamson, Lawrence") does not appear on any Fort Worth map of the period. He probably lived near the original stockyards and worked as a day laborer. Another itinerant laborer of this early period (1885-1886 directory) was Félix Gonzales (see Figure 1-2) who lived on the north side of the T&P railyard near Pine Street—east of the original stockyards.

Hijínio Aguilar, José Delagarcía, and Frank Treviño all boarded with John G. Carper, a musician who resided on the southwest corner of East Twelfth and

FIGURE 1-4   **1892 MAP OF FORT WORTH, TEXAS**

① Hell's Half Acre, earliest area of Hispanic settlement   ② *La Diecisiete*, first barrio   ③ *La Corte*, second barrio, located around the courthouse

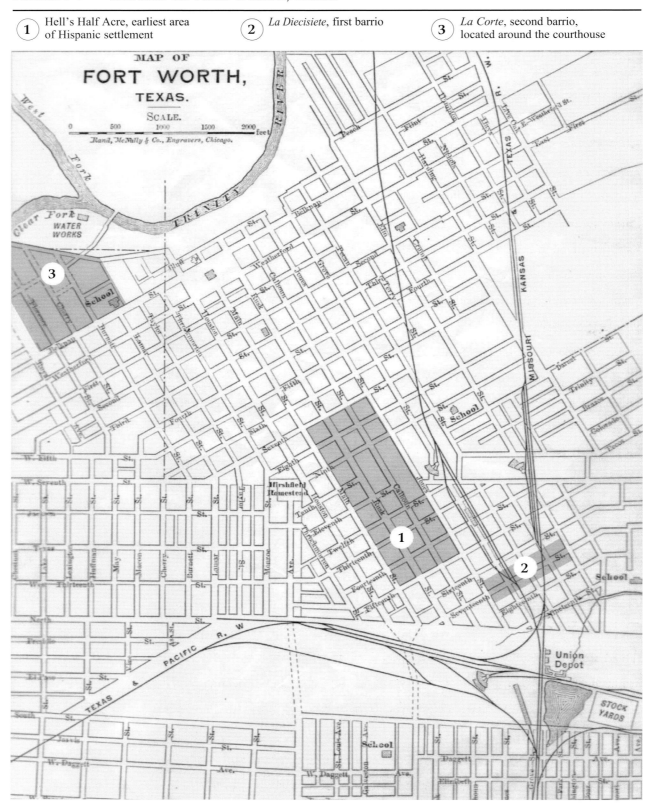

Rand, McNalley & Co., Engravers. Chicago. 1892 map of Fort Worth showing areas of the earliest barrios.

Pecan streets (see Figure 1-2). This neighborhood, located just east of the infamous Hell's Half Acre, seemed to be popular with new arrivals and transients. Not only did these three men board together, but they also sold tamales in and around the downtown district.[8] Manuel Canapa lived at the intersection of Twelfth and Rusk streets, three blocks southwest of Carper's home, and managed his neighborhood grocery business from the same location.[9] In the 1886-1887 edition of the *Fort Worth City Directory* (see Figure 1-3), two men were listed as actors or performers at local theatres. A. Gonzales is shown as "Performer" at the Fashion Theatre, while the entry for Henry Gonzales merely notes "Comique Theatre." Some sources give the Fashion Theatre's address as 1616 Main Street, but Sanborn maps of 1885 show that address occupied by a shoemaker and barber. The Comique Theater, located a few blocks south of the courthouse at 301 Main Street (corner of Main and Second streets), was owned by Alexander Wilson, who provided the town with entertainment commonly referred to as "leg opera." A precursor of vaudeville, a "leg opera" theatre featured comic skits, juggling, and singing and dancing provided by resident as well as traveling troupes. Prostitution and gambling were often ancillary features.[10] A. Gonzales lived on East Tenth Street, not too far away from Henry Gonzales' residence at the corner of Twelfth and Rusk. Henry's residence at the corner of Twelfth and Rusk streets made him either a neighbor or boarder of grocer Manuel Canapa. However, it's tempting to speculate that these two men who shared the same surname and occupation might have been brothers or cousins from a performing family, come to the new land to seek their fortune.

LA CORTE

La Corte, an area located southwest of the courthouse between Belknap and Third streets and Cherry and Burnett streets, attracted Mexicanos who worked primarily as busboys, cooks, dishwashers, maids, and laundry workers at downtown hotels, restaurants, and coffee shops. Miguel García and José Leal, however, were two early residents of *La Corte* who worked as tailors for the Dahlman Brothers clothing store located at Houston and First streets. Both men boarded at the home of Susan H. Price, the widow of Thomas F. Price, who lived on Belknap Street between Lamar and Burnett streets. This area took its colloquial name of

La Corte for its proximity to the heart and soul of the downtown district. Because of its location, conveniently close to downtown businesses, *La Corte* was the second Mexican barrio established in Fort Worth.

Another early resident of *La Corte*, Miss Millie Mendoza, was an actress at the Theatre Comique, 301 Main Street (corner of Main and Second streets). Ms. Mendoza's listed residential address is that of the theater, indicating that there were probably rooms available for some of its employees. While Millie had a Hispanic surname, it is unclear whether she was Spanish or Mexican or Anglo married to a man with an Hispanic surname.

With few Anglos, *La Corte* became a residential haven for minorities. The other racial groups to whom this neighborhood was home included five African American families and one Chinese family with five children. A resident in the 1920s, Sammy Pantoja, remembered mimicking the Chinese man who always went about "*echando madres en chino.*" Literally, this translates to "spewing out mothers in Chinese." Losing some meaning in translation, this slang phrase would more accurately mean "cussing indiscriminately in Chinese."[11]

Located on a bluff near the Trinity River, *La Corte* was divided on a topographic basis into what Spanish-speaking residents referred to as *el barrio de abajo* and *el barrio de arriba* (the lower neighborhood and the upper neighborhood, respectively). In the lower area were several wood yards, some owned by Mexicanos such as Vicente Márques, who provided customers with wood for stoves and fireplaces. During the 1920s other Latino families lived in the barrio, including those headed by Antonio Zapata, Filiberto Briones, Alfonso Jara, and Aurelio ("Earl") Bouzas. A good neighbor, Doña Josefa ("Chefa") Cruz was *la partera* (the midwife) who assisted area women with birthing. There was even a neighborhood *curandero* (natural healer), Don Pedro Molina, who helped area families deal with their health problems.[12]

EL PAPALOTE

Another barrio known as *El Papalote* (windmill in Spanish) emerged not far from *La Diecisiete* to the southwest, immediately southeast of the current I-35 and I-30 interchange. Because it was located directly east of the original stockyards and adjacent to many rail lines, it was a convenient place to live, and it became the foremost barrio in the first half of the twentieth century. The main street in this neighborhood was Presidio, and the cross streets were Kentucky, Poplar, Cedar, and Cypress avenues. There was no windmill in the area; the barrio got its name from the fact that the earliest Mexicanos had difficulty pronouncing the word "poplar" and altered it to something more familiar and easier to say.

THE NORTH SIDE

Perhaps the largest and most influential of all the Hispanic enclaves was the old North Side. Its history goes back to 1902 when Chicago-based Swift and Company and the Armour Packing Company[13] both established satellite facilities in Fort Worth. Home to at least six major railroads by the turn of the century, the city naturally had begun to attract more industry. Immigrants from Spain, Italy, Greece, Eastern Europe, Poland, and Russia poured into the old North Side to work for the slaughterhouses, making it at first a microcosm of eastern and southern Europe. But recently arrived Mexicanos in search of the same employment opportunities[14] soon made it their home as well. Shared culture and language, along with property restrictions and covenants, kept Mexicanos confined to certain well-defined areas within the city. Over the next three decades the population of Mexicanos grew larger than Eastern Europeans until the North Side became a distinctively Mexican barrio.[15]

Highlighting the new shift is a list of Hispanic names from the 1905-1906 city directory. (See Figure 1-5)

The 1905-1906 city directory was the first to note Mexicanos who worked for the two meatpacking plants. Fred García, Fred Garza, Joseph Garza, José Hernández, and Juan Leal worked for Swift and Company, while James Gonzales and Manuel J. Zepeda worked at Armour and Company. All of these individuals, except Manuel J. Zepeda, lived in what was probably a rooming house at 2012 North Grove Street.[16] The residences of these laborers in the newly established North Fort Worth subdivision—an area that would come to be popularly referred to as the "North Side"—again reflected the need to live within walking distance of work. This neighborhood, just south of the new stockyards and meatpacking plants, was defined on the west by North Main Street, on the east by North Grove, on the north by Northeast 23rd Street, and on the south by Northside Drive.

FIGURE 1-5   FORT WORTH CITY DIRECTORY, 1905-1906

Name	Occupation & Location	Residence
Acosta, Meryildo [sic]	tailor Borschow, Levin & Safferstone	
Cruz, Juan	cook Severo Lopez	rms 305 Main
Delarossa, Aleadio	restaurant 1305 Calhoun	r. same
Fuentes, Gregoria	servant Rev. Junius	r. same
García, Fred	lab Swift & Co.	r. 2012 Grove N.Ft.W
García, Juan	lab I.& G.N. Ry	bds 1318 Edward
García, Kate Miss		h. 929 E. Leuda
Garza, Fred	lab Swift & Co.	rms 2012 Grove N.Ft.W
Garza, Joseph	lab Swift & Co.	rms 2012 Grove N.Ft.W
Gómez, José		r. 1301 Calhoun
Gonzáles, Amador G.	servant E.H. Carter	r. same
Gonzáles, Elmo	jewelry stand	r. 114 W. Belknap
Gonzáles, James	butcher Armour	r. Grove
Gonzáles, Joseph M.	tailor Stonestreet & Davis	bds 404 Taylor
Gonzáles, Lupe (Mrs. A.G.)	cook E.H. Carter	r. same
Gonzáles, Riley	wks T&P Stockyards	r. 1236 Daggett
Gonzáles, Victor	peddler	rms 109 E. 13th
Govea, Jesús	chile stand 109 E. 13th	r. same
Guerraro [sic], Jesús	waiter Hotel Rosen	
Hernández, Ascensión	chile stand 1401 Jennings Av	r. 110 E.14
Hernández, Carmile	tamale peddler	rms 110 E. 14th
Hernández, Enoch	wks Mrs. S.A. Conner	
Hernández, Enrique	cook Victoria Martinez	
Hernández, José	lab Swift & Co.	rms 2012 Grove
Hernández, Sabino	waiter	rms 302 Main
Hernández, Severino	waiter Jim Kle	rms 110 E. 14th
Leal, Jesús M.	tailor A.&L.August	r. 207 E. 3rd
Leal, José A.	tailor Washer Bros	r. 207 E. 3rd
Leal, Juan	lab Swift & Co.	rms 2012 Grove
López, Eugenio	waiter José López	h. same
Lopez, José	Mex chile stand 114 Houston	r. 1113 Taylor
López, Martinas P.	barber shop, chile stand 1302 Rusk	r. same
López, Severo	chile stand 305 Main	r. 1113 Taylor
Lozano, Zeferino	chile stand W. Belknap	r. same
Martínez, Salvador	tailor	rms 310 Calhoun
Martínez, Victoria Mrs.	restaurant 311 W. 13th	r. same
Muños, Guillermo	lab I.& G.N. Ry	bds 1318 Edward
Rodríguez, Pietro	tamale peddler	r. sw cor E.10th/Harding
Rodríguez, Refugia R. (wid Fco)		h. 109 E. 13th
Sandoval, Alexander S.	driver Tex Prtg Co.	r. 824 Monroe
Treviño, Charles	lab	bds 300 E. RR Ave
Uzueta, Silverio	lab	r. 1301 Calhoun
Zapata, Benjamín	lab I.& G.N. Ry	bds 1318 Edward
Zepeda, Manuel J.	lab Armour & Co.	r. 2207 N. Calhoun

By the 1920s the Mexican population of the North Side had increased so that it was now the largest of the Fort Worth barrios. Appendix A is a block-by-block listing of inhabitants on the North Side's three principal streets—North Commerce, North Calhoun, and North Grove streets. This listing, taken from the 1920 *Fort Worth City Directory*, shows that most of the inhabitants of this neighborhood were Mexican with a few Greeks and other Eastern Europeans mixed in.

Within the North Side proper there existed two sub-barrios known as *el barrio de la garra* (of the rag) and *el barrio del pujido* (of the groan). *El barrio de la garra*, located east of North Grove between 14th and East Central, earned its name from all the cloth baby diapers that hung from clotheslines. *El barrio del pujido*, bounded by North Commerce, North Grove, 20th and 21st streets, was so named because walking up the embankment of the usually dry Marine Creek elicited groans and moans from older pedestrians.[17]

Most North Side Mexicanos lived in relative peace and harmony with each other, but there were exceptions. One of the greatest family feuds took place in *el barrio del pujido* in the summer of 1936. The Robledo family home at 2009 North Calhoun was located right across the street from the García family home at 2010. Good-looking and light-skinned (*parecían españoles*), José Robledo's sons were Benáncio, Eduardo, and Esteban. José made neighbors uneasy because he approached them on the street and somewhat threateningly asked for money. The García family resented his demands, as did others in the neighborhood, and antagonism festered. No one knows for sure who started the feud, but when it was all over three members of each family had been killed. José Robledo's throat was cut in a North Main bar near the present El Rancho Grande Restaurant, Benáncio was shot to death, and Esteban was disemboweled. Eduardo Robledo took the hint and moved to Houston.

Three members of the García clan were killed on September 16, 1936.[18] One was shot at point-blank range as he sat in his car waiting for his wife who was shopping in Leonard's Department Store. The surviving member of the García family was told bluntly by police to leave town.[19]

Few events in the North Side were as traumatic. Everyday life was difficult, especially during the Depression, but most residents were remarkably resilient and able to transcend many trials. The individuals who populated the North Side came from every region of Texas and Mexico. Those who stayed in Fort Worth found employment, raised families, and made the city their home. The North Side represents a cross-section of the migrant/immigrant experience—an experience that yielded significant contributions and ultimately changed the character of Fort Worth forever.

LA YARDA

La Yarda, a mini-barrio of 1920s North Side, was located at the east end of Terminal Road about where it intersected with Runnels Street. Railroad crews working for the Cotton Belt Railway refurbished old boxcars to give them the appearance of homes: Wheels were removed and doors and windows added for convenient access, light, and ventilation. Families usually cooked and washed dishes, clothes, and themselves outdoors. Depending on the size of the families one or even two families lived in each car.[20] During the late 1920s and early 1930s Román Soto Mercado worked for the Cotton Belt Railroad, and he and his wife, Helen Flores Soto, lived on Terminal Road in *La Yarda*.[21] Several of the Soto Mercado children, including Benito, were born in their boxcar home.[22]

LA LOMA

La Loma was a neighborhood consisting of about seven to ten Hispanic families in North Fort Worth near Meacham Field between Clinton and Ellis avenues and West Long Avenue and Northwest Thirty-sixth Street (a traditionally white area).[23] Mexicanos had formerly been limited geographically to housing in the sector just south of the new stockyards and meatpacking plants.[24] By 1923 Amado Rangel was the first Mexicano to move his family to 3602 Ellis Avenue, near Meacham Field. Over the years a few more families joined the Rangels, thereby creating a small barrio that became popularly known as *La Loma*.

EL TP

Before 1928, most men employed by the Texas & Pacific Railroad had lived south of the downtown district in and around *La Diecisiete* near the original round-house.[25] In the 1928 city directory there is evidence that crews working for the railroad had created another barrio. Figure 1-6 shows for the first time Hispanics with southwest side addresses.

A small community of Mexicans who worked for the Texas & Pacific Railroad settled in the area where Vickery Boulevard now intersects with Montgomery Street between Locke and Lovell avenues and Pulido and Montgomery streets, to be near the railroad. This new barrio naturally became known as *El TP*. The assistant engineer's office was located at 3505 Rutledge Avenue, and it is quite possible that the railroad also moved its roundhouse operations to the area about this time. In addition to the Pedro Pulido family, other families moved into the neighborhood—Toribio and Avelina Mendoza, Tony and Juanita Rodríguez, José and Panchita Mata, Augustín and Maxine Mosqueda, and Juanito and Panchita Ruiz.[26] The barrio also became home to San Mateo Mission of St. Patrick's Cathedral and Pulido's Restaurant. *El TP* scarcely exists anymore, a victim of the construction of Interstate 30 and the Vickery-Rosedale connection.

THE SOUTH SIDE

South Fort Worth seemed to grow faster than any other part of the city, partly because the Trinity River formed a geographic barrier to the north. In addition, by the early years of the twentieth century it was apparent that the stockyards and slaughterhouses that dominated North Fort Worth generated an offensive odor. Living either south or west of this area meant being upwind from the unpleasant smell; but even then, there were times when the foul odor permeated the entire city.[27] Just as the North Side was born out of the meatpacking plants, the South Side quickly developed after the establishment of the Texas Rolling Mills in 1908. Texas Rolling Mills became Texas Steel and was called *La Fundición*, the foundry.

FIGURE 1-6   FORT WORTH CITY DIRECTORY, 1928

Name	Occupation	Residence
Herrera, Pedro (Irene)	lab T&P Ry	r. 3310 Locke
Vallejo, Herminio (Santos)	lab T&P Ry	r. 3304 Locke
Gonzáles, Balliano (Sista)		r. 3508 Rutledge
Vallejo, Ovano (Loretta)	lab T&P Ry	r. 3508 Rutledge
Vásquez, José (Carmen)		r. 3511 Rutledge
Rodríguez, Elena		r. 3513 Rutledge

The defining boundaries of barrio *La Fundición* in the early part of the twentieth century were Hemphill Street on the west, Grove Street on the east, West Ripy Street on the north, and Bolt Street on the south. Most Mexicans who lived here worked for the steel company or for a few small foundries.

The city directory for 1910 lists five Mexicanos who worked for the plant in *La Fundición*: F. Fernández, Amado G. Gonzales, Dominico Martínez, Louis Martínez, and David Rodríguez. No addresses are indicated, as they probably lived in company housing conveniently located adjacent to the plant itself, by Butler and Fogg streets and Alice Street and Bryan Avenue.[28]

GROWING PREJUDICE

As Mexicans came pouring into Fort Worth eager to fill jobs offered by the expanding industries, attitudes of Fort Worth's Anglo population hardened. Mexicans encountered deed restrictions that prohibited their living in certain areas of town. Editorials in the newspapers, if they mentioned Hispanics at all, depicted them in a most indefensible manner. The *Fort Worth Record* extensively covered the situation in Mexico during the revolution. When the "Fighting Ninth" Army infantry unit passed through Cowtown by rail on their way to the border to fight,[29] an article in the *Fort Worth Record* quoted one young man eager to join the army, "Gee, I would like to get a chance at those `Greesers.'[sic]"[30]

In 1935 President Franklin Delano Roosevelt persuaded Congress to pass the Works Progress Administration bill creating thousands of jobs to lessen the effects of the Great Depression. The bill also established jobs for historians, artists, and writers. Writers and historians in Fort Worth, under the auspices of the Fort Worth Federal Writers Project, documented noteworthy events in Cowtown's development between 1880 and 1940. In gathering material for this project writers primarily relied on reprinted articles from the *Fort Worth City Guide* and local newspapers such as the *Fort Worth Record*, the *Fort Worth Press*, and the *Fort Worth Star-Telegram*. The articles provide an interesting perspective on Fort Worth's attitudes towards Mexicanos at the time and are extremely important in helping to understand the experience of a minority ethnic group during those early years. Another article in the *Fort Worth Record* reported alleged atrocities and barbarous behavior on the part of Mexican nationals.

Many stories, more or less doubted, are received from the Mexican border, telling of the cruelties practiced by both the federals and constitutionalists in Mexico, but there is one story which the people of Fort Worth are bound to believe, for some of the parties concerned, a band of Syrians, are here in person to vouch for the atrocities that were practiced upon them near [Ciudad] Juárez, by a band of constitutionalist soldiers.

These Syrians passed through Fort Worth Saturday on their way east from Mexico, and, in the offices of a Fort Worth lawyer they were induced to relate their story. They told graphically of tortures almost unbelievable, and even produced scars where they had been scarred with red-hot brands. As they mentally reviewed the tortures they had endured so recently the Syrians became almost frantic, and were so earnest and vivid in their descriptions that no one can, for the moment, doubt the truth of the statements, according to the attorneys.

The Syrians say that they fell into the hands of a half-savage band of Mexican bandits, dignified by the name "Constitutionalist." After the bandits had tortured their victims to their hearts' content and had their fill of barbarous fun, they allowed the Syrians to depart with their lives.[31]

Regardless of whether or not the above story was true, "cruelties," "atrocities," "tortures almost unbelievable," "a half-savage band of Mexican bandits," and "barbarous fun" were all vivid descriptions reflecting prevailing public opinion. Related in this pseudo-factual way, stereotypes became easy to accept, as the negative image of Mexicans seemed to be reinforced by the long-running historical perspective, where memories of the "Black Legend,"[32] the Alamo and Goliad, and Mexican banditry in general had shaped the attitudes of generations of Anglo-Texans.

Chapter 2

STORIES FROM THE BARRIOS

The lives of Mexican immigrants changed irrevocably upon entering the United States. Accustomed to hardship and scratching out a living, these new Americans began their new lives using the agricultural skills they brought with them. Most of the men who appear in this book worked as laborers in the cattle industry or for the railroads. Most of the women were employed as cooks or domestic servants. Isolated by culture and language, the new residents naturally clung together, and the communities they developed slowly began to impart a distinctly Mexican flavor to Fort Worth.

Riley Gonzales, one of the earliest permanent Mexican residents of Fort Worth, is representative of immigrants who were resilient, adaptable, and determined to provide for their families. Born somewhere in Mexico in January 1851, he emigrated to the United States (perhaps to Fort Worth) in 1880 at the age of twenty-nine.[1] Around the same time, he married Sarah, an Anglo who had been born in Tennessee in February 1849. The marriage produced one son, Thomas E., born in May of 1886, possibly at the family home at the corner of Elizabeth and Arizona streets in Fort Worth.[2] From the early 1880s, Gonzales worked for the original stockyards and lived in and around the area where I-30 and I-35 now intersect. In 1916, the sixty-five-year-old Gonzales lived with his thirty-year-old son in North Fort Worth at 2600 Ross Avenue, just west of the new stockyards where both worked.[3] After 1920 Riley Gonzales lived at 2520 Clinton Avenue, and in 1925, at the age of seventy-three, he became a machinist's helper at the Texas & Pacific Railroad. Son Thomas is not listed in the city directory after 1922, and no other records are found until his obituary notice on Saturday,

March 29, 1930.[4] In 1928 Riley Gonzales, now seventy-seven years old, worked for the Transcontinental Oil Company and lived on Denton Road.[5] He died in the City and County Hospital on October 30, 1928. His death certificate notes the cause of death as "cardiac decompen[sation]" after having been attended since October 23 by a Dr. Goldier. The document names him as "Raleigh L. Gonzalez" and describes him as a widower, aged seventy-nine (date of birth unknown), and gives his occupation, as "laborer." The elderly Mexicano died after nearly five decades of working in Fort Worth. Riley Gonzales can be considered a symbol of the city's earliest Mexican immigrants—a people who helped build the modern city and whose history has to be reconstructed from city directories and census data.

◆   ◆   ◆

Secundino and Tomasa Muñoz Martínez illustrate the effects of the Mexican Revolution on families. Born on July 1, 1874, at Villa Hidalgo, San Luis Potosí, Secundino Martínez worked *en la labor* (as an agricultural worker). In 1897 he married a fellow villager, Tomasa Muñoz, in the Catholic church of their small ranching community. The family grew with the birth of two daughters, Eufemia in 1898 and Simona in 1908. Normal life, however, was suddenly disrupted by the Mexican Revolution. Brother-in-law Gregorio Pérez sent money to enable Martínez to flee the violence spreading across *la tierra* in 1910, and he set out for Fort Worth determined to seek a better life.[6]

Upon his arrival, Martínez stayed with his brother-in-law, who found him a job at Texas Steel Company, where he worked from 8:00 A.M. to 5:00 P.M. six days a week. After two years, he had saved enough money to bring his family to Fort Worth. Together with their wives and children, all of Martínez's brothers soon left Mexico and settled in Fort Worth .[7]

◆   ◆   ◆

Salvador C. Gonzalez, Sr., was born to farming parents in September 1880, on a ranchito near Encarnación in the state of Jalisco. He served in the Mexican army for one year—1914. He then decided to leave the disorder in Mexico to make his way to Seguin, Texas, to pick cotton.[8] Beatriz Castorena was born in

Aguascalientes, where her father was a doctor. The family fled Mexico because of the revolution, settling near San Marcos, Texas. It is possible that Salvador and Beatriz knew each other in Mexico and kept in contact during and after their separate moves to Texas. They eventually married in Round Rock, Texas, around 1917. Their first daughter, Elvira, was born in Seguin in 1918 but died within six months. The family stayed in that area for about two years, then moved in 1920 to Fort Worth, where Salvador worked for the Southern Pacific Railroad on a crew maintaining and replacing rails and ties. They lived in a rental house at 504 Leota Street, a house that would become a kind of touchstone for the family. A second daughter, also named Elvira, was born in that house during the first year. She did not survive to adulthood but died at age fifteen of pneumonia. The third child, Salvador C. Gonzalez, Jr., was born on June 22, 1922, at the Leota Street house, with Ramona Vega, the wife of Southern Pacific co-worker and friend, Luz Vega, performing the duties of midwife.[9]

In 1923, for reasons that are not clear, the family, including Beatriz's brother, Leopoldo Castorena, all moved to St. Louis, Missouri, to work on a ranch. In 1924, however they all returned to Mexico. The elder Salvador was never able to adjust to life in the United States and always longed to return to Mexico. With money earned in the U.S., he was able to fulfill part of his dream—to buy a home and start a small business. The fourth child, Eleodoro, was born at the ranchito near Encarnación on April 13, 1924. As an adult, Eleodoro worked as a kitchen-and-bath tile contractor and later at a minimum-security federal prison on the South Side of Fort Worth.[10]

As a symptom of his discontent, Salvador, Sr., drank and gambled heavily; when drunk, he tended to be violent to his family. In the same year that Eleodoro was born (1924), Senior gambled away the little home he had just bought. And so, in late 1924, out of money, out of luck, and out of a job, Salvador, Sr., dragged his family back to Fort Worth. They lived in the same rented house as before—at 504 Leota Street—in an area that had been known since the turn of the century as the Rock Island neighborhood. Once again he worked hard eight-hour days for the Southern Pacific Railroad, replacing old rails and ties. His work crew consisted of about twelve Mexicanos; the crew boss was an Anglo.[11]

The fifth child, Aurora, was born in Fort Worth in 1926. She later married Juan Sánchez, had seven children, and died of cancer around 1985.[12] Child number six, Oralia, born in 1928, later married Raul Pacheco and had seven children. The seventh child born to Salvador and Beatriz, a boy, died at birth (which might have been premature) around 1930. Their eighth and last child, Alvaro, was born in 1934. He later married Juana Muñoz and had two daughters.[13]

Salvador C. Gonzalez, Jr., went to Alexander Hall Elementary School, where the total enrollment included only three other Mexicans—Salvador's brother, Eleodoro, and friends Augustín Vargas and Augustín's brother—during the six years (1930-1936) that Junior attended. In 1936 Salvador attended Jennings Junior High School for six months—long enough to convince him that he wasn't learning anything he didn't already know. Realizing that his son indeed could read, write, and count, his father permitted him to drop out of school. The boy worked a newspaper route for the *Fort Worth Press* in the Hemphill and Vickery neighborhood until 1937, then worked as a dishwasher at the Fort Worth Club. Salvador worked from ten to twenty hours a day, seven days a week, for forty dollars per month. No matter how many hours he worked, every two weeks he was paid $19.75, with twenty-five cents deducted for Social Security. Still, he held the job until 1941. Next, he worked as a fry cook for the Texas Hotel, a job that lasted from 1942 to 1945 and again from 1946 until 1948.[14]

On October 12, 1941, Salvador, Jr., married María Sánchez.[15] The two families were closely linked: María's brother, Juan, was married to Junior's sister, Aurora, and one of María's sisters was married to Junior's brother, Eleodoro. When Senior and the family moved to a rental home on the corner of Calhoun and Anne, Salvador and María lived with them there for two months, then rented a room from Hermenejildo Martínez, a successful concrete contractor who lived at 401 Third Street (on the corner of Pecan Street). Hermenejildo and his wife, Sabina, were gracious people who had a two-story house with indoor plumbing; it was one of the finest homes owned by a Hispanic in Fort Worth. Only a few other Hispanics lived in this area of Third Street.[16]

In 1945, Salvador Gonzalez, Jr., reported to Parris Island, South Carolina, for Marine boot camp. From there he went to Camp Pendleton in Oceanside, California, and then to Pearl Harbor, Guam, and China. He was honorably dis-

(April 1972) Born in 1889 in Austin, cement contractor Hermenejildo R. Martínez was the first Mexican American in Fort Worth who owned a home of substance that featured the luxury of indoor plumbing. *Photo courtesy of Sam Picazo.*

charged from the Marines in 1946 after the end of World War II with about eighteen months' service. He returned to Fort Worth to his former job at the Texas Hotel.

Reunited after the war, Salvador and María rented a three-room house from her mother at 415 Pecan Street, where they lived for about three years. This was one of the "shotgun homes" that were common at that time, so called because all the rooms were laid out in a straight line. Later Mrs. Sánchez bought a house at 1015 East Bluff Street and rented it to the couple for about one year.[17]

The Gonzalez family experienced Fort Worth's prejudice in a most visible, hurtful way. In 1947, desperately wanting to own their own home, Salvador and María Gonzalez put down their life's savings of $2,000 in savings bonds to buy a house in an all-Anglo neighborhood at 514 Wall Street, next to the Santa Fe railroad tracks. Matis Real Estate Company financed the $1,000 balance. As soon as word spread that a Mexican couple was moving into the neighborhood, almost all the houses sprouted "For Sale" signs. The Anglos wanted to move away as quickly as possible; they must have said to themselves, "well, there goes the neighborhood." By 1952 three other Mexican families were living on Wall Street. These included Tomás and Mary Yañez, 500 Wall Street, a laborer with the Texas & Pacific Railroad; Fernando and Dominga Guajardo, 508 Wall Street, employed at CVAC; and Juan and Aurora Sánchez (Salvador's brother-in-law and sister), 518 Wall Street, employed as an assistant purchasing agent with the Texas Hotel, according to the 1952 *Fort Worth City Directory*.

In 1948 the Texas Hotel brought in a new kitchen manager with whom Salvador had some trouble. He quit and went to work for Armour and Company, where he was often laid off and finally left when he injured his knee-cap. Next he found employment with the Mathis Company, 1200 block of East Broadway Street, which manufactured furniture, fans, air coolers, and air conditioners. He worked here for nine years until 1957.[18]

When Salvador left the Mathis Company his wife, María, went to work for them, first in the finishing room and later working on air conditioners. The place proved rough for a woman, especially a Mexicana, and María endured frequent verbal abuse. Because of such abuse she often would come home shaken and crying. To this day she maintains a serenity and sweet spirit that through all the years of uphill struggles has made her a successful and resilient survivor.

After quitting his job at the Mathis Company in 1957 Gonzalez went to work for the post office. He worked out of Handley for two years and then was given a route in the Meadowbrook area. On March 1, 1989, Gonzalez retired at the age of sixty-six, after having worked for the postal service for thirty-two years.[19]

He and his wife live quietly, enjoying retirement and their extensive family at the same home he bought in 1947.[20] Together they have improved and added to their home over the years. It is a beautiful home with a large well-kept yard, and their pride of ownership is quite evident. María and Salvador have seen the neighborhood change over the years since 1947, with many other minorities moving. They have noticed that Anglos, too, are starting to move back, although they are

Anglos of more humble means. The Gonzalezes, with a keen sense of humor, now say to themselves, "well, there goes the neighborhood!"[21]

◆ ◆ ◆

One of the earliest residents of the North Side, Pascacio ("Pete") Martínez was born on August 4, 1886, near Monterrey, Nuevo León, Mexico. He quit school at an early age in order to work on a hacienda, where he learned to raise livestock and to break and ride horses. Pete's parents disowned him when he ignored their objections to his marrying a woman outside his class. Undaunted, twenty-two-years old, disinherited, Pete Martínez left Mexico in 1908 in order to marry Elena Ocampo. Born on November 22, 1895, Elena was only thirteen when she married Pete and fled to a new life north of the Rio Grande. The couple arrived in Fort Worth in 1908, and Pete eventually supported his family by working for the railroad, a job he held from 1910 to 1930.[22]

Pascacio ("Pete") Martínez and his family. Second row, l. to r.: Elvira M. Garza; Richard; Helen M. Rodríguez; Johnny (in uniform); Pete, Jr.; Mary M. Garza; Gloria M. Cardona. First row, l. to r.: Robert; Isabel M. Delgado; Pete, Sr.; Elena Ocampo Martínez; Mike; Yvonne ("Kiki") Cisneros. *Photo courtesy of Yvonne ("Kiki") Martínez Cisneros and Mary M. Garza.*

The Martínez family's earliest recollections of their first home was its proximity to Marine Creek on the North Side. After he began working at the Armour meat-packing plant, Pete purchased their lifelong residence at 1419 North Calhoun,[23] an address that was home to the couple and their six sons—Mike, Pete, Jr., Jimmy, Sonny, Johnny, and Bobby—and seven daughters—Isabel, Julita, Helen, Elvira, Mary, Gloria, and Yvonne ("Kiki").[24] With rosebushes growing along the large front porch and main entrance, the well-kept, white, one-story home contained seven rooms, not including two bathrooms that had running water—a feature not found in most North Side Mexicano homes at the time. The home was equipped with the latest amenities, including a telephone, an electric refrigerator, and other appliances. A shiny new Chevrolet automobile stood out front. The backyard was home to a menagerie of animals that included two milk cows, several chickens, and the prize rabbits that Pete loved to raise and sell as a hobby.[25]

In 1930, after having worked for the railroad for twenty years, Pete Martínez found a better-paying job at Armour and Company. Honest, dedicated, and hard-working, Pete caught the attention of his supervisors when they discovered he had a natural ability with a boning knife. His youthful experience with livestock helped Martínez land the prized position of "beef-boner" at Armour—a position he held for another twenty years until the day he passed away. During the Great Depression, while the most menial jobs at the meat packing plant paid between twenty-five and thirty-five cents an hour, the highly-skilled beef-boner earned between $1.25 to $1.50 per hour. Martínez's expert handling of a sharpened knife together with his position as chief steward of the CIO union won him a legendary reputation at Armour's.[26]

◆　◆　◆

Eutimio Ayala was born December 24, 1896, at Quelseo de Abasolo, Guanajuato (west of Salamanca). Eutimio took care of *la raya* (payroll records) for a hacienda. In 1916, in either Salamanca or Irapuato, he married María Gutiérrez Ortiz, who had been born near Salamanca on June 17, 1901. She worked on the Rancho de Doña Rosa. The young couple moved to Yucatán seeking work but found the area unbearably hot. Their next home, in 1918, was Detroit, Michigan, where Eutimio worked for the Willis Overland Company. After a few years of working at the firm's steel foundry, which made car frames, they moved to Toledo, Ohio. There Eutimio worked for either a railroad or a steel foundry, and three of their fourteen children were born. Four or five years later they moved to Decatur, Indiana, where both worked in the beet and tomato fields. In 1933 the family relocated to Fort Worth, where they lived at 1313 North Grove Street. Eutimio took a job with Swift and Company in the dry salt department until a heart attack forced his early retirement in 1952. He died one year later on August 5, 1953.[27]

◆　◆　◆

Margarito Rodríguez Padilla was born on February 22, 1903, at Villa Hidalgo, San Luis Potosí, not long after his family left Mexico. Again the cause was the Mexican Revolution. Although his maternal grandmother, Regina Mascorro Rodríguez, insisted on the gracious manners that reflected the Victorian Age, she was tough and resourceful enough to risk fleeing the revolution strapped on top of a speeding train.

Born in 1850 in the Hacienda de Silos near San Luis Potosí, Mama Regina decided early on that her family would not tolerate the escalating danger posed by marauding soldiers. With her children (including her daughter, Margarito's mother, Ruperta Mascorro Rodríguez; her son-in-law, Margarito's father, Marcelino Padilla; at least seven grandchildren; and eleven other relatives), she attempted to board a train headed for the border. The train was so packed with refugees that the only space available was on the roof of the cars. Mama Regina and the others strapped themselves down with ropes to keep from falling off. In this manner, the family rode the entire trip, looking forward to a safe and stable life in Texas.[28] The family eventually found their way to Fort Worth. As Mama Regina's great-granddaughter, Hope Padilla Ayala, recounts this story, she reflects on the grit and determination that ensured her family's survival and thinks she has a lot to live up to.

◆　◆　◆

Catalina Tobías Loredo was born on February 22, 1898, in Hacienda de Silos, San Luis Potosí, to Macario Loredo and Angela Tobías. Macario and Angela had six children: Dionicia (Quintanilla), Inés (Gamboa), Francisco, Catalina, Julio, and Lina. On the hacienda Macario supervised a crew of field hands that cultivated maguey plants as well as a variety of vegetables. As a young girl, Catalina took care of the hacienda's owners, two elderly unmarried sisters. They had no heirs, and the sisters promised Catalina that she would inherit their estate. But then the Mexican Revolution began.[29]

Frequent raiding by opposing factions made life on the hacienda precarious. A lookout perched on a tower overlooking the property warned residents when soldiers were approaching. A secret chamber underneath the main house provided a hiding place for the women on these occasions. In one of these encounters, soldiers hanged Macario Loredo and left him for dead. After the soldiers left, the women cut down his body only to discover that he was still alive. He died shortly thereafter, however, and, fearing for their lives, his widow, Angela, prepared to take her youngest children, Catalina and Julio, to the safety of the United States. Catalina did not want to leave her inheritance behind and begged to stay in Mexico, but her mother would not hear of it. The three traveled by train to the border in search of Francisco, the oldest son, who had already emigrated to the U.S. Catalina was sixteen when she crossed the border at Laredo in 1914.[30]

The family settled in San Marcos, Texas, and worked in the fields. In an odd reprise of her situation in Mexico, two elderly and wealthy German sisters hired Catalina to take care of them. They taught her how to prepare and cook American foods. Becoming familiar with the cuisine, Catalina later served American-style food to her own family, along with more traditional Mexicano-style cooking.[31] For ten years, until her wedding day, she faithfully served the sisters. On January 15, 1925, in San Marcos, Catalina married Telésforo Cancino, whose family had lived in Texas for generations. His parents, Román Rodríguez and Refugio Cancino, had nine children: Juan, Teófilo ("Ted"), Telésforo ("Tele"), Roberto ("Robe"), Bartolo ("Chico"), Aniceto ("Cheto"), Rosa, Josefa, and Santos.[32]

After their marriage, Telésforo and Catalina lived and worked on an Anglo-owned farm, where he developed a warm relationship with the owners. They even nursed him back to health when he had pneumonia. Telésforo continued to work at the farm until early 1926, when he and Catalina moved to Mexia to work for the Santa Fe Railroad.[33]

Telésforo worked for the railroad for two years before moving to Fort Worth, where Catalina's family had settled.[34] In 1929 they lived with Catalina's mother at 1408 North Commerce Street. Cancino worked as a woodcutter, clearing fields near Fort Worth. In 1930 they lived briefly on Bernal Drive in Dallas before returning to Fort Worth. Telésforo worked for Swift and Company, curing hides and, later, loading meat onto railroad cars. Telésforo died before Catalina, but there are no records of his death. Catalina celebrated her one-hundredth birthday in 1998.[35]

❖   ❖   ❖

A farmer who tended his *milpa* and raised hogs, Román Pérez Mercado was born on August 9, 1901, in the village of Manalisco, Jalisco. The woman he would eventually marry, Atilana Soto, was born on October 5, 1897, in Yahualca, Jalisco.[36] Around 1920 Pérez Mercado left his wife in Yahualíca to come to the United States. Although he first found employment in Oregon and Washington, he made his way south working for the Rock Island Railroad, spending some time in Nebraska. Mercado periodically visited his wife in Mexico, as did many other Mexicanos working in the U.S. His road crew worked around Sherman and Denison and arrived in Fort Worth in 1926. Still in Mexico, Atilana experienced great difficulty getting her two baby daughters baptized due to the deterioration of relations between church and state that became known as the Cristero Rebellion (1926-1929). Catholic churches in the state of Jalisco, and in many other areas of Mexico, closed to protest government policies against the church. Atilana and children made it safely out of Mexico and to Fort Worth that same year (1926). Seven more children were born to the couple in Fort Worth.[37]

❖   ❖   ❖

While some Mexicanos encountered prejudice from Anglos, Sammy Pantoja, an early resident of barrio *La Corte*, on the other hand, experienced kindness. As a young boy in the 1920s Sammy loved to dart around exploring the dirt streets and back alleys of his barrio and of the intriguing world beyond. He'd go by the Mexican Presbyterian Church, where the dynamic pastor, Guillermo A. Walls, gladly gave him clothes and shoes, affectionately calling him *"Chapo"* because of the boy's Japanese looks. Sammy often ventured out of his barrio, toward the downtown district. The area around the farmers' market was particularly interesting because he could easily help himself to discarded fruit from the many trash cans in the vicinity. Farther on, between Fourth and Fifth and Throckmorton and Houston streets, there was an alley known as *"el callejón de las láminas"* ("the alley with the tin gates"). One winter day at the age of seven Sammy wandered into the alley to see what he could scavenge. A passing Anglo couple noticed the boy standing barefoot in snow. Taking him by the hand, they marched him to Monnig's department store and bought young Sammy a new wardrobe, including a coat and shoes.[38]

Over the years Sammy Pantoja worked for a variety of restaurants such as the Mexican Inn (1940s), El Chico's (1951-1954), and Harry's Steakhouse (1954-1966), before starting his own business. He established the first Sammy's Restaurant at the corner of Northwest 36th and Ellis streets, immediately south of Meacham Field in the barrio known as *La Loma*. In 1971 he moved the restaurant to 300 West Central Avenue in the extended North Side.[39] Sammy's Restaurant was one of the few places in Fort Worth that stayed open until 2:00 A.M. To both Anglos and Hispanics it was the place to go for late night breakfast, until it closed in the late 1990s.

❖   ❖   ❖

Few people can top the genuine good-heartedness of Mexican immigrant Benito Cardona, Jr. Born in 1898 in Torreón, Coahuila, Mexico, to Benito Cardona, Sr., and Manuela Garza, Benito had six siblings: Manuel, Cuauctemoc, Elias, Ester, Raquel, and Aida.[40] Owner of *La india* bakery in Fort Worth,[41] Benito, Jr., was an expert horseman who also raised horses and burros, rented supply wagons, and operated a stagecoach line.[42]

After Mexico suspended payment on its foreign debt, the French army took over Mexico City, Benito, Sr.'s, father, Bonifacio Cardona de la Bastida, was an officer in the French army of occupation (1862-1867).[43] In the course of his tour of duty, Cardona fell in love and married Felipa Muñoz, a Mexican woman from San Luis Potosí. Now with dual allegiances, it no longer made sense to him to challenge Mexico's democratically elected president, Benito Juárez. The story

Benito Cardona, Sr., named in honor of Mexican President Benito Juárez. A French Army officer who married a Mexicana and refused thereafter to fight against Mexico, Cardona's father went in person to ask the Mexican President for a pardon. Bennie Cardona, whose grandfather, Benito, owned *"La india"* Bakery in Torreón, Mexico, continues the family tradition. *Photo courtesy of Bennie Cardona.*

goes that Cardona secured an audience with President Juárez to ask for pardon for his role with the French army and to offer his services to the legitimate government of Mexico. He even named his first-born son Benito in honor of the president.[44]

Later, during the Mexican Revolution (1911-1917), Benito Cardona, Sr., was elected to the post of *alcalde* (mayor) of Torreón. He became known as *"el rebelde"* ("the rebel") as he became increasingly disenchanted with the policies of Mexican president Victoriano Huerta.[45] In 1913, one of his sons was wounded and taken prisoner—he was poisoned in prison and died. Benito, Sr., fled Torreón, accused of being a traitor. After a time he thought he could return to re-establish his good reputation. On his way to Torreón, Cardona's train suddenly came to a halt at Pedriceña, and *federales* forced him and nine others off the car and executed them alongside the tracks.[46]

His son, fifteen-year-old Benito Cardona, Jr., who learned the bakery business from his father, had been studying violin for two years at a conservatory of music when news came of his father's death. He immediately returned home to his terrified mother, Manuela, and the family made preparations to leave Mexico with a few of their possessions in one of his father's wagons. With his mother, sister, Aida, and brother, Manuel, on board, Benito drove the wagon for three days until they reached Laredo. They stayed two years at the home of sister Ester (Cardona) and her husband, Pasqual Ruiz, who now lived in the border town and owned a hide shop.[47]

Around 1916 Benito and his family came to Fort Worth's North Side to visit Raquel Cardona and her husband, Santos Mireles.[48] During his eight-year stay in Fort Worth Benito met Cándida Martínez, a recent immigrant herself. Her parents and brothers, who had owned a tobacco plantation in Cuba, were killed during the Spanish-American War (1898).[49] With her surviving sisters, Cándida traveled to New York City and then to New Orleans in search of a religious education. They finally came to Fort Worth, where she worked towards a degree in theology from Southwestern Baptist Theological Seminary. Cándida met Benito at the Mexican Baptist church and married him there in 1923. Over the next six years the couple alternated between living in Fort Worth and Dallas as Cándida ministered in various Mexican Baptist missions. In Dallas Benito and Cándida lived in the barrio known as "Little Mexico"[50] and, while there, had their two sons, Moises and Benito.[51]

After that Benito Cardona and his family moved frequently all over Texas—Laredo, Del Rio, Harlingen, Dilly, Pearsall, and Divine. Wherever there was a market for his baked goods, Benito set up shop and quickly established a bakery with the help of other Mexicanos. Using traditional adobe building methods, Benito and his friends could erect an oven in a matter of a few weeks. In a typical situation, the crew dug a hole, added water, and mixed the resulting mud with straw from a nearby field. Then they poured the straw-mixed mud into molds made from discarded lumber. After the adobe bricks hardened, they were removed from their molds and allowed to dry in the hot South Texas sun for about a week. Benito and his crew then built an igloo-shaped baking oven on an eight-foot square platform made of railroad ties. A highly resourceful and inventive man, Benito built the

Moises Cardona graduated
in 1941 from R.L. Pascal
High School. *Photo courtesy
of Moises Cardona.*

oven against one of the walls of his home for additional warmth. An opening in
the wall allowed for direct access to the oven from within his home. To get water
to the bakery, Cardona relied on a long spigot connected to a large barrel filled
with water. (The crew had to roll the barrel up a ramp to get access to the water.)
Thus, within days, the hard-working Benito was open for business.[52]

The family finally settled in Fort Worth in the 1930s, and opened a bakery
named after the elder Cardona's shop in Mexico, *La india*. Yet Bennie never forgot
his desire to be a musician. He continued practicing the violin, and, in the late
1930s, a grant from the Works Progress Administration sustained Cardona's position as first violinist with the Fort Worth Symphony. In the evenings, he gave
music lessons to groups of North Side children. His sons, Moises and Bennie,
both learned to play musical instruments and were excellent musicians.[53]

(1975) Bennie Cardona (Benito Cardona, III) at his bakery at 1344 N. Main Street (at Central). Cardona is married to Gloria, daughter of Pascacio ("Pete") Martínez. *Photo courtesy of*

Benito was not only a successful baker who made a wide variety of quality *pan dulce* and pastries, he was also a good and conscientious neighbor. When his friend and bakery competitor Gregorio Esparza, Sr., left for Mexico to see his ailing mother, Benito helped run his bakery. For about six months Cardona baked *pan dulce* and took care of Gregorio's meat business. Esparza returned after his mother passed away, grateful for his friend's help.

Benito Cardona, Jr., was known throughout the North Side as a generous neighbor—hungry people who came to his shop received milk and a meal. When there was death in the barrio, he always took a large box of *pan dulce* to the home of the grieving family. When Benito Cardona, Jr., passed away in 1981, people from far and near agreed that they had lost a good friend.[54]

Chapter 3

MAKING
A LIVING

From the 1880s on, the magnet that drew thousands of Mexicanos to Fort Worth was the ever-increasing number and variety of jobs the city offered. As Fort Worth gradually grew more sophisticated, new job opportunities developed, from slaughtering cattle and laboring on the railroads to service-oriented jobs such as waiting tables or tailoring. Although Hispanics slowly began their own businesses, from the 1880s to the first decade of the twentieth century, the main sources of employment for newly arrived men remained the railroads and meat-packing plants.

A careful examination of the first series of city directories (1883-1910) provides an understanding of the labor trends in the earliest barrios. Certainly Hell's Half Acre and the original stockyards (districts that were the first areas of residence for Fort Worth's newest minority group) provided newly arriving Mexicanos with a number of employment opportunities—tending livestock, working for the railroads, selling prepared foods, dishwashing, and other domestic labor. Newspaper articles during the 1920s referred to this area as "Little Mexico," for the continuous influx of Mexicanos and Mexicanas.[1] Not to be confused with North Calhoun Street, created in North Fort Worth after the turn of the century, lower Calhoun became the commercial center of Little Mexico with its barbershops, corner groceries, chile stands, and bars.[2] This first geographic core neighborhood shifted a few blocks south and became popularly known as *La Diecisiete*.

TYPICAL JOBS

Figure 3-1 illustrates emerging demographic trends: the clustering of Mexicanos around Hell's Half Acre and working in low-paying, menial jobs such as stockyard and railroad laborers or service-oriented work such as waiters and dishwashers. Dishwasher Epifanio López, waiter Charles Morales, and waiter Félix Rodríguez all worked for downtown hotels located in and around Hell's Half Acre, and the listing for Riley Gonzales shows a double occupation—the railroad and the stockyards.

Individuals arriving with marketable skills such as tailoring could find steady work at a number of haberdasheries and, as in the case of Joseph A. Leal, could set up their own shops within a few years. Good cooking and some restaurant experience could also lead to a measure of independence, as Antonio Estrada demonstrated by opening his own eating establishment.

According to the 1890 city directory (See Figure 3-2), Riley Gonzales no longer worked for the stockyards but was a wiper at the Texas & Pacific roundhouse.[3] Jesús Lópes, address unlisted, worked as a Pullman Palace car cleaner, also at the Texas & Pacific roundhouse. J. L. and J. W. Márquez are both listed as laborers who lived near the railroad tracks on the north side of a graveyard—possibly the old Pioneers' Rest Cemetery, about half a mile northeast of the courthouse. Evidence of the increasing numbers of jobs provided by the different rail lines converging on Fort Worth, the railroads listed in the 1892-1893 city directory include: The Fort Worth and Denver Railway; the Fort Worth and Rio Grande Railway; the

FIGURE 3-1   FORT WORTH CITY DIRECTORY, 1888-1889

Name	Occupation	Residence
Esquivel, Pianio	tamale peddler	r. ws Rusk bt 11th/12th
Estrada, Antonio	lunch stand 303 Main	r. 900 Houston
Gonzáles, Riley	wks T&P Ry Stockyards	r. ne cor Terry/20th
Leal, Joseph A.	tailor	r. se cor Throckmorton/W.13th
López, Epifanio	dishwasher Ginocchio's Hotel	r. same
Marcas, Pablo		r. ws Rusk bt E. 11th & 12th
Morales, Charles	waiter Tremont Hotel	r. same
Rodríguez, Felix	waiter Ellis Hotel	r. same
Rodríguez, Pedro	tamale peddler	r. ss 12th bt Rusk/Calhoun
Rubiolo, Francisco	feed hay grain 300 E Belknap & Calhoun	r.same

FIGURE 3-2   FORT WORTH CITY DIRECTORY, 1890

Name	Occupation	Residence
Cárdenas, Miss E.	chambermaid	Pickwick Hotel
Espinosa, Louis	wks FtW lime factory	r. same
Estrada, Antonio	restaurant	1513 Main
Gonzáles, Riley	wiper T&P roundhouse	r. 705 S. Crump
Gonzáles, W.	wks stockyard	r. 717 E. Front
Leal, J. A.	tailor, shop & r. cor W. 1st & Throckmorton	r. cor W. 1st & Throckmorton
Lópes, Jesus	Pullman Palace car cleaner, T&P roundhouse	
Márquez, J.L.	lab	r. ns graveyard nr rr track
Márquez, J.W.	lab	r. ns graveyard nr rr track
Vecerra, Joe	lab	

Gulf, Colorado and Santa Fe Railway; the Houston and Texas Central Railway; the Missouri, Kansas, and Texas Railway; and the Texas & Pacific Railway.

Mexicanos learned to take advantage of the skills acquired working for railroads, stockyards, and in the service sector to secure better jobs. The 1892-1893 city directory lists Joseph A. Leal, along with Jesús and Joseph Leal, in his tailor shop at 311 W. 1st Street. Ten years later Joseph A. Leal was the first Mexicano to have a telephone listing in Fort Worth (number 1076).[4] Also listed as tailors were Pablo Acosta, who worked for "Dot Leetle French Man" Charles Marcelin[5] at 109 E. 3rd Street, and Joseph Ramírez, who worked for W. S. Matney at 212 E. 1st Street (and lived with the Leals).

Educated Mexicanos began to find positions as well. The 1892-1893 directory lists the Reverend Juan G. Pérez, who worked as a Spanish instructor at the Polytechnic College. According to the 1894-1895 city directory, the Polytechnic College of the Methodist Episcopal Church, South, was located on the south side of the T&P Railway, two miles east of the city limits. The institution's name later changed to Texas Wesleyan College and today is Texas Wesleyan University.

Other occupations continued to add to the variety of listings in the Fort Worth city directories. The 1894-1895 directory listed Martín Aguilar, Antonio Estrada, Rosalio Hernández, Alejandro Losoya, and Louis Rodríguez—each either owned a chile stand or peddled the spicy condiment on the streets.[6] Joseph Cortéz operated his own barbershop at 1309 Main Street and was the first Hispanic listed in the city directory under the heading of "Barber Shops."[7] Antonio H. Valencia made his living as a photographer with C. O. Lorenz.

Notwithstanding those who possessed marketable skills such as leather-crafting, hair cutting, or tailoring that would allow them to set up their own businesses, Mexicanos frequently tried their hand at being restaurateurs. Pioneers in this category began with Antonio Estrada, the first to have a lunch stand,[8] Juan Gonzales, and Severio López. López first appeared in the 1901-1902 city directory. [9] It indicated that he had a chile stand[10] at 305 Main Street and resided at 109 North Taylor Street.[11] Several years later, his listing in the 1904-1905 city directory shows him to be the proprietor of the San Antonio Restaurant, located at 114 Houston Street. He still had his chile stand at 305 Main Street and later moved to a new residence at 1113 Taylor Street. Severio López must be the first Mexicano restaurateur to intentionally market his restaurant with a catchy name, designed to catch the public's attention. This name-recognition strategy must have had a positive effect on business because in 1904-1905 López employed a waiter, Zeferino Lozano, and, in the next year, added a cook, Juan Cruz.[12]

Hispanics were a continuing presence in entertainment as well. Adolph Gonzales, a comedian at the Andrews Theatre, and his wife, Lula, a musician at the same establishment, lived at the northeast corner of East 12th and Jones streets.

Following the city directories on a yearly basis reveals the transient nature of the early Mexicano population in Fort Worth. Equally frustrating is the lack of information on where Mexicanos relocated and for what reasons. How many of these people returned to their native homeland or moved on to other Texas cities?

STOCKYARDS, RAILROADS, AND SERVICE

Mexicanos actively sought to better their situations, even if it meant moving or changing their means of livelihood. Of the three tamale peddlers listed in the 1885-1886 directory, two left town (Aguilar and Delagarcia) and the third, Frank Treviño, found work at the T&P rail yard. Antonio Estrada, listed as a saddle girth maker in this directory, opened a lunch stand at 303 Main Street the following year.[13] "Restaurant" replaced the designation "lunch stand" in the

1890 city directory, apparently making Antonio Estrada's eating establishment the first owned by a Mexicano. We don't know if he served Mexican food or prepared the usual Anglo fare; however, we do know that he moved his restaurant several times—to 1513 Main Street in 1890, 1101 Main in 1892, and to the northwest corner of East 12th and Rusk in 1896.[14]

While Dahlman Brothers tailor Miguel García left town, Joseph Leal continued for one more year as a tailor with that firm. The 1888-1889 city directory (See Figure 3-1) no longer lists Dahlman Brothers as Leal's employer, and the 1890 directory (Figure 3-2) notes that Joseph's shop and residence were on the corner of West 1st and Throckmorton (just a block west of his old employer). By 1893 the city boasted two more tailors—Jesús Leal and another, Joseph Leal, perhaps relatives of Joseph A. Leal.[15] These data clearly demonstrate a familiar pattern in the study of immigration—a male establishes a "beachhead" in a new area, secures employment and housing, and then summons relatives once work is readily available.

LABOR TRENDS

A 1917 article from the *Fort Worth Record* explores the extent to which Fort Worth was a collection and shipping point for Mexican labor to other parts of the country.

> Demand on labor grows as many Mexicans move. Northern rush of cheap workmen and literacy test will improve the working conditions in Texas.
>
> More than 2,000 Mexicans have been shipped from Fort Worth to points in Pennsylvania and other northern cities within the last few weeks, in the opinion of Immigration Inspector W. H. Robb.
>
> By far the larger percentage of these Mexicans have gone to the iron works in Pennsylvania, Robb said, where they are given an average wage of $2.10 per day. On the railroads in that section they also receive a wage of from $1.50 to $1.80 a day. Five hundred Mexicans were shipped to the Pennsylvania iron sections at one time a few days ago, it was announced.
>
> In view of the fact that the literacy test to the immigration law

becomes effective on May 1, Robb is of the opinion that the extensive immigration of common labor from this section to other sections of the country will most probably result in a greater demand for white labor on the railroads and the farms here, with a consequent increase in wages. He points out that the average Mexican is satisfied at low wages, and never kicks at paying exorbitant prices at the commissary for his provisions. He predicts that this condition will not suit the average white laborer and for this reason the railroads will be forced to raise wages on the sections. The present average pay for section hands amounts to only about $1.50 per day. A few years ago it was not more that $1.20 on an average.

In the opinion of those who have made a close study of the situation at least 90 per cent of the immigration from Mexico and Italy will be cut off after the literacy test becomes effective. Robb asserts that these two nationalities furnish practically all the common labor used by the railroads and when it is no longer available they will be forced to raise prices and employ white labor.

He [Robb] predicts that the foreign born population of Fort Worth will be perceptibly reduced in a short time after the literacy provision becomes operative. At this time, according to statistics gathered by him, it amounts to about 12 per cent of the total population. He points out that many of those of foreign birth are returning to their native heath after having remained in this country for a few months and after having made a small "stake"[.] This, coupled with the heavy exportation of labor to the northern states, will cause an era of greater prosperity and higher wages for the American working man, he believes.[16]

This article offers a window to the past, providing a wealth of information on such issues as availability of jobs, wages, job mobility, constraints facing immigrants, as well as domestic attitudes regarding foreigners. The fact that so many different rail lines converged upon this North Texas city gave it a huge advantage as a collection point for cheap labor from all over the Southwest.

"More than 2,000 Mexicans have been shipped . . ." sounds as if they were dealing in a commonly-traded commodity, rather than people. Perhaps anticipating the inevitable increase in the demand for labor, the article appeared just two weeks before President Woodrow Wilson's war message before Congress on April 2, 1917.

When Immigration Inspector Robb stated that "the average Mexican is satisfied at low wages, and never kicks at paying exorbitant prices at the commissary for his provisions," he was voicing a widely held perception of Mexican migrants as malleable, compliant, and submissive—hard workers who rarely complained. Undoubtedly there were many who fit this description, perhaps because most had experienced a life marked by even greater hardships in Mexico.

Yet not all Mexicanos were as compliant and submissive as the popular stereotype. The following article demonstrates the willingness of Fort Worth's Mexican workers to risk losing their jobs to increase their pay and reduce the number of hours worked per day. Although not wishing to cause trouble in an alien land, Mexicanos nevertheless found it necessary at times to be more assertive to protect their rights.[17]

Approximately 100 pipe fitters and helpers walked out on strike at the Home Oil and Refining Company plant Friday afternoon. Higher wage scales were demanded by both classes. The present scale of pipe fitters is $6 per day; they asked for $7. The scale of the helpers is $4 per day and they asked for $5.

All Mexican labor at the plant also went out on strike, demanding increased wages from the Hedrick Construction Company. The Mexicans, now being paid 37 cents per hour and working nine hours per day, demanded an eight-hour day at 45 cents per hour.[18]

In the years immediately following World War I, when millions of American soldiers were returning from Europe, the demand for foreign labor dropped markedly. As the economy slowed down and jobs became scarce, nativism and xenophobia rose to high levels amidst an atmosphere charged with the resurgence of the Ku Klux Klan and widespread calls for immigration restrictions and deportation of foreigners. Local concerns are reflected in the following article.

A telegram concerning the Mexican relief policy adopted by the city of Fort Worth was sent to Alvaro Obregón, Pres. of Mexico, by Mayor Cockrell Tuesday. The telegram was sent to Obregón, as it is desired to keep in touch with Mexican authorities, hoping to speed up deportation from Fort Worth.

A trainload of 250 Mexicans, men, women and children, is expected to leave for Laredo tonight. Another trainload will probably follow Wednesday. The Fort Worth Welfare Assn. received $1,300 from the Mexican Government Tuesday. This [was] the sum the association has spent in relief work among Mexicans here and was furnished by the city. It will be returned to the municipal treasury.

The Mexicans who reported to Edward's Park Monday for the work and eat program adopted by the Municipal authorities will be more than doubled within two days. Robb stated that men will be excluded from the bread line at Wesley House, the food distribution center for the Mexican Relief work, after today. This act will cause many of the men to go to work . . . .

Regulation army tents have been erected in the park as quarters for the Mexicans. Many of them returned to their homes, Monday, however, carrying their half loaves with them, along with the other rations. American employees of the Park Department declare the Mexicans are willing workers . . . .[19]

Racism has always been a major obstacle to the progress of any minority. A "Jim Crow" mentality existed in many regions of the country before the Civil Rights era of the 1960s and manifested itself through both blatant and subtle policies of segregation and discrimination. Fort Worth was no exception. During the 1930s, the Fort Worth city telephone book listed white and colored business establishments separately. For example, all the white barbers are grouped together under the heading "Barbers;" there was a separate heading for "Colored Barbers." While separate headings did not exist for "Mexican" businesses and Hispanics were not barred from owning businesses, there did appear to be an unwritten understanding as to the limits or boundaries within which those businesses could be set up and operated. These widely understood geographic limitations dictated that Hispanic businesses remain within the confines of the barrios. With the exception of one popular Mexican restaurant on Camp Bowie Boulevard, all other establishments observed the unwritten rule. In addition, Mexicans felt that they were not to venture out of their barrios, unless they were working for an Anglo employer, at the risk of bodily harm. North Side Mexicanos could not cross North Main Street unless they were working, for otherwise Anglo gangs would attack them.[20]

At the start of the roaring twenties, Fort Worth served Texas and the Southwest as an extensive marketplace for Mexican labor. The following article demonstrates the extent to which Mexicanos flocked to Cowtown in hope of being employed somewhere in the United States.

A week ago there were around 3000 Mexicans awaiting jobs down in Little Mexico. Now there are but 500.

These are the estimates of Juan Flores, who operates a prominent Mexican labor bureau at 5th and Calhoun sts.

There's been a dimunition [sic] because beet field labor demands from Colorado, Wyoming, and Nebraska have gulped up hundreds of the peóns, who centered here from points all over Texas and Mexico.

But right now demands for the single men—and it's mostly they who make up the pack that's marking time—has fallen off and the demand for families perceptibly quickened, says Flores.

But it won't be long ere [sic] the available families will be exhausted the agent predicts. Then the single men will have their chance. However, many aren't waiting for the Fort Worth bureaus to call them, Flores said. They're moving on to Kansas City at their own expense.

Others have dismissed the beet field entirely and are waiting for jobs when cotton chopping starts in Tarrant-co two weeks or so hence.

The influx hasn't stopped according to Flores. He estimates from 25 to 50 are pouring in each day.[21]

Juan Flores did not operate the only Hispanic employment service (5th and

Calhoun) in town during the 1920s. The demand for cheap, reliable labor necessitated the presence of several employment agencies devoted solely to channeling Mexican laborers into other regions of the country. Eduardo Aldrete had his office at 215 East 14th Street, and Manuel Robles ran his agency from 210 East 12th Street.[22]

Slowdowns in an economy, especially during an era of post-war readjustments, typically provoke nativist sentiments. Anxiety about being overrun by foreign groups soon surfaced, as seen in the following 1927 article from the *Star-Telegram*.

Federal probe of the reported wholesale influx of Mexicans into Fort Worth began Thursday morning.

United States District Attorney Henry Zweifel, who is conducting the investigation, declared that Chief of Police Lee called on him during the morning and asked for the probe of the asserted dumping of Mexicans in Fort Worth.

In recent weeks, it has been charged, hundreds of peóns have been brought into this city. Zweifel said Lee told him many of the Mexicans had entered this country without passports and that there was an organized plan in operation of bringing the Mexicans into this section on false pretenses that jobs awaited them . . . .[23]

A NEW INDUSTRY ARISES

In 1904 the South Side received a considerable boost with the establishment of a new industry—the Bolt Works, a small nut-and-bolt manufacturing facility located on Hemphill Street. That same year one of the charter investors bought out the other stockholders and became sole owner of what grew into Texas Rolling Mills. By 1905, George W. Armstrong purchased rolling-mill equipment, making his company the first of its kind in the Southwest.[24]

Initially the railroads were the biggest customers of Armstrong's Texas Rolling Mills, but the advent of the automobile completely revolutionized the entire transportation industry. The construction of streets, roads, and highways demanded certain steel products, especially reinforcing bars. Armstrong's repeated efforts to lobby the Texas State Highway Department for new business paid off, and Texas Rolling Mills began selling reinforcing bars to the State of Texas for use in highway construction.[25]

With a marked increase in both domestic and foreign competition and the subsequent fall in the demand for steel, the post-World War I era brought a significant downturn in the volume of business, and Armstrong declared bankruptcy in 1923. In the same year an old friend, Texas industrialist John H. Kirby, bought Armstrong's properties in Fort Worth and Mississippi. Kirby then reorganized Texas Rolling Mills as Texas Steel Company and made George W. Armstrong manager of his former properties.

By the 1920s there were Mexicanos working for Texas Steel Company. Over the years their numbers increased steadily, reflecting Armstrong's preference for a steady and dependable work force. Mexicanos who worked for *La Fundición* lived in sixteen company houses located immediately across from the plant on Alice, May, and Pafford streets. The company also built houses on Fogg Street that were referred to as "*las casitas amarillas*" (the little yellow houses).[26]

Since 1920, Armstrong's oldest son, Allen, had worked for the Mexican Gulf Oil Company in Tampico, Mexico. At the end of the 1920s, Allen was appointed secretary of the Association of Producers of Petroleum in Mexico, a lobbying group representing the interests of American oil companies. In this capacity, he became familiar with many facets of Mexico's economy and politics and reported to his father on conditions there. Allen returned to Fort Worth with his family to work at Texas Steel Company in 1937. His fluency in Spanish was a real asset in dealing with an increasingly Mexican workforce. Another son, George, Jr., remained closer to home, to help his father manage his Mississippi holdings and other interests. George, Jr., assumed management of Texas Steel Company in 1934.[27]

The abundant volume of business generated by the World War II finally made Texas Steel Company a profitable operation. From 1941 through 1945 Texas Steel was awarded contracts from the army and navy to manufacture mortar shells. This tremendous surge in business provided the capital for expansion for the next two decades, and in turn led to increases in the hiring of more personnel, especially Mexicanos.[28]

Compared to conditions in Mexico, life in Fort Worth proved bearable in spite of long hours, hard work, paltry wages, and substandard housing. While a few people longed to return, most took comfort in the stability and opportunity for employment available in their newly adopted country. A network of relatives and friends beckoned many to come to Fort Worth's various Hispanic enclaves. The networks served to aid newly arrived kinfolk in securing jobs and housing. Once individuals had established themselves as reliable employees, no matter in what industries, Anglo supervisors often asked these workers if they could recommend a friend or relative to fill open positions. Newly arrived immigrants usually stayed with relatives or friends until they could support themselves.

Resilience was the quality that allowed Mexicans in Fort Worth to persist under the worst of conditions. As historian Arnoldo De León observed:

> To argue that the decade wrought disorientation and devastation distorts history and does a disservice to a community that proved resilient. As other people in other places and times have done, residents of the colonia took stock of adversity and kept going. . . . In the 1930s, indeed, a sizeable portion came to look to the United States as their home instead of condemning it for the poverty and misery which accompanied the 1930s.[29]

THE RISE OF THE ENTREPRENEURIAL CLASS

Having enough money to ride out the first few lean years in America was difficult enough for Mexicanos; amassing enough to start a small business was almost hopeless. With the catastrophic effects of the Great Depression, the 1930s proved to be one of the worst possible times to consider self-employment. Most Hispanics had arrived from Mexico or other parts of Texas with little money and were forced to seek employment wherever they could find it. Low wages and long hours left little time to devote to starting and maintaining independent ventures. Some worked for years before being able to scrape together enough money to start a business. Local banking institutions were not in the habit of approving loans to people without established credit, let alone poor Mexican immigrants.

Education proved to be yet another barrier. With few exceptions, most people arriving from Mexico during the first thirty years of the twentieth century came with little or no formal education. Most possessed skills associated with farming, ranching, butchering, or baking. These skills, together with a language barrier and a lack of capital, dictated that they work for someone else. In Fort Worth, nothing suited Mexicanos better than to work for any of the various slaughter and packing houses that dotted the North Side. Once established in any one of Fort Worth's many barrios, the children of these workers had an opportunity to attend school, but before World War II, few went past the sixth grade. The pressing need to help their parents forced children to earn a living and help with household expenses, either by working in a family-run business, running errands, shining shoes, or by having a paper route. Hence, most were content to be able simply to read, write, and count. When asked by his grandson why he did not continue on to high school in order to get a better job, Mario Trujillo responded, "It did not matter how much education you had, you'd wind up doing manual labor. You didn't stand a chance if you were Mexican."[30] For all these reasons, most Mexicans did not place a high value on or give priority to education. Yet, despite barriers of racial prejudice and lack of money and education, small enterprises did spring up in the various Hispanic neighborhoods of Fort Worth.

Because of capital, language, educational, and geographic limitations, Hispanic businesses begun before or during the 1930s consisted of small mom-and-pop establishments usually located within or in front of the family home. Creating extra income in order to supplement meager wages motivated some enterprising individuals to consider going into business for themselves. For others, the skills they had acquired in Mexico such as running small grocery stores, butcher shops, or bakeries, gave them the incentive to begin similar operations in their new surroundings. A few eventually became successful restaurateurs at the insistence and encouragement of friends or acquaintances who had sampled their cooking.

At first, Hispanics faced little or no competition to the small businesses they established within their own little enclaves. Virtually all of these concerns gave credit to neighborhood families for essential goods. All this changed by the mid-1930s when large chain stores like Safeway, which offered cheaper items on a cash-only basis, moved into the territory of small neighborhood stores. According to sociologist David Montejano, "the introduction of 'cash and carry' chain stores throughout Texas in the early twentieth century, for example, put credit stores on the defensive, for goods purchased in cash-and-carry stores like Piggly Wiggly and J. C. Penney were cheaper than those in credit stores."[31] The larger chain stores therefore had a severe effect on Hispanic small businesses. Within a few years, many Hispanic small business owners found themselves unable to meet the competition of these chain stores, and began to fold.

THE GREAT DEPRESSION

Fort Worth's economy suffered when ranchers began to send their cows to market on the trains, rather than the trails—affecting most profoundly the poorest ranks of society. It wasn't until the turn of the twentieth century, when B.B. Paddock, editor of the *Daily Democrat*, called upon the city to industrialize in order to diversify its economic base that a more stable climate emerged. Paddock's farsightedness led to the development of the packing plants, the utilities, the Fort Worth Brewing Company, and a host of other industries that increased the number of jobs in the city.[32] But the 1930s were to have a shattering effect on Mexicanos.

The stock market crash in October 1929 heralded the arrival of the Great Depression. Between 1931 and 1934, the Fort Worth City Council appropriated money for emergency services and soup kitchens. In 1933 the council applied for federal aid to establish public works projects.[33] Over fifteen million dollars of New Deal[34] money helped to construct the Ballinger and Daggett Street overpasses, improve Rosedale Street, provide a lighting system for the municipal airport, and build a new city hall, library, and the Will Rogers Memorial Auditorium and Coliseum complex.[35] While most of this work was given to needy Anglos, some Mexicanos and African Americans also participated in the road and construction crews.

During the Depression, the number of people (mainly men) scrambling for fewer and fewer jobs created an atmosphere in which some Anglos advocated the deportation and repatriation of Mexican citizens, especially in rural areas where drought and plummeting crop prices took a heavy toll. Many Mexicanos in Fort Worth, with good jobs and children who had been born in the United States, refused to leave. When immigration and naturalization officials intimidated the head of one household in the North Side, the Mexicano boldly retorted, "I'm coming back, so come back in thirty days and get me again." The government officials gave up on the spot and moved on.[36]

Of the estimated 5,000 Mexicanos who lived in Fort Worth in 1930, almost half returned to their homeland. Decisions to leave centered on the difficulty of finding work, the intimidation of some disgruntled Anglos, and offers of jobs and land from the Mexican government. Approximately 250,000 men, women, and children left Texas during the 1930s, leaving a Mexican-Texan population of at least 500,000.[37]

Many Mexicanos faced hardship and danger to come to America. Once they arrived, however, they sometimes found life was far from ideal. Jobs were often scarce and low-paying. Mexicans were forced to move frequently in search of better-paying jobs or more hospitable communities. Fort Worth in the late nineteenth and early twentieth centuries proffered a unique confluence of industries—cattle, steel, and railroads—which were incentives for immigrants to make Fort Worth their home. In the stories of these early immigrants lies the foundation of the vibrant community of Mexican Fort Worth.

STORIES FROM THE BARRIOS

The oldest Hispanic-owned restaurant still in operation, The Original Mexican Eats Café, opened for business in 1926 at 4713 Camp Bowie Boulevard. Begun by Gerónimo and Lola (San Miguel) Piñeda, the business was unique in that it was not located within any of the Hispanic enclaves in the city.

Born in Barcelona, Spain, in 1871, Gerónimo Piñeda served in his country's army for twelve years[38] until discharged in August 1898, about the time the Spanish-American War ended. He made his way to the United States where he eventually secured a job selling insurance in South Texas.[39] Lola San Miguel, whose parents hailed from Múzquiz, Coahuila, Mexico, was born in Laredo, Texas, on December 18, 1881. Gerónimo and Lola were married in Austin, Texas, on April 29, 1911.[40]

While in Austin, Lola gave birth to two daughters, Eva in 1912, and Ruth in 1914. Gerónimo Piñeda kept traveling from town to town, selling insurance, until the early 1920s when he moved his family to Waco and used their savings to start a restaurant. They opened the Texas Café in downtown Waco; it was successful enough to allow them to build a home and purchase an automobile with their profits. The 1920s boom in business allowed the Piñedas to open a second restaurant called the Villa Valencia. Unfortunately the good times did not last. In 1929, about the same time that Eva graduated as valedictorian of her class at Waco High School, the stock market crashed. Overextended with payments for their home, car, and restaurants, the Piñedas lost everything for which they had worked. Determined to start anew, the family moved to Fort Worth in 1930 to open a new restaurant, this time using borrowed funds.[41]

Having lost all his capital, Gerónimo could not get a loan from a bank to finance his business and resorted to borrowing funds from a gambler. Although it took several years to repay the loan, Gerónimo and Lola succeeded in establishing their new restaurant—The Original Mexican Eats Café. The restaurant began with one room and a kitchen separated by a door. Between the two rooms was a window through which plates were passed. During the Depression, there were just two employees—a cook and a busboy. Patrons ordered at the window and when their order was ready, they carried their own plates to the table. When they were finished, a busboy cleaned up. Eventually expanding to accommodate seventy-eight patrons, The Original opened every day for lunch and dinner.[42] Lola San Miguel Piñeda served her mother's traditional northern Mexico recipes. At first the entire family waited on customers, but as the volume of business grew they hired Mexicanos as waiters. Over the years former waiters at the Original moved on and opened their own restaurants, e.g., Jim Martínez from Del Rio, Manuel Marroquín (Casa Linda), and Sam Becera.[43]

Because they have had the same cooks for many years, the Original has had remarkable consistency in food quality. Mrs. Inés Richardson worked there thirty years or more and was personally instructed by Ruth Piñeda in all aspects of food preparation and presentation. She mentioned that the Piñedas were strict and very businesslike in their dealings with all employees.

In spite of the Great Depression, the Piñedas soon developed a thriving business and drew a large Anglo clientele that included the cream of Fort Worth society—the Leonards, the Moncriefs, and the Carters. Franklin Delano Roosevelt's son, Elliott, regularly dined at the Original during the late 1930s.

(c. 1940) Gerónimo, Lola (San Miguel), and daughter Ruth in front of their home, not far from their restaurant, the Original Mexican Eats Café. *Photo courtesy of John J. Kane.*

Elliott lived in Benbrook with his new bride, Fort Worth socialite Ruth Googins, and managed his radio and ranching interests in the area.[44] A regular customer, Elliott always ordered one enchilada, one taco, and one chalupa without the usual side order of refried beans and rice. The Piñedas permanently dubbed this combination plate "the Roosevelt Special" in his honor, and it is still on the menu today. Other well-known personalities who have visited and tasted Lola Piñeda's recipes include actor Jimmy Stewart and former Speaker of the House Jim Wright.[45]

In the late 1930s, the Piñeda family bought a home at 1709 Ashland Avenue, in the Arlington Heights subdivision. Located within walking distance of the restaurant, the comfortable residence allowed the older Piñedas the opportunity to come home and take a restful nap after the frenzied lunch business. In 1940, when everything seemed to be going well for the family, Gerónimo Piñeda suddenly developed stomach cancer. He passed away on January 18, 1941, at the age of sixty-nine, leaving Lola Piñeda and her daughter Ruth to manage the restaurant. As a child, Ruth was incapacitated with rheumatic fever, a condition that seriously impaired her heart valves and limited her activity. The constant companion to her mother, Ruth remained single all her life.[46]

Eva, meanwhile, had found employment as a bookkeeper at the downtown Stein's Credit Jewelers. In November of 1942 Eva met John J. Kane at a USO reception at the Texas Hotel. Kane was a United States Marine stationed at Eagle Mountain Lake, undergoing training as a navigator with the glider squadron. Formerly of Holyoke, Massachusetts, the young serviceman began a courtship, and the couple married on May 12, 1943.[47] Eva, who learned to cook from her mother, prepared superb *menudo*, flour tortillas, and hogshead tamales that melted in the mouth at *Noche Buena*, family members recall. [48]

In the early 1960s Lola and Ruth decided to sell the restaurant to their accountant, Gordon Sheffield, and his wife, Louise. Ruth, who had suffered so long from ill health, passed away at the age of fifty-two on September 12, 1966. Surviving both her husband and daughter, Lola Piñeda died on October 2, 1974, at the age of ninety-three. [49]

The Sheffields operated the restaurant until August 1972 when they sold it to Joe Holton (Louise's son by a previous marriage).[50] At first Holton hated the restaurant business, but the Original was so profitable that now he would never consider disposing of it because one "never sells a goose that lays golden eggs." [51] Today the restaurant serves about seven hundred to a thousand customers per day, maintains a staff of about thirty-six, and has been expanded to include two more dining rooms and a bar.[52]

◆   ◆   ◆

The oldest bakery in the North Side belonged to Gregorio Esparza, Sr., who was born in 1899 in San Luis Potosí, where he had worked as a baker in his youth. In 1921, Esparza emigrated to Dallas to escape the Mexican Revolution. He worked at the Adolphus Hotel as a busboy and in 1924 met and married the former Consuelo Cabello. The couple eventually had four children: Alice, Mara, Gregorio, Jr., and Socorro. In 1927, they moved to Fort Worth's North Side, where Gregorio set up a bakery on Northeast 23rd and North Commerce streets. Esparza later moved diagonally across Northeast 23rd Street to establish a small grocery store still in operation today. The store sold not only freshly baked goods and basic staples but also carried an array of herbs and spices used as *remedios caseros* (home remedies) for a variety of ailments. Esparza's stock was invaluable to North Side residents who lacked the funds to pay doctors.[53]

◆ ◆ ◆

Joe T. García's, the most famous Hispanic enterprise to emerge out of the old North Side, has an interesting history. José Tafolla García, born March 5, 1898, in La Piedad, Michoacán, Mexico, was the only child of Refugio Tafolla and María García.[54] Refugio owned a *carnicería* (meat market) and a ranch, on which he raised cattle, chickens, wheat, corn, and *maismilo* (chicken feed). When Joe T. was only three months old, his father passed away, leaving his mother and uncle, Juan Saldaña García, responsible for operating the ranch and meat market. Tío (Uncle) Juan raised Joe T. and in 1912 brought him to Fort Worth, fleeing the Mexican Revolution. They had been working at the Bluebonnet Packing House for a year when they received news of the death of Joe T.'s mother. For many years, García dreamed of one day returning to his *patria*, and he always harbored ambivalent feelings about living in the United States. He felt American values and morals were inferior to those more traditional ones found back in his *tierra*.[55] Nevertheless, sometime in the early 1920s, when he had saved enough money to start a business, Uncle Juan Saldaña García opened a small grocery store and meat market on the southeast corner of Northeast 22nd and North Calhoun streets.

In 1929, Tío Juan returned to Mexico leaving his nephew Joe T., now thirty-one, in charge of the business. By this time, Joe had married Jesusa ("Mama Sus") Torres and produced several children. In addition to groceries, the store brought truckloads of pottery from Guanajuato, Mexico—*casuelas, jarros marranitos* (piggy banks), pots, and vases—to sell. The store also stocked many herbs and spices such as *manzanilla* (used to treat upset stomach and colic), *canela* (cinnamon for making tea and for sweet bread flavoring), *anise* (for bread), and *gordo lobo* (an herb good for the kidneys). The dry herbs and spices came from Mexico, but the fresh ones were raised on ranchitos around Fort Worth. Straw hats and vanilla also came from Mexico, and hats for children proved to be the best sellers.[56] Joe T.'s daughter, Hope, as astute a businessperson as her father, managed the grocery store until 1955 (Joe T. passed away in 1953), when the decision was made to close it.

In the early 1930s, Joe T. García had begun to sell meat wholesale, using a truck to deliver beef to Leonards' Everybody's Store downtown on First and Throckmorton streets. He also made deliveries to the police department and to many small grocery stores. The wholesale meat operation continued until the mid-1930s, when Joe T. decided that the time was right to open a restaurant.[57]

Mama Sus had been serving hot Mexican food to the workers of the City Packing Company, located right across the street from the store. The delicious homemade food drew rave comments, which gave Joe T. the idea of opening a restaurant. Several years later, in the early 1930s, Joe T. sold the Northeast 22nd and North Calhoun property to Antonio ("El Arabe") and moved the operation that he now called "Joe's Place" one block east to 2140 North Commerce, located on the southeast corner of Northeast 22nd and North Commerce (diagonally opposite the restaurant's present-day location).[58]

On July 4, 1935, Joe T. García, Mama Sus, and their five children, Josephine,

1935 grand opening of Joe T. García's, with his four daughters ready to assist. *Photo courtesy of Hope García Lancarte and Mary García Christian.*

(c. early-1950s) Joe T. García showing Texas Governor Allan Shivers a sample of his barbecuing skills. *Photo courtesy of Hope García Lancarte and Mary García Christian.*

Ralph, Pauline, Mary, and Hope, opened the family restaurant for business under the name "Joe T. García's." The building sagged so badly it had been condemned, but the family repaired it, cleaned it up, and gave it a new coat of paint. They lived in the back and operated the restaurant in the front of their home. The restaurant consisted of a kitchen and a large room with eight tables—two tables for six and six tables for four persons. Both kitchen and dining room were kept clean and spotless under Mama Sus' close supervision. Joe T. and his daughters all pitched in to help Mama Sus prepare and serve the hot dishes, such as *carne de chile adobada*, enchiladas, tacos, and *tamales de puerco y de dulce*. These dishes are traditional Michoacán-style from Mama Sus's native state.[59]

Joe T. García even experimented with Texas chili and southern-style barbeque recipes obtained from his African American friend, Stanley Woodard. Stanley's brother, an excellent chef, owned Jack's Barbeque on Angle Street. Joe T. added his own special Mexican spices to the recipe and served barbequed brisket, ribs, chicken, and turkey. Every Thanksgiving, Joe T. prepared at least fifty turkeys for the Fort Worth Boat Club. He supervised the slow cooking in a huge, specially built grill, a process that took from 8:00 P.M. until 8:00 A.M.[60]

García could very well have been the first Mexicano who actively courted Anglo business. To promote his restaurant Joe T. asked daughter Mary to take sample dishes to the downtown offices of lawyers, judges, and bankers. Along with the Mexican food, Mary gave each prospective customer a complimentary flower, usually a cape jasmine. Joe T. also prepared special banquets and invited the public to sample his dishes, in part to demonstrate his gratitude for their continuing patronage. All these efforts, especially word-of-mouth recommenda-

Pauline and Hope García proudly displaying a platter full of delicious *enchiladas* at Joe T. García's. *Photo courtesy of Hope García Lancarte and Mary García Christian.*

tions, paid off and helped elevate Joe T. García's to the status of a premier Fort Worth institution and landmark.[61]

The family of Joe T. García was successful because they served a quality product, marketed it aggressively, and were always present to ensure good service. Joe T. García succeeded because he was gregarious, outgoing, and a good businessman who know how to treat his customers and keep track of expenses. There is an old saying in Spanish, *"bajo el ojo del dueño engorda el caballo,"* which literally means, "under the eye of the owner the horse fattens." In plain English, this old proverb means that a business will prosper if the owner is present, alert, and working hard. Today, the third and fourth generations of Garcías are still personally involved in the business. Esperanza's, a restaurant and bakery serving Mexican-style breakfast and lunch, opened in the early 1980s. At least three family members are involved in the daily operations of this enterprise. Many in Fort Worth consider Joe T.'s the best Mexican restaurant in the entire city.

◆   ◆   ◆

Diagonally across from where Joe T. García and his uncle established their famous restaurant on Northeast 22nd and North Calhoun Streets, Orencio and Elisa Cagigal tore down two shotgun houses[62] and built a two-story home with a little grocery store in front.

Orencio Doce Cagigal, born in September 1885 in Palencia, Spain, in the northern Basque country, came from a family that included five boys and two sisters—María and Francisca ("Paca").[63] In 1905, when Orencio was twenty, he left Spain with his older sister, Francisca, her husband, and their daughter Lisinia, bound for Havana, Cuba.[64] After a few years, they moved to Mexico City for a short while before finally settling in northern Mexico. In 1912, he met Elisa Acuña, the daughter of Simón Acuña, a traveling merchant who used a horse and buggy and was based at La Rosita, Nuevo León.[65] Orencio and Elisa married in 1915 in San Antonio, Texas. After a short stay in San Antonio, the couple moved near Thurber, Texas, where Orencio worked in the mines at Strawn and at Beargram. It was in this community that Elisa gave birth to three of her four sons: Artemio, 1917; Orencio, Jr., 1919; and, Simon, 1921. In 1922 Orencio moved his young family to Fort Worth, where a fourth son, Francisco, was born in 1924. A

(April 1965) Fiftieth wedding anniversary of Orencio and Elisa Cagigal, celebrated by their children. L to R: Simon, Orencio, Jr., Orencio, Sr., Elisa (Acuña , Artemio ("Temo"), and Frank. *Photo courtesy of Frank and Maggie Cagigal.*

carpenter by trade, Orencio plied his craft throughout the North Side neighborhoods[66] while his wife ran their newly built store at 2201 North Calhoun Street.[67]

Elisa took after her business-minded father and not only managed the store but also cooked and sold hot lunches, usually *guisos* (stews) and vegetables, to the workers of the City Packing Company located across the street. In addition to groceries and meals, Elisa sold sodas for two cents, several flavors of ice cream, and *raspas* (snow cones with fruit flavoring). Elisa had a small booklet (*libreta*) in which she carefully recorded the purchases on account—most people bought from her on credit. Although she never learned English well, Elisa somehow managed to communicate with the Anglo vendors who regularly called on her store. Orencio Doce Cagigal passed away in 1965 at the age of eighty; Elisa survived him by twenty-two years, passing away at the age of ninety-three in 1987. [68]

◆   ◆   ◆

One of Fort Worth's most long-lived Mexican barbershops was owned by Amador F. Gutiérrez. Amador was born in 1896 in Chihuahua, Mexico, where his father owned a *tienda de abarrotes* (grocery store). Between 1905 and 1910 Gutiérrez arrived in El Paso, Texas, in search of employment. He worked for the Texas & Pacific Railroad until 1915, when he and his new bride of one year, Paula García, moved to Fort Worth's North Side. Gutiérrez worked for Swift and Company preparing and salting bacon until his retirement in 1946. Amador and Paula raised seven children—Celia, Esther, Amador G., Gilberto, Leonor, Ernesto, and Raymundo.[69]

Even while working for Swift and Company during the day, Amador also operated his own barbershop at 2221 North Commerce, on the corner of Northeast 23rd and North Commerce (across the street from the Esparza Grocery). He conducted this "moonlighting" operation in the late afternoons and evenings after his regular job at Swift in order to earn extra income. The barbershop was in a room fourteen by twenty feet, and the family home was located in the rear of the shop. In 1945, after his retirement from Swift, Gutiérrez moved his barbershop to a better location at 1424 North Main Street. As the barbershop was actually the side room of Rafael ("Ralph") Y. Valle's pool hall, Gutiérrez had greater visibility and attracted more walk-in traffic.[70] Amador's clientele remained with him until his death on September 7, 1962.[71]

◆   ◆   ◆

Born on July 4, 1921, in Fort Worth, Alejandro Gallegos, Sr., inherited a love for doing business from his parents. During the first decade of the twentieth century, his father, Vicente Gallegos, began his career selling merchandise out of a wagon. Soon tiring of this itinerant life, Vicente opened a butcher shop with his brother. He quickly expanded the business to include general merchandise as well as homemade *masa* and tortillas.[72]

Around 1910 Vicente Gallegos married Rosa Sánchez, who was born in 1886 in Guadalajara, Jalisco, Mexico. Even though her family owned and operated a successful meat market, Rosa had always longed to move to the United States. Vicente and Rosa raised a family that included Benjamin, Ester, Catalina, Alfredo, Vicente, Jr., and Alejandro.[73]

During the Mexican Revolution the store burned down and Vicente moved to another location to establish a second store, one that sold *abarrotes* (groceries). This store was burned down as well, and his family decided it was time to leave Mexico and head north. After passing through Laredo, Texas, the family made its way to Fort Worth in June 1918 to meet Rosa's uncle-in-law, Bernardino Santoyo, a cobbler. [74]

Vicente found work as a bricklayer. He helped to build the Santa Fe Railroad terminal and the Texas Hotel. Vicente also set up a little grocery store and *pandería* (bakery) on Belknap Street. In 1924, the Gallegos family bought a house at 1400 North Calhoun on the North Side, where they established a grocery store, a meat market, and bakery. Vicente also set up a mill for making tortilla *masa* from ground corn and hired four ladies to make fresh tortillas to sell. In 1925, Gallegos bought a new truck for the large deliveries he made each day. In the Prohibition era, Vicente even indulged in a little bootlegging to help make ends meet.[75]

In 1940 the Texas Hotel kitchen staff included Alejandro Gallegos, Sr., (far left) and Salvador Gonzalez, Jr. (fourth from left). Alejandro's two sons, Alex, Jr., and Alfredo own Los Alamos Mexican restaurant. *Photo courtesy of Sara Barajas Gallegos.*

Rosa S. Gallegos passed away in 1927 and her husband, Vicente, died in 1933. Economic hardships at the height of the Great Depression made it difficult for the family to continue their house payments, and the First National Bank repossessed the home. The property was subsequently acquired by J. J. Domínguez, Sr., and it became the site for the *Mutualista San José*. Vicente's and Rosa's oldest child, Benjamin, soon left Fort Worth, but his brothers and sisters remained. Because the North Calhoun Street house was dear to them, the remaining Gallegos children tried repeatedly to buy it back but were unsuccessful. Instead, Alejandro and his siblings pitched in and purchased a home on the opposite side of the street at 1405 North Calhoun.[76]

In 1935, fourteen-year-old Alejandro began working at the downtown Texas Hotel as a dishwasher. Before long he was promoted to fry cook. Helping his siblings to make ends meet, Alejandro worked for the hotel until 1942, when he was called to active duty by the army. Before leaving Fort Worth Gallegos married Sara Barajas in June 1942. Born on January 25, 1920, in Dwight, Illinois, Sara Barajas Gallegos was the daughter of Librado Barajas and María Infante. Alejandro and Sara had six children over the next twenty years—Rosemary, 1942; Ester, 1944; Alex, Jr., 1953; Frankie, 1954, Alfred, 1956; and Robert, 1962.[77]

Within months of the December 7, 1941, Japanese surprise attack on Pearl Harbor, Alejandro Gallegos reported for desert training in California, expecting to be sent to North Africa. Instead, Alejandro was sent to England and participated in the massive D-Day invasion of June 6, 1944. During the amphibious landing, Gallegos received a concussion from the blast of a shell and was dispatched to England to recuperate in an army hospital. His wife, Sara, received a telegram informing her that he had been injured. Alejandro, unable to write any letters home during his six-month recuperation, was finally discharged. In November 1945 the Gallegos family was reunited.[78]

Alejandro Gallegos returned briefly to his old job at the Texas Hotel, but it was not long before he began planning to go into business for himself. In 1949 he rented a space at 1438 North Main Street, just south of the Marine Theater, from his friend Raymond Burciaga. Alejandro's brother Mike, who worked for General Motors in Michigan, lent him $200 to start the venture.[79] Relying on the recipes of his mother-in-law, María Infante Barajas, of Morelia, Michoacán,

Alejandro established a restaurant that he called La Villita. The business continued for ten years until a series of rent increases caused Gallegos to look for a property he could call his own. With additional loans, Alejandro planned the construction of his new restaurant, Los Alamos, just north of the Marine Theater,[80] and in 1959 the tin structure located on this corner was demolished to make room for Los Alamos. The particular block on which the restaurant was located was also home to a number of bars, and their patrons sometimes were involved in altercations. There were even a few killings. As a result, Alejandro closed Los Alamos by seven or eight in the evening in order that his customers might avoid the rowdy bar crowd.

The menu at Los Alamos featured standard entrees such as enchiladas, tacos, tostadas, and flautas,[81] all accompanied by rice and beans. Tamales and menudo, a typical Mexican soup consisting of tripe and hominy, were usually available as well.[82] Burritos (flour tortilla tacos) could be ordered with either *carne guisada con frijoles*, *chorizo con huevo*, *papas con huevos*, *machacado con huevo*, or *picadillo*.[83] However, the restaurant's specialty was the deliciously seasoned pork chops *rancheros*; the recipe was a closely guarded secret.

❖   ❖   ❖

Another restaurateur-to-be, Pedro Pulido, Sr., was born on August 11, 1907, near the town of Ecuándureo, Michoacán. At an early age Pulido helped his father, Dolores Pulido,[84] work the fields. Sharecroppers of some substantial acreage, young Pulido and his father raised corn on their *milpa* (small acreage of tillable land), half of which belonged to the hacienda de Ucácuaro. In 1925, at the age of eighteen, a friend of Pedro's told him about all the good jobs available in the United States. The friend gave him the name of some *renganches* (labor agents or contractors) located in the border town of Laredo, Texas, who would help him find work.[85]

When Pedro arrived in Laredo, the labor agents sent him to Montana to work for the Northern Pacific Railroad. Wearing his traditional clothing and *huaraches* in freezing weather, Pedro wound up assisting the cook of a road maintenance gang in Montana for about a year. As part of the obligation of being the eldest[86] child (there were nine siblings in all), Pedro sent most of his money to help support the rest of his family in Mexico. Montana was so far from home and so cold that Pedro decided to migrate south to Argyle,[87] Texas, where he lived for one year in a section house (railroad workers' housing) and worked on a railroad maintenance crew. In August 1927 he found a job working for the Texas & Pacific Railroad and moved to the Fort Worth barrio of *El Papalote*.[88] At the Texas & Pacific Railroad roundhouse, Pedro's responsibilities included washing the engines, filling them up with sand for traction, and loading them with coal (before the change to diesel). Pedro Pulido worked for the T&P for thirty-one years until his retirement in 1968. [89]

In 1935, Pedro Pulido married Dionicia Márquez, the daughter of Mauricio and Eufemia Cruz Márquez. Dionicia was born on April 9, 1911, in the small agricultural community of Lagos de Moreno, Jalisco. While his family was still in Mexico, Mauricio Márquez came to Texas and worked on a road crew for the Santa Fe Railroad. In 1919 he returned to Mexico to bring his family to Texas. Before finally settling in Fort Worth in 1930, the family followed jobs, continuously on the move, living mostly in section housing in places like Robstown, Mexia, Coolidge, and Eastland. Widowed since 1930 (she married in 1924 at the age of thirteen), Dionicia had three children—Vincent, Philip, and Shannon ("Chano") Pulido—whom Pedro adopted.[90]

From 1935 to 1941 Pedro, Dionicia, and their three sons rented a home on Presidio Street in the heart of *El Papalote*. The family grew to seven children in all with the birth of Mary in 1936, Pedro ("Pete"), Jr., in 1938, Rodolfo ("Rudy") in 1939, and Robert in 1941.[91] In 1941, the same year as Robert's birth, the Pulidos moved from *El Papalote* to the barrio that would forever be associated with them— *El TP*.[92]

The family purchased a roomy two-story home at 2921 Spring Street for $1,200. On the first floor were three bedrooms, two baths, a living room, and a kitchen; the large room on the second floor served as a dorm for the children. Although this house no longer exists, it was across the street from the original Pulido's restaurant. [93] Over the years, the Pulidos bought land and houses in the barrio to rent out for additional income. Pedro's family and other TP families attended the Catholic mission of San Mateo, the spiritual center of the barrio, established in 1941.

A veritable menagerie of animals populated the Pulidos' spacious backyard that sloped gradually to a creek.[94] Most of the time, there were two horses, four to five milk cows, and about fifty to sixty chickens. A reflection of his agricultural roots in Mexico, Pedro Pulido enjoyed raising these animals, and the money he received from the sale of his dairy products supplemented the family's income. Pedro also raised corn, onions, potatoes, squash, and jalapeño peppers. Twice a week Dionicia made forty to fifty little spheres[95] of Mexican *asadero* cheese from the cows' milk. The children made the rounds of the neighborhood selling the homemade cheese as well as milk, which was poured, unpasteurized, into re-usable quart milk bottles. Dionicia made and sold pork and chicken tamales and sold eggs by the dozen as well. [96]

The Pulido boys helped their father raise the animals. Stumbling out of bed every day at five, the brothers all took turns milking the cows. After a hearty breakfast of *papas con huevo* they pastured the cows wherever there was vacant land. One favorite field was the land on which the Ramada Inn is located today. The boys drove the cows to pasture, staked their ropes firmly in the ground to keep them from wandering, and dashed off to school.[97] After school, they led the cows back to the family's backyard and milked once more. The parents insisted that all the children complete their homework before their nine o'clock bedtime.[98]

The children also took turns delivering his favorite lunch to their father—*taquitos*,[99] which might contain *guiso de carne de puerco* (pork stew), *frijoles refritos* (refried beans), *chorizo con huevo* or *papas con huevo*. All the laborers, whether Anglo, African American, or Mexican, ate their lunches together, and so it did not take long for Pedro's fellow workers to notice, and envy, the delicious aromas coming from his lunch bag. They began bartering their desserts for his wife's mouthwatering tacos. The craving did not end at lunch. After work Anglos began calling at the Pulido home to purchase Mama Dionicia's freshly made tamales to take home for supper. [100] A quiet revolution was being unleashed—thanks to the Pulidos and others, Mexican food gained acceptance by Anglos and was well on its way to transforming the American culinary experience.

The idea of a restaurant began as an attempt to ensure the financial security of the second generation of Pulidos. In 1962, Robert Pulido married Carol

Rodríguez, and they soon began their family.[101] With plans for dental school derailed because of lack of funds, Robert began working for his brother, Pete, in his upholstery shop but did not earn enough to support his growing family adequately. To learn the restaurant business Robert apprenticed at El Chico restaurant on Berry and Lubbock streets managed by his brother-in-law, Edward Gámez. Edward Gámez taught the Pulidos all the important aspects of managing a restaurant. In 1965, family members began construction of a restaurant building using timbers salvaged from the dismantling of the Texas & Pacific roundhouse. Pete Pulido upholstered all of the booths.[102]

On July 1, 1966, the flagship restaurant on Spring Street was formally opened with all family members proudly present. While Pedro Pulido, Sr., still worked for the Texas & Pacific, the rest of the family ran the restaurant. Mama Dionicia and Robert handled all the cooking, and Carol and Mary took turns as cashiers and hostesses. Two teenage cousins from Mexico, George and Javier, worked as busboys, as did Tony de Anda, another cousin from Laredo. Pulido's Mexican restau-

The Pedro Pulido family at their tortilla factory. L to R: Rudy, Edward Gámez, Robert, Sr. (with glasses), Dionicia, and Pedro Pulido. The hard-working Pulidos exemplify the classic rags-to-riches American experience. Grandfather Pedro began working as a Texas & Pacific Railroad maintenance worker and opened the first Pulido's Mexican Restaurant in 1966. The entire Pulido family became involved in making their business the success it is today. *Photo courtesy of Rudy Pulido and Edward J. Gámez.*

rant started out as a family affair and that tradition continues today.[103]

The new restaurant was fortunate to have a good clientele from the beginning. Mexicanos and Anglos, primarily from the Arlington Heights section of Fort Worth, came in droves to patronize the establishment. Open for lunch and supper, the restaurant had an original seating capacity of about eighty. Early menu entrées included tamales de puerco, cheese and chicken enchiladas, and beef or chicken tacos—all served with refried beans and rice. For dessert, there were New Orleans-style pralines that Carol made fresh daily from her own personal recipe.[104]

Encouraged by the tremendous response to their first restaurant, the Pulidos decided in January 1967 to incorporate. The following month they opened their second restaurant on Highway 377. Restaurant number three opened in 1968 in Arlington, followed by number four on the Jacksboro Highway in 1969. Most of the units are managed by family members, including some who came from Mexico over the years. Pedro ("Don Pete") Pulido finally retired from his railroad[105] job in 1968 to help with the family business. Both he and his wife continued to report to work daily, until he was well over ninety and she was . . . well, never mind. [106]

Today the corporation that Pedro and Dionicia began encompasses thirteen area restaurants, tortilla and tamale factories,[107] and has about three hundred employees. In addition to supplying the needs of their own restaurants, the factories sell their products to other area restaurants as well. Chips made at the tortilla factory make their way to Reunion Arena and the Ballpark at Arlington. With Edward Gámez as chairman of the board and Robert Pulido, Sr., as president, the family enterprise boasts annual gross sales in excess of ten million dollars. [108] The family of a hard- working railroad laborer managed to succeed in making the American dream a reality.

◆   ◆   ◆

The Menchaca family's story is one of ability, coupled with determination, passed down from generation to generation. Anacleto ("Francisco") Menchaca was born in 1877 in the state of Michoacán. Starting as a peón working in agricultural fields, Francisco soon impressed his employer with his ability to break horses. But at the age of fifteen he left the fields of his *tierra* for work in the coal mines of New Mexico. After seven years in the coal mines, Francisco returned to his native land to care for his parents. His aptitude, experience, and confidence earned him a position as a *caporal* (foreman) on a large farm. This enhanced status allowed Francisco to dress well and to ride a good horse with silver trim on the saddle. Wherever he rode, self-assured Francisco attracted attention. [109]

In 1902, he married Romana Candelária de Várgas, who was born in 1887 in Pénjamo, Guanajuato. After four years in Mexico Francisco and Romana emigrated to Fort Worth. In 1906 the Katy Railroad hired him as foreman of a road crew. The Menchacas lived in *la sessión* (sidelined boxcars), where most of their ten children were born.[110] For a few years Francisco also worked for both Armour and Swift, arranging non-overlapping shifts with each employer.[111]

An independent-minded man, Francisco did not like working for others, and in 1919 he rented acreage between the West Fork of the Trinity River and

(c. 1945) Anacleto ("Francisco") Menchaca farmed the area of present-day Rockwood Park Golf Course and gained fame for his shrewd horse-trading abilities. The bulge on the top pocket of his overalls is the wad of money he always carried with him. *Photo courtesy of Leonard Menchaca.*

Jacksboro Highway[112] from a veterinarian named Cardona.[113] An excellent land-lord, Cardona built a four-room house for the growing Menchaca family On this river-bottom land Francisco planted wheat, onions, squash, sweet potatoes, beans, potatoes, melons, and two varieties of corn—one for animal and the other for human consumption. Francisco loved to negotiate the purchase of mixed-breed cattle to raise and sell. To assist him in taking care of his growing enterprise Menchaca hired Mexicanos from the North Side. Even Joe T. García worked for Francisco before he started his restaurant. Mexicanos soon came looking for work, and those who were hired lived in tents on the property.[114]

Using a one-horse wagon sons Juan and Leonard helped their father by selling surplus fruits and vegetables throughout the North Side's Anglo neigh-borhoods. The door-to-door peddling proved difficult because some Anglos displayed open hostility toward the boys. Once, when a Mexicano was killed downtown, an unruly crowd of North Side Anglo vigilantes proceeded toward the Menchaca home with the intention of stoning the family.

An Anglo lady who lived on Grand Avenue on a bluff overlooking the Menchaca homestead knew the family and succeeded in stopping the angry mob. "They are good people, leave them alone!" The crowd dissipated and a few weeks later the Menchaca family relocated to the North Side barrio.[115]

Francisco rented a shotgun house at 1213 North Grove Street and rented river-bottom land between North Grove and the Trinity River. The property was ideal for the Menchacas, because in the back of the house was a barn suitable for Francisco's dairy herd of forty Holsteins. Francisco's two brothers who lived in California urged him to relocate there, and in 1927 he sold everything except one milk cow and two horses. In the midst of these preparations to leave, the cou-ple's seven-year-old son, Santos, became ill and died. The wake was held at the Menchaca home.[116]

It seemed as if the family was destined for bad luck, for, hardly had they recovered from the death of Santos, when they lost their home and their life sav-ings. Francisco had purchased an organ from a friend to use as a bank, secreting all of his money in a hidden compartment. This included the money he had made selling his dairy herd for the move to California. Shortly after Santos' death the Menchacas returned from their fields to discover that their home had burned down. Initially the cause of the fire was thought to be a fallen candle, but in sifting through the ashes Francisco never found any evidence that his money had burned along with the organ. This led him to suspect that the fire had been started deliberately to cover up a robbery.[117]

Once the family settled into the house next door Francisco began negotiating for a new herd of dairy cows. To accommodate the seventy Holsteins just purchased, he leased both sides of river-bottom land between Samuels and North Grove streets. On the east side of the Trinity he planted milo maize for cattle feed. A natural-born trader Francisco also made money buying and selling livestock and with the profits from the dairy he provided well for his family throughout the decade of the Depression.[118]

Even before the start of World War II Francisco had found another source of income. Behind the dairy barn was a series of gravel pits where people had been dumping their trash. Francisco bought all of the pits and began to charge ten cents a load for dumping trash. Although people initially complained, Francisco called a city official who verified Menchaca's claim of ownership, posted a sign, and stopped the complaints. Just before the start of World War II Fort Worth City Inspector Grammar recommended the passing of a city ordinance allowing junked parked cars to be brought to people like Menchaca to be sold as scrap metal. The Japanese were buying all the scrap iron they could get their hands on. During the last years of the Great Depression Francisco hired Mexicanos like the Holguines, Ruperto García,[119] and Antonio and Luis Zapata to help him in the scrap metal business.[120]

The start of World War II heralded several changes for the Menchaca family. On December 7, 1941, Leonard was in basic training at Fort Sill, Oklahoma, when the Japanese attacked Pearl Harbor. His older brother, Juan, had moved to Colorado to pursue a career in painting. With both of his principal helpers gone Francisco could not continue leasing the river-bottom land; he sold his herd of Holsteins and quit the dairy business.[121]

On returning home from the war, Leonard worked as a truck driver for a series of freight and moving companies. He began dating Anglo women until a Mexicana on the city bus got his attention. While he was going downtown to meet a date, Ramona Alvarez was going to church on the same bus. When he finally mustered enough courage to talk to her, she invited him to her home at 1220 North Calhoun, where she served him a bowl of soup. On July 29, 1944, Leonard

Menchaca and Ramona Alvarez[122] married and eventually raised a family of fifteen. His father, Francisco Menchaca, whose livestock-trading instincts had served the family well, passed away in 1950; his mother died a decade later. In 1982, after having worked for Red Ball Lines for thirty-one years, Leonard retired and bought a few acres of land north of Fort Worth in Montague county. He and his wife enjoy living a quiet life in the country.[123]

◆   ◆   ◆

In the early 1940s Michael Ayala's brother, Louis, supplemented the family's income by shining shoes at Jack Mead's barbershop on East Central Avenue. In 1943, Jack asked Louis if he would like to go to Texas Barber College on Throckmorton Street, and Louis jumped at the opportunity. The following year he was cutting hair. A master barber familiar with the styles of the past five decades, Louis Ayala has cut the hair of several movie stars including Jason Robards and members of the cast of the popular TV series *Dallas*. Fort Worth's proximity to the movie studios at Las Colinas provided Ayala a steady stream of famous clientele. When Oliver Stone began filming *JFK* in 1991 Louis gave actors such as Kevin Costner the look of the late 1950s and early 1960s. When asked about these stars, Louis replied that they are people like everyone else and he doesn't react to them any differently.[124]

◆   ◆   ◆

North Side grocer José Jesús Domínguez, Sr., was born in 1893 near Celaya at Purísma del Rincón, Guanajuato, Mexico. His father, Prisciliano Domínguez, owned a large fruit orchard, and his mother, who had given birth to four boys and a girl, died shortly after José Jesús was born. Prisciliano raised his five sons and one daughter on his own. In 1913, at the age of twenty, José Jesús and his older brother, José Angel, emigrated to Fort Worth in order to escape the Mexican Revolution—the *federales* and other warring parties were forcibly conscripting young men.[125]

In Fort Worth the brothers stayed at a North Side boardinghouse and found work at Libby's Packing House. One day, around 1920, while at work, José Jesús accidentally cut off the index finger of his right hand. As compensation for his injury, the company gave the young man a rather decent settlement. With the money José Jesús and his wife, María Concepción Gonzalez, bought a shotgun house at 2113 North Calhoun.[126] The couple had already started a family that eventually included six children: José Jesús, Jr., Celia, Dolores D., Prisciliano,[127] Virginia, and Concepción. About 1926 Domínguez constructed a twelve by fifteen foot room in front of the shotgun house and opened a grocery store. He called it "*El faro*" ("The Light") because of the bright light on the front of the store. It was a true family enterprise—mom, dad, and all six children helped to run the store. They stocked groceries bought wholesale from the Waples-Platter Company and purchased meat wholesale from City Packing Company.

José Jesús recalled that tortillas were five cents a dozen; saltine crackers—five cents a sleeve; a twenty-ounce Nehi or Big Red soda—five cents; a quart of milk—ten cents; one pound of bologna—ten cents; a pound of longhorn cheese—ten to fifteen cents; and a pound of round steak—fifteen cents. The store also carried a wide variety of Mexican items that included spices, chiles, garbanzos, and *camarón seco* (dried shrimp).[128]

Almost all customers bought on credit and paid their bills on payday; unfortunately, some didn't settle their accounts. The 1932 opening of the Safeway store on the corner of North Main and Northeast Twenty-Third streets had a terrible effect on all the small stores in the North Side. When business began to be slow, Domínguez supplemented the family income by working for Armour. Because of increasing competition from the large supermarket chains, Domínguez's store closed in the mid-1940s.[129]

◆　　◆　　◆

The family of Rodolfo and Juanita Rodríguez lived one of the most amazing success stories of the North Side. In 1919, at the age of eleven, Rodolfo Rodríguez, his older brother, Eulogio, and their father, Florencio, left their home in El Infiermillo, near Pénjamo, Guanajuato, Mexico, to start a new life north of the Rio Grande. Warring factions in the Mexican Revolution had destroyed Florencio's rancho, where they had raised cattle, hogs, and other livestock. With proper immigration papers in hand, Florencio and his two eldest sons worked their way from Laredo to North Texas. They picked cotton in Hillsboro and then moved to Dallas, where Florencio heard of possible employment at the packing houses of North Fort Worth. With his knowledge of livestock as an asset, he applied for work at Swift and Company, where he stayed for about a year and a half before returning to his homeland to bring his wife, Felicitas, and his six other children to America.[130]

When Florencio left to go back to Mexico, Eulogio stayed with a friend who lived in *La Diecisiete*, while Rodolfo stayed on the North Side with Jose Tafolla García[131] and worked in his little restaurant. When Florencio returned with Felicitas and the other children, the reunited family lived on the 2100 block of North Calhoun.[132]

After two or three years Rodolfo and Eulogio both began working for the Hotel Texas. When he was a little older, Rodolfo worked for Swift, icing down railroad cars to keep the meat cold during shipping. Florencio had worked for Swift and in later years worked for City Packing Company, located on North Grove and Northeast Thirty-Fifth (or Thirty-Sixth) streets. He worked in the "hide house," curing cowhides in a process that involved immersing them in vats of salt water.

Rodolfo Rodríguez married Juanita Trujillo the same month and year as the great stock market crash, October 1929.[133] Born on June 24, 1910, in Francisco del Rincón, Guanajuato, Mexico, Juanita was the second child of Lino Trujillo.[134] Lino came to the United States in search of work, leaving Juanita behind to be raised by his cousin, Hilarión Franco, and his wife. In 1914, Hilarión Franco brought Juanita to Fort Worth for a brief reunion with her father before moving on to Kansas City to work for the Armour plant there. By 1925 Lino Trujillo, who had remarried several years before, went to Kansas City to bring his daughter back to Fort Worth. Juanita was in the eighth grade at the time.[135]

After their marriage Rodolfo and Juanita settled in a shotgun house at 2205 North Calhoun Street, where they brought up six children: Rudy, Ernesto, Ester, Alice, Raúl, and Charles.[136] A dear family friend, Dr. Raúl López Guerra, delivered all six children. Rodolfo and Juanita grew tomatoes and green beans in their small backyard garden and kept a goat and several dogs as pets.[137]

Although Rodolfo supported his family by working for Swift and Company, he had always wanted to go into business for himself. In 1939, he opened a pool hall on the southwest corner of North Calhoun and Northeast 22nd streets. After only a year in business, a fire destroyed the building. Undeterred, Rodolfo bought a corner grocery store, which formerly belonged to his first employer, Joe T. García, across the street from where the pool hall had been.[138] The store was especially appealing because it had a four-room house in back. During World War II, Juanita took care of the store while Rodolfo served his tour of duty from 1943 to 1945 in the navy stationed in the Aleutian Islands. Because of his experience managing a grocery store, he was put in charge of a navy commissary in Attu. After two-and-a-half years, Rodolfo was honorably discharged and returned to manage the business.[139]

In 1956, with money saved and his son, Rudy, out of school,[140] Rodolfo and Rudy opened Rodríguez and Son Food Mart in the 1400 block of North Main, just south of the Marine Theater. They operated from this location until 1960, when they moved to a larger facility and opened a supermarket on North Main Street and Central Avenue.[141] Five years later they opened Rodríguez Tortilla Factory adjacent to the supermarket on Central Avenue. At first, the Rodríguezes made only corn tortillas; they added flour tortillas in 1968 and chips, tostadas, salsa, and chorizo in 1969.[142] Father and son incorporated in 1969, creating the present corporate entity, Rodríguez Festive Foods, Inc.

Over the next three decades, the operation expanded at an exhilarating pace. By 1970, they had outgrown their facility on North Main and Central. The Rodríguez family built their first processing plant at 913 North Houston, adjacent to their present location. In 1979, they purchased a meat processing plant at 500 East Central Avenue to grind meat for burritos, enchiladas, and tamales. Next, in 1986, came the acquisition of the old J.W. Nichols Poultry plant, located at 899 North Houston. This former chicken-processing facility was immediately transformed into a large-scale tortilla factory. The Rodríguez family purchased yet another building at Northwest 28th and Decatur streets, a former grocery supermarket now used exclusively for making tamales.[143]

Today, Rodríguez Festive Foods, Inc., offers a product line that includes corn and flour tortillas, chips and salsa, tamales, tacos, enchiladas, and burritos. The tamales, tacos, enchiladas, and burritos are packaged and frozen at the plant for distribution to thirty-five states and seven foreign countries—Spain, Portugal, France, Belgium, Germany, the United Kingdom, and Lebanon.

All wholesale business is presently handled through a system of regional distributors. Thirty-five food brokers represent the company nationally, while one represents it internationally.[144]

Rodolfo Rodríguez, who worked hard seven days a week throughout his life, left an impressive legacy to his family, his North Side community, and to the city of Fort Worth. He passed away in February 1988, and his sons proudly carry on the family tradition of excellence and hard work. Rudy is now the chairman of the board and chief executive officer of Rodríguez Festive Foods, Inc. Ernesto is president of the company, while Raúl serves as senior vice president and Charles is secretary-treasurer. The company earned the Golden Tortilla Award in 1995, an honor bestowed at the annual meeting of tortilla producers in Los Angeles. At present, they employ 450 workers, most of whom live on the North Side, and the corporation generates annual gross sales in excess of thirty million dollars.[145]

◆   ◆   ◆

Hermenejildo R. Martínez, an independent and successful concrete contractor, lived with his wife, Sabina, and their children at 701 East Second Street.[146]

Hermenejildo Rodríguez Martínez was born on April 13, 1889, in Austin. On July 22, 1909, Hermenejildo married Sabina Vázquez, who was born on December 30, 1893, in Seguin. The family soon grew with the birth of three children: Amalia Martínez Romero, Francisca Martínez de León, and Pedro Vázquez Martínez.[147] The family lived in Georgetown where they operated a restaurant. Sabina also made and sold Mexican candies such as pecan pralines and *leche quemada*,[148] while Hermenejildo repaired shoes and cut hair. The Martínez family came to Fort Worth in 1928, and Hermenejildo learned to be a concrete contractor while working for the Mitiletic Company.[149] Martínez soon became known for high-quality work laying concrete foundations and by 1946 had formed his own contracting business, H. Martínez and Sons. Hermenejildo and Sabina were gracious people who had extra rooms in their home to rent. Their two-story home, considered luxurious at the time because it had indoor plumbing and several bathrooms, was one of the finest residences owned by a

Mexicano in all of Fort Worth. Salvador Gonzalez, Jr., while working for the downtown Fort Worth Club, rented an upstairs room from them when he and his wife María were newlyweds.

Hermenejildo eventually passed the business on to the couple's son, Pedro. Hermenejildo R. Martínez worked until he was eighty before he retired. He passed away on November 5, 1984, at the age of ninety-five.[150]

❖   ❖   ❖

Antonio Vásquez Zapata was born in June 1883 in Baxter County to Jesús and Isabel Vásquez Zapata, originally from Del Rio. Zapata's wife, Antonia Elena Miranda, born in June 1895, came from a ranching community near Valle de Santiago in Guanajuato, Mexico. Antonio and Elena married in Fort Worth on January 1, 1919. The marriage produced five children: Jesús, Consuelo Z. Narvaéz, Josefina, Carmen, and Luis,[151]

A jack-of-all-trades, Antonio Zapata settled his family in *La Corte*. Zapata, fluent in both English and Spanish, was often hired as a court interpreter and sometimes helped immigrants with their paperwork for citizenship. Near the courthouse, Antonio established his first restaurant next to a feed store. He opened a second restaurant close to the barrio of *La Diecisiete*, across the street from the Gayety Theater on the southwest corner of 15th and Main streets. An enterprising man, Zapata opened his first grocery store in the early 1920s on the northeast corner of Valley and Mills streets, next to his residence at 500 Mills Street. From their store the Zapatas sold all the regular grocery items—sodas, *raspas* (snow cones), *pan dulce,* five-cent Washington fruit pies, and other staples.[152] They sold beans by the pound out of large ceramic barrels. In an era when few people could afford electric refrigerators, Antonio Zapata delivered blocks of ice from house to house on his horse-drawn wagon. He purchased the ice in bulk from one of the city's icehouses and wrapped the blocks with a heavy tarpaulin to minimize melting.[153] People usually bought on credit until payday, a courtesy he extended to all. There were only a few customers who never paid their bills. His daughter, Consuelo, sometimes helped at the store, but her frank manner with certain customers earned her a strong rebuke from her mother, *"quítate de aquí, porque te corres a los clientes."* (Translation: "Get out of here, for you are going to scare the customers away.")[154]

Antonio Zapata raised his family in their *La Corte* home until his death in December 1941. Antonia sold the property to Petra Zavala,[155] and the Zapata family moved to a duplex at 906 West Weatherford Street. This property, located on the northwest corner of Weatherford and Henderson, was sold in 1946 to the Kinnard brothers for a used-car dealership. Antonia Miranda Zapata passed away in 1974.[156]

FAMILY LIFE

Throughout the history of Mexican immigration to the United States, the importance of family has been evident: young and not-so-young males come first and then send for the rest of their families. Relatives provide homes for newly immigrated families. Families secure jobs for others or run businesses to hand down to family. The triple burdens of culture, language, and discrimination add layers to the depths of these connections. From courtship to cooking, from traditional to folk medicine, the Mexican experience in the United States demonstrates the importance of family.

◆　◆　◆

Although Fort Worth had several businesses owned by Hispanic families, the Caro family's story offers a unique perspective on the importance of family and how traditions passed down through the generations often end up as lucrative business opportunities. María de Lourdes ("Lou") Caro was born in the late 1920s in Río Grande City, Texas, to Juan Bautista and Modesta Cavázos Caro. Juan Bautista Caro was the son of Eduardo and Felipa Caro and the grandson of Dr. Juan Caro, a U.S. Army doctor from Pensacola, Florida, who was assigned to Fort Ringgold, Río Grande City, Texas, in the late 1800s. Dr. Caro married a woman from Río Grande City and eventually they had nine children—eight boys and one girl. The family acquired land and ranches and sold hides, an important business at that time. One of Dr. Caro's eight sons, Eduardo, married a woman named Felipa who was an excellent cook. Felipa owned a large ranch on the Mexican side of the Río Grande. On this ranch, they raised cattle, goats, chickens, and vegetables such as corn, squash, onions, tomatoes, and peppers. There were plenty of fresh ingredients with which to prepare fine border cuisine, and the family thrived on admirable meals. Eduardo and Felipa had only one son, Juan Bautista Caro, who lived the life of a playboy—attending the opera, betting on horse races, and playing second base for the Mexican baseball league team called *Los alacranes* (the Scorpions).[1]

While Juan was playing baseball and traveling with *Los alacranes* in Durango, Mexico, some admiring ladies invited him to their home for supper. They prepared unique "puffed" tacos that were so delicious Juan Bautista never forgot this culinary experience or how to make them. This manner of making tacos or chips[2] is actually more labor intensive because they are made directly from the corn *masa* (corn dough) and not from the finished corn tortilla.[3]

In 1918, Juan Bautista visited relatives and friends in the small community of San Vicente near Herreras in the state of Nuevo León. At a dance given by the town judge, Juan's host pointed out all the lovely young ladies and asked, "Whom do you choose to dance with?" Surveying the room from one end to the other, Juan's eyes alighted on a tall, blue-eyed, blond beauty. The judge introduced seventeen-year-old Modesta Cavázos to thirty-two-year-old Juan Bautista, and the two danced the night away.[4]

Two years later in 1920, Juan Bautista Caro married Modesta Cavázos. Modesta was born in San Vicente on February 22, 1901, to Jacinto and Bernardina Hinojosa Cavázos. Her parents owned large tracts of land on which they raised various kinds of livestock. They had nine children, all having either green or blue eyes. Area residents called Modesta *la gringa* (the Anglo), because she did not look like a typical Mexicana. In addition to her psychic-like gifts, Modesta's other talents included baking bread, delivering babies in her role as a *partera* (midwife), and traditional folk healing, as a *curandera*.[5]

Modesta learned to cook from her mother-in-law, Felipa Caro, a master of border culinary arts. Felipa taught Modesta how to make most of the traditional border and northern Mexican dishes: *picadillo, guisos, fideo* (vermicelli), *calabacita, cabrito en sangre, cabrito asado,* Mexican-style rice, *frijoles refritos o borrachos,* and *tortillas de harina* (flour tortillas).[6] Felipa also demonstrated how to prepare the soup-like *pompurrado—carne seca con fideo y especias* (dried meat with vermicelli and spices), her son's favorite dish.[7]

During the 1920s and 1930s, Juan and Modesta had six children: Rosario in 1921, Eduardo in 1923, Carmen in 1925, María de Lourdes in 1927, Argentina in 1929, and Juanito in 1931.[8] By 1932 Juan Bautista had begun to make plans to open a restaurant in Río Grande City.[9] In preparation for the restaurant's opening, he made the sign, "Caro's," that would hang over the restaurant, but on November 30, 1934, Juan Bautista Caro suddenly passed away.[10]

Left alone to raise six young children, Modesta Cavázos Caro did what she could to survive. She took in people's laundry and cared for children whose mothers had just given birth and needed time to recuperate. She even cleaned rooms in a small tourist court. The Martínez family, owners of the motel, asked Modesta to help them manage the place, in addition to cleaning the linens and rooms. In time, they agreed to her proposal to open a restaurant in the twelve-by-twelve-foot motel office. Modesta installed a stove, an icebox, brought some *masa* and other ingredients from home, and proceeded to make taquitos and those Durango-style "puffed" tacos. Initially selling three tacos for ten cents, she gradually introduced other menu items that included hamburgers, enchiladas, *tamales de puerco* (four for a quarter), and *caldo de res* (beef soup).[11]

Modesta did so well in her restaurant that in four years she was able to buy five lots[12] on which to establish a larger freestanding restaurant. María de Lourdes ("Lou") became her mother's right-hand woman, working wherever needed throughout the 1930s and most of the 1940s. After the war, feeling adventurous, Lou Caro decided to leave home and explore other career options than the restaurant business. She headed for Houston, where she worked for a year in the perfume department of Foley's department store. One day her roommate arranged a blind date for Lou with John Day Whitten—a date that changed her life.[13] Whitten was working in Houston but planning to leave for Saudi Arabia on business. Whitten postponed the business in Saudi Arabia in order to pursue a courtship, and the couple married on October 9, 1949.[14]

John and Lou returned to Río Grande City to help run Caro's Restaurant after growing tired of unfulfilling jobs in Houston and Atlanta. Cheerful and energetic, John breathed new life into Caro's. He remodeled and upgraded the restaurant and installed air conditioning. Yet, in spite of the fact that the restaurant was flourishing, Lou wondered if their future there in Rio Grande City, with a population of only 2,243, was secure. After the birth of their first child, John Day Whitten, Jr., on December 27, 1951, the couple's concern for financial security grew sharply. When they took a much-deserved break in early March 1954 to visit her sister, Argentina, in Fort Worth, they liked what they saw. Lou remembers impulsively blurting out, "John, go look for a place to open a restaurant. I'm tired of working for nothing at Mother's!"[15]

In May 1954, they leased a building from Aaron Rashti on Bluebonnet Circle and opened Caro's Restaurant. Initial menu items included chalupas, arroz con pollo, enchiladas, tamales, *tacos de pollo* (chicken tacos), and, most importantly, their signature puffed tostadas and guacamole. The Whittens also rented the house in the back of the restaurant for their growing family. Their second child, Maudie (Lourdes Modesta), arrived on their tenth wedding anniversary. A year later, Mary Margaret was born in January 1961.[16]

For a few years, the Whittens expanded their operations, opening a second restaurant at 5930 Camp Bowie Boulevard in 1956 and a third in Arlington in 1958. The late Sid Richardson and newsman Jim Lehrer were among the many notable Fort Worthians who loved to eat at Caro's. Because of rapidly increasing rent, the Whittens closed the Arlington location in 1968 but kept the Camp Bowie location open until late 1985. John Day Whitten had passed away the year before on October 27, 1984, and the burden of two locations on Lou and her daughters proved to be too much. To this day, the entire family is involved at Caro's, and they still serve traditional border fare and especially puffed tostadas.[17]

◆   ◆   ◆

Fathers often played a dominant role in the household. When Secundino and Tomasa Muñoz Martínez gave birth to their third daughter, Dominga, it was in "*las casas coloradas*" (the red houses), in *La Fundición*.[18] The neighborhood *partera,* María Cisneros, came to the family home to assist in the delivery. Tomasa preferred the name Adelita, but the father objected because he did not want her to have the name of "*esa vieja soldada de Pancho Villa*" ("that old female soldier of Pancho Villa"). Adelita is called the Woman of the Revolution for her bravery. She was actually linked to Zapata, not Villa. Because she was born on a Sunday and possibly because Secundino had been celebrating the birth of his daughter a little too much, they named her *Dominga*. She has never liked the name, preferring "Minnie," as her friends called her in school.[19]

Minnie Martínez remembered going to the baseball games on Sunday afternoons at La Grave Field on the North Side when she was a girl. Families from all over the North Side came to see the Anglo team, the Fort Worth Cats, which played there on a regular basis. But, more importantly, it was a great place for girls and boys to meet. On one of these Sunday afternoons in 1940 Minnie Martínez met North Side resident José Gutiérrez.[20] They started dating and married on January 18, 1942. José was excused by medical reasons from joining the U.S. Army during World War II. The couple made their home in the South Side and began their family.[21]

❖   ❖   ❖

Fort Worth movie star Pilar del Rey (born Pilar Bouzas) comes from a flamboyant, adventurous family. Pilar's father, Aurelio ("Earl") Bouzas, was born on August 1, 1902, in Pontevedra, Galicia, Spain, in a well-educated, middle-class family. His father received an engineering degree from the university at Pontevedra.[22]

Adventurous at heart, Earl left Spain at the age of twenty-two (1924) to join two of his brothers already living in Gary, Indiana. One brother, Dom (Domingo), owned a restaurant/bar across the street from the large steel plant where his other brother Nemésio worked. Earl worked for his brother Dom in the restaurant and learned to be a good cook. Some months later a friend in Gary decided to head for Texas, which seemed like an interesting idea to Earl. He accompanied his friend to Fort Worth, where he obtained immediate employment as a cook for the Worth Hotel (1924-1930). Earl loved to play cards and had a regular poker game going—morning, evening, and during his lunch break—with the Fort Worth police at their downtown headquarters, near his home on Henderson Street in *La Corte*.[23]

Earl married Juanita Barrera, who was born on December 27, 1897, in San Antonio, Texas. When her father passed away in 1908, Juanita (age eleven), her sister Mary, and her brother Arthur moved to Fort Worth; they lived on the North

Side. Eventually Juanita and Mary, with their other sister Genevieve, bought a house at 1407 North Jones Street and a Model-T Ford with the money they earned working for Swift and Company. Arthur worked as an interpreter at the courthouse and sometimes hired people to work as contract labor in other states.[24]

Juanita and Earl met at a party celebrating the baptism of her brother Patricio. The couple married in 1927. Juanita was outgoing and loved to sing and play the guitar; Earl, a gregarious six-footer, was European-looking—in fact, he resembled western movie star Tim McCoy. Police almost arrested Patricio Barrera for "arguing" with his brother-in-law Earl. They thought that Patricio, a Mexican, was bothering Earl, an Anglo. "Naw, he's just my brother-in-law," Earl retorted.[25]

Pilar's brother, Arthur, was such a terror that his worried parents thought he might be insane. They finally took him to see Dr. Raúl López Guerra for an expert medical opinion. After carefully observing the boy the good doctor called in Juanita, who was patiently waiting out in the hall.

"Let me tell you something," he told her. "You and I are crazier than this kid. What you're going to have to do is start `baptizing' him." Puzzled, Juanita replied, "Well, I've baptized him."

"No I don't mean baptizing that way; I mean *así*," the doctor made a spanking motion with his hand. "*Lo vas a tener que comenzar a bautizar*" ("you'll have to begin baptizing [spanking] him").[26]

◆   ◆   ◆

The Padilla and Ayala families demonstrate the central role of family in the lives of Mexicanos. In the early 1930s, Hope Padilla Ayala's family began a tradition of annual reunions that continues to this day.[27] The original clan has expanded dramatically and now includes numerous families of Rodríguezes, Padillas, Herreras, Hernándezes, Ayalas, and Garcías. Reunions, which attract three to four hundred people, are usually in June and last an entire weekend— a dance on Friday evening, a Mass at 5:00 P.M. followed by a reception on Saturday, and a picnic at twelve noon on Sunday. A festive atmosphere permeates the picnic with face painting for children, balloons, and a variety of games. Each branch of a family wears a specially-made T-shirt with an assigned color—yellow for Rodríguez, red for Herrera, blue for Ayala, etc.[28] The reunion is also the time to introduce new family members, exchange recent news and laugh over old stories, take group photographs, and eat wonderful food. Everyone has a memorable time passing on a cherished tradition.

One branch of the family, the Ayalas, serves as a case in point for the

(1930) Hope Padilla (Ayala) posing at family home at 2106 N. Calhoun. *Photo courtesy of Michael and Hope (Padilla) Ayala.*

importance of family grounded in church and community service. In 1934, Michael Ayala attended second grade at M. G. Ellis Elementary, but his parents became convinced that a Catholic school would better prepare the boy for communion and confirmation. In spite of the family's modest finances, the following year he transferred to San José School, where he stayed until the sixth grade. Michael then enrolled at J. P. Elder Junior High. In 1944, he graduated from Northside High School and attended Texas Wesleyan College for one year. The following year, with the World War II winding down, he joined the Merchant Marine.[29]

Michael worked in the Merchant Marine as a helmsman and quartermaster between 1945 and 1947. While he was serving in the Merchant Marine, Michael sent money to his family to enable them to buy Anderson Grocery, a North Side business establishment begun in 1911. After leaving the service in July 1952 Michael worked at the renamed Ayala Grocery, located at 411 E. Central. The family purchased stock items from wholesale grocers and the farmers' market located between 13th and 14th streets near the present-day Fort Worth Convention Center and meat from Swift and Company and Murphy's Meats. Of course they always stocked Mexican products such as pinto beans, peppers, oregano, *cominos* (cumin), *canela* (cinnamon), and *garbanzos* (chick peas). They purchased spices in bulk from Mexican Chili Supply on Belknap Street. Considering their clients *"gente de palabra"* (trustworthy people), the Ayalas extended credit to practically all of them. On payday, most people came to settle their accounts. The family finally sold Ayala Grocery to Rafael Saldaña in 1956.[30] Michael later went to work for the U.S. Postal Service.

On April 24, 1949, Michael Ayala married Esperanza ("Hope") Padilla at San José Catholic Church. They have three children: Carlos Ayala, married Norma Villarreal; Dolores, married Ramón Ríos; and Teresa ("Terry"), who married Charles Michael Bruton.[31]

Hope worked at All Saints Catholic Church as the receptionist and office manager, retiring in 1994 after thirty-three years. In the 1960s, she actively participated in the Home and School Association (the PTA for All Saints School). In the 1970s, Hope served on the boards of the North Side Boys' Club and All Saints Catholic School. She possesses a wealth of information on the history and people of the North Side and appears on television programs speaking on a variety of cultural and historical topics. Not to be outdone by his wife, when Michael retired from the postal service he began to volunteer his time as a tour guide at the North Fort Worth Historical Society's museum located at the Stockyards.[32]

◆　◆　◆

Pasacio ("Pete") Martínez was another person who valued community and family bonds. North Side Mexicanos came to appreciate Martínez's open-door policy of help on a variety of issues, such as in the preparation of immigration papers for citizenship. Despite his lack of a formal education,[33] Martínez possessed a keen intelligence and a willingness to help that benefited his family and his neighbors. Even while he was a union boss, Pete's leadership qualities extended to organizing a local chapter of *Los Hacheros del Mundo* (Woodmen of the World), and speaking regularly at many *fiestas patrias*. Martínez also joined the Masons and

(October 11, 1936) Los Hacheros (Woodmen of the World) with their uniforms and axes in front of M.G. Ellis Elementary School. Eufemio Guajardo holds sword at far left. *Photo courtesy of Ramon Angiano.*

was an active member of the Julian Feild Lodge. Because of all these commit-
ments, Pete instilled in his family an appreciation for education, hard work, and
maintaining good credit. He was also a loving and tender father: when his
youngest daughter, Kiki, broke her arm, Pete was so upset that he cried as he
rocked her gently in his arms to comfort her.[34]

Pete Martínez worked hard until the time of his death on November 8,
1950. Although he was entitled to a free Masonic funeral, the family elected
instead to have a Roman Catholic service. He was perhaps the first Mexicano
interred at the historic Oakwood Cemetery.[35]

Pete's youngest daughter carries on the family banner with perseverance and
hard work. Yvonne ("Kiki") Martinez married John Valentine Cisneros, Jr., in
1960. After working for others in the food service business, they went into business for themselves in 1978, renting a little house on Sylvania Avenue and 28th
Street, across the street from Mount Olivet Cemetery. With her brother Johnny as
their partner, the Cisneros opened their first restaurant, Mi Casita. Over ten years
they built up a loyal customer base, allowing them to buy the property on which
their restaurant was located. As the North Side, the stockyards, and Billy Bob's
began attracting thousands of visitors and residents to the area, John and Kiki
wanted to benefit from the boom and opened their second restaurant, Los
Vaqueros, on February 12, 1983. Their two sons Johnny and Michael have now
taken over management of this restaurant, which is located on North Main
Street.[36] Without a doubt, Pete Martínez would have been most proud of all of
his children's many accomplishments.[37]

HEALTH CARE

Wesley Community House on the North Side, has been a source of support for
the Hispanic community since the early twentieth century. Among its many functions was, and is, ensuring that adequate medical care is available to all, regardless
of ability to pay. In 1928, one of two cottages on the property, originally the quarters of the janitor, was transformed into a free medical clinic, with area doctors
donating their services and dispensing medications without charge. Dr. C. Pearre
Hawkins treated as many as thirty patients twice a week, and Dr. W. C. Lakey
administered the free clinic on Saturdays beginning at nine in the morning.[38] Dr.

H. V. Helbing tended expectant mothers and deliveredmany of the children in the community.[39] The doctors and the Wesley House staff worked to raise public awareness of a number of serious diseases, especially tuberculosis, an endemic scourge that resulted in a high death rate in the North Side. [40]

◆   ◆   ◆

No one in any of the Fort Worth barrios occupied a higher position of honor and respect than Dr. Raúl López Guerra, Sr. For almost thirty years, from 1927 to 1956, Dr. López Guerra fulfilled multiple roles as medical doctor, community leader, counselor, good neighbor, and trusted friend. During this period, he was the only Mexican doctor in Fort Worth, if not in all of North Texas.[41]

The paternal roots of Dr. López Guerra's family can be traced to Rancho el Nido, [42] between León and Silao, in the state of Guanajuato, Mexico. The doctor's paternal grandparents, Juan López and Genoveva Valdívia, raised corn, poultry, and rabbits, and tended orchards of apple, peach, fig, lime, lemon, orange, and *membrillo* trees.[43] Son Francisco López de Valdívia, was born in Unión de San Antonio, Jalisco. He eventually raised corn and other staples at the Hacienda de Pedrito, located near Lagos de Moreno, the village of his future bride. In this rural setting Francisco met, courted, and married Basilisa Guerra Sánchez.[44]

Born on May 27, 1898, in León, Guanajuato, to Basilisa and Francisco, young Raúl López Guerra entered into a traditional world shared by nine other siblings.Of fourteen children, four died in early childhood.[45] Raúl was the only one of the children to learn a profession and come to the United States.[46] Upon completion of *la primaria y la secundaria*,[47] in León, Raúl aspired to study medicine at the Universidad national autónoma de México. After graduating from medical school in 1923,[48] Dr. López Guerra fulfilled his internship requirement at the Hospital Juárez in Mexico City (1923-1924). The following two years he practiced medicine in his hometown of León, where he also became involved in helping the Red Cross.

There are two different stories about how Dr. López Guerra came to live in San Antonio. One version describes how, following a flood in León, as the city's representative, he traveled to San Antonio to accept relief funds raised by that city's Mexican community.[49] The other version focuses on his desire to study general surgery with Dr. Aureliano Urrútia, a political exile living in San Antonio, which had become a popular haven for political exiles at that time.[50]

Whichever story is true, in order to practice medicine in the United States López Guerra had to prepare for a state medical exam. A close friend and a one-time Mexican ambassador to Italy, Dr. Francisco Del Río, encouraged López Guerra to take the Texas Medical Board examination, which he passed with the help of interpreters on July 15, 1926.[51] While living in San Antonio, López Guerra met and courted Aurelia Avila, an accomplished pianist enrolled at Our Lady of the Lake University.

Born in San Pedro de las Colonias, Coahuila, on May 1, 1905, Aurelia grew up with all kinds of music, dance, and poetry. Her father, Antonio Avila Delgado,[52] encouraged his thirteen-year-old daughter's musical talents and in 1918 sent her to study in San Antonio. Two of her older sisters,[53] Elisa and Evangelina, already lived there. In 1919, Antonio Avila's premature death at the age of forty-eight led his widow, Aurelia Várgas Treviño,[54] to move the rest of her family to San Antonio.[55]

Aurelia Avila organized musical and theatrical benefits that included recitals, zarzuelas,[56] dances, and fiestas patrias. In the mid-1920s, Aurelia played the piano and sang on an historic first radio transmission between the United States and Mexico initiated by the new San Antonio radio station XEQ. She also collaborated with the San Antonio Symphony on numerous radio performances. Her experience in the performing arts later proved to be an invaluable contribution to the rich cultural diversity of Fort Worth.[57]

In San Antonio, Aurelia stayed with her mother's oldest sister, Adela Várgas de Meave, who did not have any children of her own. Assuming responsibility for her niece's welfare, Adela rejected two suitors for Aurelia's hand before finally giving her consent to Dr. Raúl López Guerra. Aurelia's dentist brother-in-law Dr. Enrique Ostos[58] introduced the couple at a community social. Ostos had married Adela, also known among the family as "La Tía China." Raúl and Aurelia exchanged vows before a large crowd at San Antonio's San Fernando Cathedral at noon on October 30, 1927.[59]

Sometime during or after their honeymoon, a Mrs. Fay asked Raúl to treat an ailing cousin of hers in Fort Worth. Upon his successfully treating this Cowtown resident, the North Side community of Mexicanos implored the doctor to stay. While Dr. López Guerra was walking along North Main Street, he came across a horseshoe on the street and concluded that staying in Fort Worth would bring good luck. [60]

The couple's first home, located at 801 Woodland, across from Our Lady of Victory School in the South Side, had sentimental value because their first child, Basilisa, was born in 1929, shortly after they had moved there. It was too

(c. 1939) On the front porch at their 1509 Ellis Street home (Northside) L to R: Raul, Jr., Dr. Raúl López Guerra, Sr., Basilisa("Basi"), at age 10, and Aurelia ("Pichuga"). The home was conveniently located across the street from Marine Park. *Photo courtesy of Basilísa López Guerra.*

far from the clinic to be practical, however, and sometime in the early 1930s, the family moved to 1545 North Main where Dr. López Guerra had a clinic in part of their small home. Dr. and Mrs. López Guerra moved to their third and final Fort Worth residence at 1509 Ellis Avenue, which they purchased for $2,000 from an Anglo doctor in 1934.[61]

The comfortable three-bedroom, one bath, brick-veneer home, located directly across from Marine Park, represented a milestone of sorts for the López Guerra family. Before 1934, no Mexicano had ever lived west of North Main Street. Conditioned to stay within their own North Side barrio, Mexicanos rarely ventured into any other areas unless business or work took them there.[62]

The Ellis Avenue home also provided Dr. López Guerra with ample space for his clinic. Patients entered through a door about ten feet to the right of the home's front entrance. Patients waited their turn to see the doctor on a first-come-first-served basis in the small waiting room. On average, Dr. López Guerra saw twenty to thirty patients per day and gave advice or treatment, regardless of one's ability to pay. While waiting, some patients, especially those from other barrios or from out-of-town, ate their lunch picnic-style across the street in Marine Park.[63]

The doctor worked seven days a week, cultivating lasting and valued relationships with his patients. Highly dedicated to their welfare, Dr. López Guerra made frequent house calls at all hours and in any kind of weather. Unable to afford a hospital, many Mexicanos had no choice but to have their children at home, and Dr. López Guerra delivered many of these babies. As most of his patients worked during the week, Saturdays and Sundays were the only days they could see the doctor. On Sundays, Dr. López Guerra examined a steady stream of patients from 8:00 A.M. until 5:00 P.M. Only after he had seen the last patient did he join his family for their traditional Sunday meal.[64]

Mexicanos comprised nine-tenths of his patients, while other immigrant groups[65] and Anglos made up the remaining tenth. Dr. López Guerra's reputation as a first-rate diagnostician spread quickly and soon patients flocked from all over—Dallas, Paduca (near Amarillo), Wichita Falls, Mineral Wells, Weatherford, and even from as far as South Texas and the Rio Grande Valley. Basilisa recalled the time that a certain lady's illness had been misdiagnosed by several physicians as appendicitis. Dr. López Guerra correctly diagnosed the woman's condition as salpingitis (an inflammation of the fallopian tubes), necessitating an entirely different course of treatment and a welcome restoration of her health. A practitioner at Saint Joseph's Infirmary and a member of the Tarrant County Medical Society, Dr. López Guerra was an esteemed and respected colleague among Fort Worth's physicians.[66]

In addition to counseling many of his patients on issues ranging from raising children to financial problems, Raúl López Guerra was occasionally called upon to help someone in trouble with the law. In an effort to resolve problems affecting the local community of Mexicanos, he often collaborated with Fort Worth's Mexican Consul. Galvanized by the discrimination that prohibited Mexicanos from enjoying an afternoon or evening of entertainment at local theaters such as the downtown Palace, Dr. López Guerra lobbied local officials and theater owners to allow his compatriots into their establishments.[67]

Like others of his generation, Raúl López Guerra firmly believed education to be the critical factor in the empowerment of Mexicanos. Taking full advantage of his stature as a positive role model, the doctor often urged his patients to continue in their studies despite the pervasive pessimism that, in an Anglo-dominated environment, education would make no difference in getting better jobs. Dr. López Guerra offered hope and encouragement that education would positively affect lives and would open the door to higher opportunities.[68]

A devout Roman Catholic, Dr. Guerra was active in the local San José parish, which, by 1927, was ministering to the North Side community from its own new building. Every time a new priest arrived at San José, he paid a courtesy call on the doctor. As a mark of the respect and esteem in which he was held by his constituency, Dr. Guerra often gave the *grito*, or traditional proclamation, at the *dieciséis de septiembre* festivities that San José parish sponsored.[69]

Aurelia Avila readily volunteered in organizing the programs for these *fiestas patrias*, doing her part to preserve the native culture by teaching young girls regional Mexican dances such as *Las Chapanecas*, *El Jarabe*, and *El Tapatío*, while accompanying them on her piano. She also instructed her own children in varying aspects of Mexican culture and helped them do a program exclusively for their father.[70]

Working round the clock seven days a week was exhausting, and Dr. López

(early 1940s) Greatly respected by Northside residents, Dr. Raúl López Guerra, Sr., and his wife Aurelia (Avila) pose outside San José Catholic Church. *Photo courtesy of Basilísa López Guerra.*

Guerra badly needed vacation time. As soon as the school year ended in May, the family packed the car and drove to León, Guanajuato, to enjoy three months of well-deserved rest and relaxation. *"Ya llegué a mi tierra,"* ("I have arrived at my homeland.")[71] was the doctor's triumphant and proud announcement every time he entered his beloved hometown. The fact that he never became an American citizen reflected his intense love for his native land. From the time he first came to San Antonio until the day he died, Dr. López Guerra remained a citizen of *Los Estados Unidos de México.* The yearly retreats were his way of keeping in touch with his Mexican roots and culture and a wonderful opportunity to enjoy his immediate and extended family in his native country. Basilisa, Raúl , Jr., and Aurelia—the López Guerra children—also cultivated a love for their father's homeland and their relatives there.

The summer hiatus also allowed the doctor to monitor the many real estate investments he had made around his hometown. While Fort Worth provided him with a handsome living, León was where he hoped to retire at the end of a long and rewarding career.[72] But, each August, the doctor and his family made their way back to Fort Worth to resume their respective responsibilities.[73]

The years of his demanding medical practice and community work began to take their toll. In the summer of 1956, an exhausted Dr. López Guerra journeyed to his beloved homeland, this time never to return to Fort Worth. The pillar of his North Side community died peacefully in bed on September 18 at his grandfather's home in the same room where he was born fifty-eight years earlier.[74]

DIET, HOME REMEDIES AND FOLK MEDICINE

For most families, diet was fairly predictable: *papas con huevos* for breakfast, *huevos con papas* for lunch, and *papas a huevo*[75] for supper. To economize, households bought larger quantities of basic staples: rice in ten- to twenty-pound bags, twenty-five-pounds of flour and pinto beans, five-gallon tins of lard, and potatoes by the bushel. Joe Aguilera, *el hielero*, delivered blocks of ice to homes. *El lechero*, an Anglo from Foremost Dairy, replaced the empty milk bottles left on the front porch with full containers, often even taking them inside to the icebox. People were more trusting in those days—in the 1930s, 1940s, and even the 1950s, people left their windows open, their doors unlocked, and often left their keys in their cars.

Many people raised chickens in their backyards to supplement their diet with fresh eggs and meat. Sunday meals were special, for it was the one day that most people ate meat. Cold watermelons were always a welcome treat in the summer months.[76]

Representing a savings of time and money, *remedios caseros* (home remedies) were the first aid of choice for most minor ailments. A combination of *petrolio* (kerosene) and spider webs helped stop bleeding. Smoothing garden soil (sometimes mixed with lard) on a bad burn prevented blistering, while mud on a bee sting eased the pain. Red meat applied to bruises and black eyes was said to lessen their effects. There were two common remedies for earache. Some people used a brand of medicine called "Dr. J. H. McLean's Volcanic Oil."[77] This *aseite de volcánico* was warmed and applied drop-by-drop into the ear. When store-bought medicines were not available, mothers placed a funnel made from rolled up newspaper in the sufferer's ear, then lit it with a match, causing a small explosion that eliminated the earache.[78] Families also used inexpensive and usually on-hand herbs and spices for various ailments: *té de hierba buena*[79] (mint tea) for stomachaches and *té de estafiate* (*artemisia mexicana*, also known as mugwort) for constipation. A frightened person could chew *canela* (cinnamon stick) for nerves. A drop of *mercurio* was swallowed to take care of coughs, asthma, or fevers. It was dispensed a drop at a time by an eyedropper. If placed on the hand, it would form a tiny silver-colored sphere about the size of a BB. Liquid *arnica* cleaned and treated cuts on the skin. To help induce labor, *parteras* boiled *cominos* (cumin seeds) in water, and the expectant mother drank the resulting infusion. Another medicine available at drug stores, *la lídia* was a tonic used to counter anemia.[80] Once when Sammy Pantoja fell out of a truck in his backyard and broke his arm, the neighborhood *curandero* Don Pedro Molina set his arm using the wood from a tomato crate. He also used an *untúra* made of axle grease to ease the swelling. Axle grease was also ideal for burns and bee stings.

Curanderas and *curanderismo* (the practice of traditional healing) can be traced back to the first Spaniards in the southwest. A set of folk beliefs, rituals, and practices, *curanderismo* addresses the physical, social, psychological, and spiritual needs of the patient. The forms vary from region to region, but the principles are the same: it is a holistic medicine addressing the mind and the body; methods are passed from generation to generation, reassuring the patient and reinforcing cultural beliefs, as well curing the ailment. *Curanderas* believe their ability to heal comes from God and that it is God's will whether or not a person is healed. They often do not charge for their services, but clients gratefully leave offerings of food or money on the altar of the particular saint that serves as intermediary for the *curandera*. Other examples of the *curandera's* art include warm horse manure on broken bones and a combination of vinegar, potatoes, and mud to break a fever. Neighborhood *curandera* Ramona Cerda prayed over the sick and rubbed a fresh egg over the entire body to draw out the heat (and the bad spirit). The egg was placed under the afflicted person's bed and several minutes later was removed, fully cooked. [81]

The *curandera* challenges the normal role of women in Hispanic cultures, as she displays confidence, courage, and learning instead of being submissive and passive. Although the practice is fading today, there are still *curanderas* in many communities.

◆   ◆   ◆

Marysol Garza is not a typical traditional *curandera*, but her longtime spiritual consulting business nevertheless offered her clients many of the benefits of traditional folk healing. Born and raised in Monterrey, Nuevo León, Garza was the daughter of rancher Rafael Garza Gutiérrez and Ofelia Saldivar. When she was a small child, Marysol realized she had certain "gifts" that set her apart from other girls. She kept this a secret from her parents fearing that they would not understand her peculiar gifts but was surprised to find that her parents actually encouraged her once they knew of her abilities. At the age of sixteen, they sent Marysol to study part of each day with Alicia Casso, a distant cousin of Marysol's father. Under the tutelage of Tía Alicia, Marysol worked from 10:00 A.M. to 6:00 P.M. learning exorcism, black magic, tarot card reading, and divining by crystal balls, water, tobacco leaves, smoke, wind, air, and noise. For example, water reading discerns spirits through the movement of water in a small glass container. Marysol said that methods such as this harmonize her energies and permit her to see beyond the normal human scope.[82]

On May 17, 1964, Marysol married in Monterrey and eventually had two sons and two daughters. She helped support her family by tailoring men's clothes and creating bridal dresses. In 1970, the family left Monterrey in hope of a better life in San Antonio. They spent four years in San Antonio but never formed close ties with their neighbors. This lack of community and the promise of a better life farther north led the family to move to Fort Worth in 1974.[83]

Marysol's husband strongly disapproved of her "powers," causing her to practice her special gifts secretly without her husband's knowledge. The marriage ended in divorce. She believed that she had a God-given mission and that it was important to serve the people who needed her gifts. In Fort Worth she began a small spiritual consulting business, maintaining a presence in the same Hemphill neighborhood for fourteen years. Here she counseled clients on a variety of concerns: marriage and relationships, feelings of inadequacy and inferiority, sicknesses, nervousness, insecurities, emotional pressures, and depression. Consulting time varied according to the individual's need and the ultimate achievement of peace of mind. Sometimes, hours passed and Marysol was so engrossed with counseling a client that she forgot about food and other personal needs.[84]

She also had expertise in sensitive issues of love and jealousy—the lack of consideration or concern among family members, yearning for the love of a spouse or children, or the desire of an older woman for a younger man. In this situation, Marysol counseled the older woman to give up her desire because she has already lived and loved and the young man deserves someone his own age. She gave this same advice to older men consumed with younger women.

Marysol also had some experience with exorcism. It was her policy for professional reasons never to visit the homes of clients requiring an exorcism—to protect the client as well as herself. She merely made suggestions and shared remedies for the exorcism of an object or person who could not come to her place of business.[85]

Marysol Garza also helped her clients observe *velaciones* (vigils) dedicated to various saints, principally: *Santa Marta*, to overcome the impossible; *Santa Bárbara*, to tame a rebellious nature; and *San Antonio*, to attract a sweetheart or find a spouse.[86]

She recommended the use of votive candles to petition for one's own health or the health of a loved one; for special petitions to God; and to dedicate prayer or thanks to Jesus or other saints and spirits. To ward off evil spirits or hexes, she used the candle with the Ten Commandments, the Star of David, or the 10,000 virgins imprinted on its side. The colors of the votive candles are significant and are to be used on specific days to symbolize such powers as God Almighty, the sun, the blood of Christ, or the occult. Candles in the form of nude human figures of both sexes represented the desire for love, a satisfying relationship, or a successful marriage.[87]

Clients often sought Marysol to conduct *ruedas espirituales* (séances) to communicate with the dead, especially with a relative or friend who died violently; to ask pardon for past wrongs, faults, or sins; to attain peace of mind on a particular issue; and to eradicate bouts of extreme nervousness or uneasiness. [88] Sessions could last up to six hours, and Marysol witnessed many surprises and unforeseen situations during séances. [89]

For example, a few of her clients wished to communicate with the long-dead Mexican revolutionary General Pancho Villa to ask his advice on certain matters. Their reason for consulting the wily general was his great strength of spirit and his aura of domination, confidence, and self-assurance.

Marysol believed that more people are turning to traditional medicine and herbal cures because they appreciate the natural approach as opposed to the approach of medical doctors (see Appendix D). While Mexicanos and Mexican-Americans constituted the bulk of her clientele, Marysol found that other races came to her for help. Anglos, blacks, Vietnamese, East Indians, and even seven Frenchmen came on a regular basis to seek herbs and advice (using tarot cards) on how to improve their lives and what crucial decisions to make with respect to their businesses, love life, and their children. [90]

Reading tarot cards was the primary method of her consultancy. Marysol recalled the time that an Anglo doctor visited her because he was troubled about something and wished to consult the tarot cards. After looking at his cards, Marysol told the doctor that several friends would soon invite him on a fishing trip to the Gulf Coast. She predicted that while driving to the coast, they would be involved in an accident in which all would be seriously injured and the doctor would be killed. She advised the doctor not to go. A few weeks later, several of the doctor's close friends invited him to go on a fishing expedition. On the day they came to pick him up, the doctor remembered Marysol's prediction and declined to go at the last minute, pleading a forgotten surgical appointment. There was, indeed, a terrible accident and the men were seriously injured.

Marysol was surprised one day when three dozen roses were delivered to her place of business. At first, the mystic was overwhelmed because she did not know who could be sending her such an obvious token of affection. "Who am I to be receiving such a splendid gift? I am just a simple, humble person who does not deserve this kind of attention." When she read the attached thank-you note, Marysol realized that what she had predicted had in fact happened, and the doctor was profoundly grateful to her for having saved his life.[91]

Chapter 5

RELIGION
AND EDUCATION

Whether it was the North Side, *La Fundición*, *La Corte*, *El TP*, or *La Loma*, most of Fort Worth's barrios were served by institutions that helped to define, unite, and motivate their residents. Churches and schools helped Mexicanos adjust to a strange new land and culture. They gave them hope, comfort, jobs, and a new identity in Fort Worth. The Roman Catholic Mission of San José, the Methodist Church's Wesley Community Center, the Presbyterian Mexican Mission, and other smaller missions scattered wherever there was a Mexican population looked after the spiritual needs of the community and also provided support services—food and clothing distribution, health clinics, kindergarten, English classes, sewing, and other useful crafts. They also offered Americanization programs, organized sports, and children's programs.

These institutions subtly molded and transformed the character, views, and values of this first immigrant generation. The next generation of Mexican Texans, unfamiliar with the mores of the old country, attended American schools—either public or parochial—and learned American values. Jovita Gonzalez, a Mexican American folklorist from South Texas, stated in the late 1920s that:

> Young Texas Mexicans are being trained in American [schools]. Behind them lies a store of traditions of another race, customs of past ages, an innate inherited love and reverence for another country. Ahead of them lies a struggle in which they are to be the champions. It is a struggle for equality and justice before the law, for their full rights as American citizens. They bring with them a broader view, a

clearer understanding of the good and bad qualities of both races. They are the converging element of two antagonistic civilizations; they have the blood of one and have acquired the ideals of the other.[1]

SAN JOSÉ CATHOLIC MISSION

At the turn of the twentieth century, many of the immigrants pouring into North Texas not only from Mexico but also from southern and eastern Europe were Catholic. Catholic priests had been celebrating Mass and delivering the Sacraments to believers scattered throughout the plains of North Central Texas since the 1860s. Around 1870 several Fort Worth area families established a chapel on the Thomas Carrico homestead—the genesis of Fort Worth's first Catholic parish, St. Patrick's Cathedral.[2] But by 1900 church officials were increasingly concerned about the spiritual needs of the laborers who settled north of the Trinity River. Fort Worth's second Catholic parish, All Saints Catholic Church, organized in the spring of 1902, grew out of this concern.

Mrs. H. A. ("Annie") Mulholland hosted the first Mass, celebrated by Father Campbell, in her home at 1305 North Commerce Street. The Mulhollands and twelve other families selected a site at the northeast corner of Northwest 20th Street and North Houston Avenue[3] and began to raise funds to construct a wood-frame building. The church was dedicated in 1903 and served the needs of its English-speaking parishioners until December 1952, when a modern and much larger brick-veneer facility replaced it.[4]

But there was no church for the increasing number of people from Mexico and the Southwest who spoke little or no English. All Saints parish decided to dedicate a chapel to serve the Spanish-speaking community of the North Side.[5] In 1909 the Mission Chapel of San José opened, possibly in a building behind the main church.[6] By 1919 the mission had relocated about four blocks east of All Saints, on the southeast corner of Northwest 14th and North Commerce streets. For the next thirty-six years, San José, under the supervision and guidance of the Claretian[7] order of priests, cared for the physical, educational, and spiritual needs of North Side Mexicanos.[8]

The Claretians had been serving North Texas' Mexicanos since 1902 when priests began to travel to the mining camps between Weatherford and Mineral

Wells and to the agricultural fields scattered throughout North Texas. They offered Mass early in the morning so the field workers could be at their jobs on time. The priests also established itinerant schools to teach reading, writing, and religion to the workers' children during the day. Impressed with the Claretians' missionary work, the Most Reverend Joseph P. Lynch, Bishop of Dallas, invited them to minister to the Mexicanos in Fort Worth's North Side beginning in June 1926. In a May 18, 1942, letter to Father Camillo Torrente, Bishop Lynch recalled the history of the Claretians in his diocese.

> . . . in 1926, I invited Father [Andrew] Resa, then Provincial of the American Province, to take over the Mexican parish of San Jose [sic], in North Fort Worth. To minister to this charge, the provincial sent Reverend Eugene Herran [sic], a most energetic and self-denying missionary . . . . Under the jurisdiction of these Fathers a suitable rectory was constructed and a parochial school founded. [9]

Not many years after taking charge of the San José mission, Father Eugenio Herrán and his assistant, Father Miguel Noval, recognized that the congregation was rapidly outgrowing the original wooden structure built in 1919.[10] Fundraising began in earnest and on June 16, 1930, the old wood-frame building was demolished; groundbreaking ceremonies for the new church were held on June 29.

The blessing and dedication of the new church—a Gothic design constructed of brick and tile—took place on October 26, 1930. An overflow crowd turned out for the historic event. Bishop Lynch officiated and the Very Reverend Father Eustace Flamenco, C.M.F., of Los Angeles, provincial of the Claretian Missionaries, preached the sermon.[11] After four years Father Herrán transferred to a parish in San Antonio, and the Reverend Sebastian Ripero succeeded him at San José.

San José parishioners were proud of their new church and worked hard to sustain it—raising money, supporting activities, or maintaining the building. Those who had no money to give in *la colecta* helped the church by doing volunteer work; some cleaned the church every week. The Holy Name Society—the parish men's club—worked to take care of the physical needs of San José, making repairs, constructing sidewalks, and painting. Longtime member Michael Ayala recalled that "the Claretian priests had the knack of making it seem as if it were your idea, and ultimately it was, for the entire North Side community benefited from the improvements."[12] Society members included Michael Ayala, Ramón Anguiano, Juan Pérez, Félix Narváez, Sisto Herrera, Domingo Martínez, Vincent Martínez, Andrés Morales, Vincent Pérez, Francisco ("Paco") Cruz, Alfonso Rodríguez, and Gus Gómez, to name but a few. The men's club met monthly for early Sunday morning Mass followed by a hearty breakfast. They helped in the *jamaicas* (festivals usually held in the summer on Sunday evenings and on Mexico's patriotic holidays), setting up and manning booths, selling drinks, *raspas* (snowcones), and running the bingo games. Their wives helped decorate and prepared a variety of Mexican foods to sell. The society also organized and participated in the annual Christmas *posada*. The money raised at these events helped defray the costs of maintaining San José's physical plant.[13]

The club for women, *Corazón de María*, met regularly in the basement hall. One of its main functions was to organize pilgrimages. In gratitude for answered prayers, the faithful made *promesas* to visit the Virgin Mary at several sites in Texas and Mexico. The most popular regional destination was *Virgen de San Juan* located in San Juan, in the Lower Rio Grande Valley of Texas. Members of *Corazón de María* also liked to visit the *Basílica de la Virgen de Guadalupe* in Mexico City and *San Juan de los Lagos*, about ninety miles northeast of Guadalajara in the state of Jalisco. Opportunities for sightseeing allowed pilgrims to re-acquaint themselves with their former *patria* and gain a new appreciation of their cultural roots.[14] During the years of the World War II and the Korean Conflict, many relatives of servicemen made *promesas*[15] to the *Virgen* for the safe return of their loved ones.

Juanita Rodríguez, the mother of Rudy, the owner of Rodríguez Festive Foods, organized many of these trips. To raise money for the club and for the pilgrimages, members made and sold tamales just before Christmas. Anita Reza served as president of the organization that included such members as Margarita Pérez, Julia Padilla, Francisca Rico, María Ortiz Ayala, and Juanita Rodríguez.[16]

SAN JOSÉ SCHOOL

The sisters of Saint Mary of Namur also operated San José School on the North Side. The principal of St. Joseph School during the 1930s and 1940s, Sister

1946 school photo taken on the side of San José Church. L to R: Michael Medrano, Alice Berber, Mario Trujillo (partially hidden), Sister Lawrencia, Margarito Padilla, Jr., Raquel Trujillo (face turned), Angelo Ayala, and Daniel Trujillo. *Photo courtesy of Michael and Hope (Padilla) Ayala.*

Lawrencia, SSMN, took a special interest in Mexicanos. In a 1984 interview celebrating her retirement, Sister Lawrencia expressed her affection for her former students, "I love those Mexican . . . . I do. I'm a gringo myself, but they don't think of me as a gringo. I love them. They know that deep down, I'm a Mexican."[17] Sister Lawrencia was resourceful in obtaining badly needed supplies. She organized the yearly Good Fellow program that helped needy families during Christmas. Little girls received a doll and a bag of candies, while little boys collected a toy car or truck and a bag of candies.[18] On occasion she would schedule all-day picnics for the children at Forest Park and didn't hesitate to ask Swift and Company for hot dogs and Mrs. Baird's Bakery for the buns. Because most of the school children were poor and in need of particular items of clothing, she often went on "shopping trips" on their behalf. Taking the streetcar to the downtown district, the determined nun went from store to store, especially Leonard Brothers, asking for shoes and clothing for her poor students. Her earnest and persistent demeanor made it difficult for any merchant to refuse her. Sister Lawrencia also persuaded wealthy individuals to donate money for the children and the school. CBS News anchor Bob Schieffer's father-in-law, Neville G. Penrose,[19] became a major benefactor of San José as a result of the good sister's public relations abilities.[20]

There were few extracurricular activities in the early days and the nuns received virtually no salary—only the twenty-five cents per child per month for tuition.[21] After Father Celestino Iglesias raised enough money to purchase the necessary equipment, students like Román Soto Mercado were able to play football. San José's team competed well against area Catholic schools like St. Ignatius, St. Mary's, and St. Alice.[22] They also played in the Dallas city championships.

From its establishment as a mission in 1908 to 1955 when it was absorbed into All Saints Catholic Church, San José was central to the process of building

1949 Champion San José Football Team. First row sitting L to R: Benny Soto Mercado, Alfred Uranga, Jesse Galván, and Mike Borbolla. Second row kneeling: Arturo García, Román Soto Mercado, Jesse Ayala, Gilbert Ruiz, and Frank López. Third row standing: Jesse Aguirre, Father Antonio Bandrés, C.M.F., and Rudy Herrera. San José Church and School can be seen in the background. This hardy team earned the championship three years in a row—1948, 1949, and 1950. *Photo courtesy of Benny Soto Mercado.*

community among the residents of the North Side. The Claretian fathers united the Mexicanos, ministering to their spiritual and temporal needs until 1992 when the Franciscans took charge. Generations of Mexicanos and Mexicanas were baptized, confirmed, taught, married, counseled, and buried thanks to the selfless service of the Claretian order.

THE WESLEY COMMUNITY HOUSE

In 1908, with so many foreign newcomers making their homes on the North Side, local Methodist Church officials decided to establish a mission dedicated to serving the needs of this growing community of seventeen nationalities.[23] The Wesley Community House was opened as a settlement house with a Christian orientation. It mirrored a national pattern of similar institutions. In 1889 the first settlement houses made their début on the American urban scene in New York and Chicago. Social reformer Jane Addams founded Hull House in Chicago to meet the social and material needs of newly arrived immigrants from southern and eastern Europe. Settlement houses emphasized programs to help foreigners adapt to life in the United States, such as instruction in English as a second language, American culture and customs, and practical arts and crafts. Wesley House combined aspects of the social reform movement of the late nineteenth century with principles of the Social Gospel movement,[24] which motivated many Christians to take a more active role in addressing the physical needs of the less fortunate members of society. A 1930s report summed it up:

> A settlement house, such as the Wesley Community House, is able to mean much to the people because the workers live among them as neighbors—visit in the homes, come to know the deepest needs, and gain their confidence, so that they are constantly called upon, day and night, for counsel and assistance in all types of situations pertaining to individuals and family life.[25]

The City Mission Board, composed of area Methodist pastors, appointed Miss Lillie G. Fox as part-time director. In a rented four-room house on the North Side that also served as her home, Miss Fox organized and supervised weekly sewing classes and Sunday afternoon religious services for people of various nationalities.[26] By 1911 the ministry had expanded to the point that it required the services of a full-time director, and its supervisory council, the Women's Council of Southern Methodism, appointed Miss Eugenia Smith deaconess to oversee the North Side mission full-time.[27] Deaconess Smith promptly rented a house to serve as her home and a temporary center for her ministry, but the need for a permanent center soon became evident.[28] In 1913 the board purchased a lot at 2131 North Commerce, in the heart of the North Side, on which to build the first permanent facility, described in an unpublished history of the Wesley House.

> The building was two stories high and had twelve rooms. The upstairs housed the workers and contained bedrooms, a living room, kitchen, dining room, bath, hall, and porch. A large sleeping porch on the south was added later. Downstairs there were the office, assembly room, club and class rooms, all used for the community work.
>
> A few years later the Wesley House workers felt that they must have a playground for their children. For this purpose two lots were

Wesley Community House, circa 1920. *Photo courtesy of Wesley Community House.*

bought, the cotteges [sic] which were located on these lots were moved, and a playground begun.[29]

One of Deaconess Smith's first efforts was to organize and direct the Sunday school, which quickly grew from only two boys on the first day. Attendance the following three weeks increased to seven, fourteen, and twenty-nine.[30]

Referring back to these years, an early 1940s report commented on the background and spiritual condition of Mexican immigrants:

> These people had come to Texas to make their homes, unfamiliar with the laws, customs and language. Especially the Mexicans had come from a country in which they were virtually poverty-stricken, looking for work. Also many of them had broken from the Catholic Church, which had kept them in ignorance and poverty, and they really had no religion. These things appealed to the women of our Methodist Churches, and they felt they wished to help in this situation.[31]

In 1914, using Wesley House's front porch as a speaking platform, Reverend Dennis Macune of the Boulevard Methodist Church led a small North Side congregation in song and worship. Twelve people were converted and the Mexican Methodist Church was formally organized. Deaconess Smith gave the following description of the founding of the church:

> Juan los Santos joined with us and was licensed to preach and became our first pastor. Following him, Benito Hernández was converted, licensed to preach, and became our second pastor. Reverend Eugenio Vidaurri was also licensed to preach and is now my pastor in Houston. In 1921 we bought the old corner saloon that had been such a menace to the community and tore it down and built a Church on the same spot, using the heavy lumber from the old in the new building.[32]

On April 11, 1914, the building was formally inaugurated as the Jerome Duncan Wesley House, after the presiding elder of the Fort Worth District at the time the facility was planned in 1911. After 1919 two other small buildings were added at the back of the original lot. One of these served as the Goodwill Industries center from 1927 to 1931. People could purchase clothing items for a nominal amount or in exchange for work. However, club activities required more space, and Goodwill moved out after 1931. A 1940s report recorded:

> The used clothing which is sent in, we do not hand out, for our people do not expect it, and there are other relief agencies in the City. We have rummage sales, which our people eagerly attend, and while the things are sold for a very small sum, they feel they are paying for them. We try always to avoid doing anything which might pauperize.[33]

Wesley Community House, circa 1930. Staff distributing coats to a waiting crowd. *Photo courtesy of Wesley Community House.*

Young boxer taking advantage of Wesley Community House's popular sports programs, circa 1950. *Photo courtesy of Wesley Community House.*

During the 1930s the Wesley House operated with an annual budget of $7,000, raised from voluntary contributions by the Women's Missionary Council and other area Methodist missionary societies. The Fort Worth Community Chest also took notice of the center's charitable work and began substantial yearly contributions.[34] Every dollar was put to good use by a dedicated staff that usually consisted of a director, kindergarten instructor, club coordinator, visiting helper, janitor, and housekeeper. In addition to dispensing food, shelter, clothing, fuel, medical help and supplies, and family counseling, the Wesley House also initiated and maintained a daily schedule of various activities for all ages. (See Appendix B) Over the years volunteers, eventually as many as forty each week, came from various area churches, the Junior League, Texas Wesleyan

College, Texas Christian University, and other civic organizations, and gave generously of their time and talents to help those in need.[35]

Furthermore, Mexicanos, or any other immigrant group who faced hunger, homelessness, lack of clothing, sickness, unemployment, despair, or domestic problems, could find help at the Wesley House. Education, recreation, advice on hygiene, nutrition, or child raising were all available to a North Side population estimated to be approximately four to five thousand.[36]

In addition to its social services and it popular sports programs, Wesley House also sponsored other activities—woodworking and scouting were especially popular with boys, sewing and scouting for girls.[37] Wesley House sponsored a variety of programs for girls that reflected traditional values and domestic skills. Members of the Girl Reserve Club learned to sew their own uniforms, for example. One of the most popular and well-attended programs, the sewing school, offered classes for all age groups. The total number of girls enrolled at Wesley House was eighty, and approximately fifty-five of this eighty, aged six to thirteen, met on Wednesday afternoons. The following is a brief description of their activities:

> Last year the girls six years old made gowns, and the ones seven and eight years old made aprons and bloomers. In addition, the eight year olds made slips. The girls from nine to thirteen years made dresses with the younger girls making more simple dresses. The Wesley House furnished all of this material. It would be impossible to conduct this sewing school without volunteer helpers. The class had fourteen teachers most of whom were Texas Women's College girls and women from the different missionary societies of the city. From five to five thirty this class had a devotional period which was conducted by T.W.C. girls.[38]

The Mothers' Club met every Monday afternoon from two-thirty to four to make elaborate quilts and linens that they sold for less than a dollar to any mother who wanted one. Sometimes they participated in musical programs or heard lectures covering health, hygiene, and other relevant domestic topics.[39] Some women took this opportunity to learn to read English or Spanish. In the mid-

1930s the wife of the Mexican Consul assisted the Wesley House by teaching the Spanish class. The class relied on a textbook used in schools throughout Mexico entitled *Learn One, Teach One*.[40]

The Wesley House, with the Central Methodist Church, sponsored a chapter of the Campfire Girls. Fees and dues were underwritten by the sponsoring agencies, ensuring wider participation. Campfire Girls met on Monday afternoons for singing, storytelling, crafts, and games. They also shared in devotionals consisting primarily of Biblical stories that underscored character-building traits.[41]

In its amazing variety of program offerings, Wesley House did not overlook the importance of musical instruction. A lay volunteer, Mrs. Pat Matthews, organized and directed a choral club for girls and boys that met Tuesday evenings.[42] Mrs. Matthews also offered music lessons on Wednesdays, Thursdays, and Saturdays. Instructors, like Alice De León Contreras, volunteered their time to teach approximately twenty women and children, who took full advantage of these free piano and voice classes.[43] Miss Contreras did so well that she earned a piano scholarship at Texas Women's College.[44] She later returned to volunteer her services to Wesley House. A 1940s report acknowledged the bitter contrast between the preparation that the young received and the circumstances that Mexicanos encountered in the surrounding communities:

> We have a number of splendid boys and girls equipped and ready for work, but I am sorry to say that through this section prejudice is very strong, and our hearts are hurt many times when we see them deprived of positions, proper hospitalization care, and other advantages which they deserve. However, we are feeling better about this for we feel in many ways this is being broken down—though it is very gradual.[45]

Although monthly attendance during the early 1930s was around 1,600 persons, Wesley House's impact in the community grew to be widespread and profound. Mexican immigrants who had lived on the North Side for years finally took the initiative to learn to read and write English, either at Wesley's night school or with a volunteer worker, to help them prepare and apply for United States citizenship.[46] The history of the Wesley House reported that "The night classes in English have been a bright spot in the work especially as the mothers have declared to their families their determination not to be shut out of many things because of the language barrier."[47]

All of these activities which the Wesley House sponsors are sponsored in order that the Mexicans may become better American citizens. By their advice and help the Wesley House serves as a friend to the Mexican. The Wesley House is the "open door" to American life for the Mexicans.[48]

The Wesley Community House operated at the North Commerce location for almost sixty years. At the end of World War II new attitudes led to a gradual easing of property restrictions affecting minorities, and Mexican Americans began to live outside their traditional enclaves. This demographic shift became the subject of concern to the Wesley staff by the mid–1950s:

The question that we had to take care of first was whether or not Wesley House would stay in this location. Even our board wondered as to the advisability of stay [sic] here. In a study of the problem, we couldn't help but think about a question asked of us by the Local Board of Education. They asked our help in the language problem because so many of the Latin-American children were failing in the public schools. Spanish is spoken in the majority of homes and the children do not know the English well enough. We learned from them how the Latin-Americans have moved all over Fort Worth and it is impossible to reach them all from any one place. We decided then that we would try to do more extension work, keeping this as our base.[49]

The center's concern for the continuing erosion of its constituency again resurfaced in a 1959 annual report:

Our enrollment this year in kindergarten was not as high as heretofore due to the fact that there were not enough children to walk [from their homes to the center]. Our neighborhood is moving away from us because of the fact that this area has been classified for heavy industry and the houses are falling apart in many cases. When they become city-condemned the people hunt other locations. That means that the children have to be picked up. For this reason our Board was very anxious to do more extension work in Washington Heights which seemed to be a very promising area. With the help of the Woman's Division we were able to rent a small house in Washington Heights and as soon as we can get it in readiness, we hope to carry on more girls and boys work.[50]

In 1967 the Wesley Community House moved from its facility on North Commerce to 3600 North Crump, in the Diamond Hill area of Fort Worth. They raised $180,000 through the generous donations of Methodist women from all over the United States and from proceeds of the sale of the old building to the Pan American Golf Association, which bought the six lots of the North Commerce property. The association kept the corner church building but tore down the two-story wood-frame structures that had served as the old Wesley Community House.

The center succeeded in gaining the confidence and trust of the community, despite the fact that most Mexicanos were Roman Catholic. In fact, priests occasionally warned their parishioners to stay away from Wesley House, as this excerpt from the 1953-1954 Annual Narrative Report describes:

> Mary Ann with a long sad face come [sic] one day to inform me that she had been ordered not to come to Wesley House anymore. She was getting ready to [m]ake her first communion and the priest had told her to stay away from us. I told her I was very sorry, that I would miss her and assured her that she would be welcome any time she wished and could come back. I don't know how she managed but she is back every day as usual.[51]

To this day the Wesley Community House Center, directed by Irma Valencia, continues its mission of social work that includes childcare, after-school

Photo of Wesley Community House kindergarten class graduation on the steps of the house, circa 1940. *Photo courtesy of Wesley Community House.*

activities and sports, counseling, and case management. Personal enrichment programs teach topics such as modeling, art, public speaking, sewing, and music that are designed to build character and self-esteem. Until 1995 the center also assisted resident aliens with immigration processing and paperwork.[52]

WESLEY COMMUNITY CENTER SCHOOL

Absorbing the first waves of immigration after the turn of the century, Americans believed that the best way to deal with the newcomers was to teach them to understand the dominant language, culture, and customs. Peace, stability and prosperity would be more likely to thrive in an atmosphere in which differences in language and culture could be minimized. Americanization programs were designed to help immigrants become self-sufficient as well as productive members of American society. As most of the children from the North Side were sons and daughters of immigrant Mexicanos in the 1930s, the Wesley Community House concentrated on curriculum and programs designed to Americanize this younger generation. Reflecting on the center's primary goals, Jennie C. Congleton, head resident at Wesley Community House in 1937, noted that

. . . [f]or years I heard much of the work in Mexican
Communities, and how those working there loved it. Now I can understand, for I, too, have the "Mexican Fever." These few months of getting acquainted have been happy ones; the people patient with [sic],
and considerate of the new-comer in their midst . . . . With the help of
a splendid corps of volunteers, and other interested [sic], the Wesley
House is taking its place with the other Social Agencies of the City, as
an important factor in the building of American Citizens, with high
Christian ideals.[53]

The kindergarten opened its doors to all children between the ages of four
and six Monday to Friday from nine to eleven-thirty in the morning.
Approximately fifty children took advantage of the program at Wesley House.[54]
Although teaching English to prepare immigrant youngsters to enter first grade
was the kindergarten's primary emphasis, the children also received instruction
on a variety of topics such as health, citizenship, culture, and nature. Over the
years teachers and their assistants provided an often overlooked
community service by paying attention to any illness or physical problem that, if
not treated, could have become serious,

The kindergarten program at Wesley House offered other benefits as well.
At mid-morning the children took a short break while each received a glass of
milk and a graham cracker. This small treat supplemented a diet that in general
was insufficient for the children's proper nutrition. In addition, a registered nurse
examined each child once a week.[55]

The children occasionally were treated to a picnic at a park or an educational trip to the zoo, a factory, or other place of business in addition to their regularly scheduled recreational activities. Kindergarteners appreciated the monthly
birthday observances and also participated in dramatic presentations that
revolved around special holidays such as Thanksgiving, Christmas, and Easter.[56]
A 1953 annual report noted that the

The Christmas party is always a high light [sic] and this year the
Christmas story was dramatized by eighty children while one hundred

and forty brothers and sisters and mothers and fathers looked on. The stage was the center of the room and a spotlight was used to focus attention on the scene in action. A real bale of hay made the manger scene more realistic and travelers crowded the inn while the maidservants hurried to and fro. Herod's soldiers were present with swords and armor made in the shop and could be seen on the streets for several days after Christmas.[57]

Kindergarten graduations also featured dramatizations that included popular children's stories such as *Goldilocks and the Three Bears* and *Little Red Riding Hood*.

A parent-teachers club consisting of kindergarten mothers held monthly meetings. In addition to time set aside specifically for recreation, mothers heard lectures on sanitation, health, the preparation of foods, and other topics.[58] As a direct result of the kindergarten experience, Wesley House workers realized the necessity of providing additional services to the North Side community. In the words of an anonymous staff member, the most urgent needs often included "better housing, better streets, play-ground[s] where Mexican boys and girls feel they are welcome, adequate hospitalization for our Mexican people—prejudice responsible for lack of facilities—we are working toward this and other situations."[59]

Interacting daily with the kindergartners, the teachers soon realized that a large number of them were malnourished. It was often the case that grocery stores did not stock the ingredients for native dishes, and local grocery products were unfamiliar. Without their customary foods the children became malnourished, and Wesley House workers decided to offer American-style cooking classes. Separate classes were offered to housewives and girls. Held every Tuesday afternoon from two-forty-five to four, the Young Mothers' Cooking Class was taught by Miss Enlow, the director of the home economics department at Texas Christian University. Miss Enlow also supervised the Girls' Cooking Class immediately following the adult class from four to five-fifteen.

The response from the community proved overwhelming; eighty-five girls applied for a class originally intended to accommodate only ten. In the class the girls learned the essentials of preparing and serving typical American dishes for breakfast, lunch, and dinner. At the end of each year the mothers' class prepared a delicious Mexican dinner in honor of Miss Enlow and her assistants, and the girls' class cooked and served an American-style dinner for their mothers.[60] Convinced of the center's positive impact, Katherine Arnold, head resident from 1934 to 1935, stated,

> . . . [w]e believe that one of the outstanding results of the operation of Wesley House is the improvement in living conditions in the homes of the foreigners that has been brought about by the teaching at this community center." Needy North Side families could count on the frequent charitable donations of foodstuffs from Fort Worth's Methodist community; and, during the Great Depression, Wesley House served as a distribution point for government flour to families living north of the Trinity River. Every afternoon from 4:30 to 5:30, two workers distributed Red Cross flour to approximately 1,700 families, of which twenty percent (340 families) were Mexicanos, twenty percent were African Americans, and sixty percent were Anglo Americans. The distribution of the twenty-four-and-a-half pound sacks of flour was tightly controlled and was linked to the number in each family. Records were kept on index cards, signatures were required, and the date on which the family received the flour was stamped on the card.[61]

Many people in the Hispanic community, such as Margaret Molleda, Pete Zepeda, Paulita Gutiérrez, and Amador Gutiérrez, Sr., responded to the spiritual principles of the Methodist denomination and became active members. Deaconess Eugenia Smith, the first head resident, said it best: "It is a joy to work with the Mexicans, they make the finest, most unselfish Christians, and they are so appreciative of every little kindness. I love them."[62]

LA PRIMERA IGLESIA PRESBITERIANA MEXICANA

Fort Worth's First Mexican Presbyterian Church was the center of religious and social life in *La Corte*. The history of this organization began with the arrival of Pastor Guillermo A. Walls on September 15, 1925.[63]

Guillermo Alexander Walls was born on December 25, 1886, in Matamoros, Tamaulipas, Mexico, of Scottish and Mexican parents—William Alexander Walls[64] and Concepción ("Concha") Aguilar. In 1916 Guillermo studied at Union Theological Seminary in Richmond, Virginia, and shortly thereafter accepted a position as instructor at the Austin Presbyterian Theological Seminary, where he completed the requirements for a B.A. in Christian education. In April 1919 Walls was ordained into the Texas Mexican Presbytry and assumed the post of director of Christian education at a church in San Benito (1919-1921). Guillermo then came to Fort Worth where he earned a B.A. from Texas Christian University and married Raquel Rocha on August 15, 1921. Originally from Mexico, Raquel had attended the *Escuela normal de Saltillo*, a teacher training institute in the northern state of Coahuila.[65]

In 1922 Walls took his new wife to Austin where he worked as an evangelist with that city's Mexican Presbyterian Church until 1925. During this time

(1935) Young people's Sunday school class at the Mexican Presbyterian Church, 901 Florence St. (*La Corte*). Guillermo A. Walls, who pastored here between 1927 and 1950, is seen at the far corner. *Photo courtesy of Herlinda Balderas García.*

Guillermo and Raquel started a family that included three children: Billy, Raúl, and Elizabeth. Walls briefly ministered as an evangelist in San Antonio's extensive community of Mexicanos before accepting similar work in Fort Worth, where he remained until 1943.

When Guillermo A. Walls and his family arrived in Fort Worth in 1925 he had neither property, facilities, nor equipment. Undaunted, Walls immediately began a Presbyterian mission for Mexicanos near the heart of the city. The first religious services took place under the shade trees in the yards of private homes in *La Corte*.

A friendly, outgoing, and resourceful man, Walls quickly garnered the assistance of local Anglo Presbyterians. Lay people such as Mrs. R. B. Rawls, representing the local ladies' missions organizations, and Dr. M. E. Gilmore, president of the Tarrant County Medical Association, supplied volunteers, funds, furnishings, and equipment.[66]

During the first year area Presbyterian churches raised $8,000 to fund the construction of the initial mission building. On December 31, 1926, the *Primera Iglesia Presbiteriana mexicana* was organized and chartered.[67] The first church officials were Juan Frías (elder), Josías Balderas (elder), and Francisco Vega (deacon). Most of the church membership came from *La Corte* and other Fort Worth barrios, but Josías Balderas and his family traveled thirty-two miles from Cleburne every Sunday to attend services.[68]

The church built a larger and more formal building next door in 1928, and the original church building became the Mexican Presbyterian Center. The building was soon converted to a medical clinic and kindergarten. Open weekday mornings from nine to twelve the clinic was under the direction of Dr. L. M. Whitsitt, a volunteer and member of the Westminister Presbyterian Church. The center treated mainly minor injuries, ailments, and burns and supplied inoculations and birthing services. Dr. Whitsitt also gave advice on health and proper hygiene. Reverend Walls had an automobile to transport the very sick to a doctor or hospital.[69]

The pastor's wife, Raquel, took care of the kindergarten class, with an initial enrollment of over thirty children. The goal of the kindergarten program was to help prepare the young for Anglo schools. Here, children took the first steps to learn English, which would change their lives. Many volunteers, Anglos and Mexicanos alike, worked at the Presbyterian Center: Mrs. W. L. Foster (in charge of area education), Mrs. M. S. Gilbert (intermediate teacher), Luisa Frías (intermediate club coordinator), Teófila Vega (children's club coordinator), and E. Luna and M. Campirano (volunteer university students). Elisa C. Martínez was the first and only secretary of the Mexican Presbyterian Center, serving *La Corte* for over fifty years.[70]

Donations from Fort Worth's Presbyterian community and additional funding from the Community Chest supported the Mexican Presbyterian Center's ever-increasing range of services. Like the Wesley Community House in the North Side, Walls' ministry in *La Corte* followed the model of a typical Christian settlement house. The primary objective of the center was to enable Mexicanos, young and old, to become Americanized as quickly as possible to function more effectively in their new environment. In view of that goal the center provided early childhood education in English and other special services to ensure that the young Mexican American generation would grow up literate. English classes were also available to working Mexicanos at night. Pastor Walls felt that a command of English was the springboard to greater opportunities and a better life for Mexicanos in the United States.[71]

Instruction at the Mexican Presbyterian Center was not limited to English and early childhood education. With Americanization in mind it offered classes in American customs, cooking (including reading recipes in English), art, music, sewing, and miscellaneous crafts.[72] Pastor Walls was available to Mexicanos who needed help preparing for American citizenship. This process entailed learning U. S. history, politics, laws, and customs. Walls encouraged anyone who wished to stay in this country to begin the process of securing U. S. citizenship and become familiar with all the rights, laws, and privileges that come with naturalization.

Even with such strong emphasis on Americanization, Walls never forgot the customs, language, or dignity of the Mexican community. Throughout the calendar year Walls and the center's staff actively promoted the feeling of *Mexicanidad* (pride in Mexican heritage) by a variety of programs. The center taught Spanish language classes to Anglos and to Mexican Americans who wished to stay proficient in their mother tongue. Mexican cooking classes appealed to the public. The center celebrated *las fiestas patrias* such as *cinco de mayo*, *dieciséis de septiembre*, and *día de la raza* (October 12) by staging modest productions that included Mexican national music, dance, and colorful native costumes made by the center's clients. Popular dances included *Las Chapanecas* and *El Jarabe Tapatío*; much of the music was from the era of the Mexican Revolution. Such well-loved and nostalgic pieces as *Guadalajara*, *La negra*, *Jalisco*, *Allá en el Rancho Grande*, *Las mañanitas*, *Las golondrinas*, and *Cielito Lindo* were especially appreciated. These programs reminded Mexicanos of their roots and instilled pride in their unique culture.[73]

In addition to classes held during the regular school year, the Presbyterian Church also sponsored vacation Bible school. Usually held the first three weeks of June, the program attracted about sixty to seventy-five neighborhood children of all ages. The cost of refreshments and miscellaneous supplies for the entire three weeks was about thirty-two cents per student. Luisa Frías, Teófila Vega, and Raquel Walls planned, coordinated, and taught during vacation Bible school, assisted by two other volunteers—María Mena and E. Luna.[74]

The Mexican Presbyterian Center also doubled as a labor clearinghouse, where every day Walls and his staff matched unemployed Mexicanos with jobs in Fort Worth, the North Texas area, or in the agricultural fields of other states. During World War II Guillermo Walls became directly involved in the *bracero* (hired hand) program, designed by the Roosevelt administration to alleviate domestic manpower shortages by actively recruiting and arranging transportation for Mexicanos, especially from San Luis Potosí. The U.S. government issued temporary visas to Mexican workers. Employers often took advantage of *braceros*, forcing them to work long hours for low pay and to live in poor conditions.

Walls regularly distributed food and clothing, cared for the sick, sheltered the homeless, and counseled those in trouble. Frequently he went to court to interpret for people who did not speak English. He also became a moral crusader against bootlegging and moonshining, which were prevalent in all of Fort Worth's barrios. A notorious site for bootlegging in *La Corte* was under the Henderson Bridge; police periodically raided this area and often met gunfire there. Anxious to promote neighborhood peace and safety, Pastor Walls never hesitated to call the police to patrol the area and eliminate potential danger, and he often spoke out against the practice. He did his best to promote safety for all who lived in *La Corte*, regardless of race, creed, or color.[75]

Because he was of mixed parentage, the son of Scottish and Mexican parents, Guillermo Walls was a natural bridge builder between two sometimes antagonistic cultures. Confident and equally at ease among Anglos or Mexicanos, Walls was a true social pioneer, prefiguring a later era characterized by a growing trend toward mutual understanding and respect. Walls had the ability to mingle with Fort Worth's Anglo community, win their respect, enlist their help for his work in the mission, and harness their resources. A firm believer in education as the great equalizer, the bridge builder urged his fellow Mexicanos to take full advantage of Fort Worth's educational opportunities.

By the late 1930s the Mexican Presbyterian Center even had a curio shop selling Mexican arts, crafts, and other products. Walls encouraged area residents to consign their crafts to the shop, which also received periodic shipments from the interior of Mexico. The store stocked such typical items as *sarapes*, *guitarras*, *jarros*, *huaraches*, *piñatas*, and small colorful chairs for children. Local Anglos saw the center as a superb place to purchase interesting gifts.[76] In 1938 Eleanor Roosevelt, accompanied by Secret Service agents, visited the center and inspected the curio shop.[77] According to the church secretary, Elisa C. Martínez, the First Lady bought four large *molcajetes,* which she intended to use as ashtrays for the President and his visitors. Mrs. Roosevelt also bought a few handmade pottery dishes and vases.[78]

Over the years the *Primera Iglesia Presbiteriana mexicana* and the Mexican Presbyterian Center have served generations of Mexicanos.[79] Some came to worship, while others learned to read and write or to fill out their citizenship papers. Still others sought medical help, food, clothing, shelter, or jobs. The center and its staff quickly became the heart of *La Corte*, providing indispensable services to the entire community. From 1925 to 1949 Guillermo A. Walls and his wife, Raquel, worked ceaselessly to better the lives of Mexicanos and Mexicanas and to foster goodwill by bridging the gap between two great cultures.

When Walls retired in 1949, the leadership of the *Primera Iglesia Presbiteriana mexicana* passed to his former student, C. S. Guerrero.[80] After retirement Walls worked out of his home at 401 West First Street and continued to assist at the church. From 1944 to 1949 he held the position of Honorary Fort Worth Mexican Consul. In 1948 Walls also helped organize Fort Worth's Mexican Chamber of Commerce. During this period he dabbled in real estate and helped people prepare their income tax returns. He engaged in civic work, serving as president of *La federación regional de organizaciones mexicanas y latinoamericanas*, an association that kept in touch with diverse *latino* organizations throughout the city of Fort Worth. In 1949 Walls accepted a position at a Mexican Presbyterian Church in San Bernardino, California, where he died in 1957. Raquel died in the early 1960s.[81]

SANTUARIO DEL CORAZÓN DE MARÍA

If Texas Steel Company was the undisputed corporate and employment center of the South Side, then the Immaculate Heart of Mary Catholic Church (*Santuario del Corazón de María*) was its spiritual base. Within a few years after North Side's San José Mission was established in 1909 the Claretian missionaries saw the need to serve the city's other major Mexican barrios. Initially they accomplished this by sending missionaries from San José to administer the Sacraments in private homes. With the steadily increasing number of Mexicanos working for Texas Steel Company, establishing a satellite mission in *La Fundición* was the next logical step. On January 3, 1927, the Claretians purchased a lot and by the following month had contracted to build a small chapel dedicated to Saint Ann (later to be renamed Immaculate Heart). On July 10 of that year, the Most Reverend Joseph P. Lynch, Bishop of Dallas, dedicated and blessed the *Santuario de Santa Ana*. From that day the fathers held regular services, and later the Church Extension Society presented a statue of St. Ann to the chapel.[82]

As the population of *La Fundición* grew, a resident pastor was assigned to the mission, and the Claretians began to explore options for enlarging the church. In the summer of 1947 the resourceful fathers bought the army chapel building of a former military camp in Gainesville and moved it to the lots next to the original chapel. On August 22, the feast day of the Immaculate Heart of Mary, shortly after the former army chapel came to rest on a newly poured concrete foundation, Bishop Lynch dedicated and renamed it *Santuario del Corazón de María*. A few years later, on December 9, 1951, the chapel building suffered $20,000 damage in a fire caused by faulty electric wiring. Fortunately, the insurance proceeds allowed construction to begin on a new brick facility. Immaculate Heart was re-blessed and dedicated on March 1952.[83]

A contingent group of St. Mary of Namur nuns from Our Lady of Victory School consistently helped with a variety of tasks around the church, such as teaching catechism classes. Claretians like Father Antonio Bandrés looked out for the spiritual and temporal interests of the people of *La Fundición*. In addition to celebrating Mass and fulfilling his pastoral duties, during the mid-1950s Father Bandrés made repeated requests to city leaders to pave area street and requested better lighting and police protection.[84]

Through its religious and spiritual mission and community-building activities, the church succeeded in uniting the people of the South Side, giving them hope, purpose, and focus. Just as the parishioners of the Mexican Presbyterian church celebrated *Mexicanidad*, the Claretian fathers in the South Side mission went out of their way to promote Mexican culture. The entire community of believers encouraged the observance of all the *fiestas patrias*, special church holy days, and feast days of saints with much traditional pomp, creating a feeling of solidarity among the parishioners.

During the 1950s, José and Minnie Martínez Gutiérrez went on various religious pilgrimages along with other members of their South Side Immaculate Heart of Mary Catholic Church. When José recovered from an illness, they made a pilgrimage of thanksgiving to the *Virgen* at her shrine at San Juan de los Lagos in the state of Jalisco. They traveled on a church-sponsored, specially chartered bus that took forty-four pilgrims almost fifteen hundred miles to the shrine. Minnie recalled staying at "bad hotels" and enduring the suspicious stares of "mustachioed old men" and other natives. After a few days of devotion, prayer, and sightseeing, the church group returned by train to Fort Worth. On another occasion they went to give thanks for the recovery of their seven-year-old daughter from the effects of rheumatic fever. The Gutiérrezes felt that God had intervened, especially after doctors failed to help her recover.[85]

Today Immaculate Heart of Mary Catholic Church continues to be the heart and soul of *La Fundición*, providing religious services and instruction to the South Side community. After 1961 the Claretian fathers turned over the administration of the church to the Franciscan Capuchin order of priests.[86]

SAN MATEO MISSION

As Hispanics began to populate the west-central Fort Worth barrio *El TP*, the Claretian fathers of San José responded to pleas from residents of the area to form a mission. Consequently, in 1941 they established the San Mateo Mission Chapel, dedicated to the New Testament evangelist Matthew, at 2930 Spring Street.[87] The original chapel building measured twenty by forty feet and had pews on both sides with one central aisle. The Texas & Pacific Railroad donated the church bell. At first, priests from St. Patrick's Cathedral and San José Church provided bi-monthly services, depending upon their availability. Claretian fathers also organized Saturday morning catechism classes taught by Mexican nuns from Our Lady of Victory School. In the early 1950s the original church building was demolished in order to make way for the widening and paving of Vickery Boulevard. The parish immediately built a new structure on adjacent property and held mass every Sunday until the current brick church was built sometime in the 1990s.[88]

SAN JUAN MISSION

With San José caring for the North Side and Santa Ana (Immaculate Heart) covering the South Side, the Claretians felt that the eastern part of the city needed to be addressed. They began construction of a small chapel in October 1927. On January 8, 1928, the Most Reverend Joseph P. Lynch, Bishop of Dallas, dedicated the little chapel, naming it San Juan after one of the four New Testament evangelists. Although it became an active religious and social center for area residents, the chapel was torn down because it stood in the way of the construction of the North-South Freeway.[89]

OUR LADY OF GUADALUPE MISSION

Our Lady of Guadalupe Mission began in 1948 when the pastor of San José Church, the Claretian Father Aloysius S. Dot, planned to establish a center for teaching the catechism in *La Loma*. Veterans returning after World War II were eager to avail themselves of the G.I. Bill and purchase homes so they could start families. A building boom rapidly expanded the old city limits and new subdivisions sprang up north of the North Side in *La Loma* and Diamond Hill areas. Mexican Americans, no longer limited to certain geographic areas within the city, delighted in the opportunity to build their homes wherever they pleased. These new areas to the north of the stockyards became the concern of Father Dot.[90]

Photo of class of 1953-54
Our Lady of Guadalupe
School, Grades 4, 5, and 6.
*Photo
courtesy of Sister Mary Patricia,
Our Lady of Victory School.*

In late summer 1949 construction on the first catechist center began on North Ellis Street, immediately southeast of Meacham Field in the barrio known as *La Loma*. The center was completed on October 22, 1949, and by the end of the month thirteen children enrolled in the first kindergarten class. Catechism classes were taught after school from three to five o'clock. The building became a true neighborhood center, available for Boy Scout meetings, mothers' club functions, and for teaching art, music, and sewing. On December 11 of that year the Bishop's Auxiliary, the Most Reverend A. Danglmyar, blessed and dedicated the center, naming it in honor of Our Lady of Guadalupe. Danglmyar also encouraged Father Dot to consider expanding the range of services at the center.[91]

At Father Danglemyar's urging Father Dot purchased eleven lots at the corner of East Long and Ross streets in April of 1950. On February 15 of the following year the center moved the two blocks from North Ellis to its new address on East Long. However, the area's exploding demographics quickly necessitated a church with an entire range of services.[92] Over 180 people attended the first Mass held at the Guadalupe Center on October 19, 1952, with more than two hundred people on the following Sunday.[93]

Bishop Thomas K. Gorman initiated the fundraising campaign by donating $15,000 and challenged area residents to match or exceed that amount through their own efforts. By 1955 the architectural plans[94] had been finalized and a contractor had agreed to a cost of $50,000 to build a brick structure capable of seating four hundred people. On April 22, 1956, Bishop Gorman and the Claretian Provincial, the Very Reverend Emeterio de la Rosa, blessed and dedicated the newly completed Our Lady of Guadalupe Catholic Church.[95] Guadalupe's first pastor was Father Raymond Martínez.[96]

OUR LADY OF VICTORY SCHOOL

Sisters of Saint Mary of Namur, the Roman Catholic order responsible for establishing Our Lady of Victory School, was founded in 1819 in Namur, Belgium. In 1863 the order sent five nuns as missionaries to America to work with Native Americans in St. Louis, Missouri. Civil War skirmishes diverted the five nuns instead to Lockport, New York. Lockport's Bishop Timon, who had been a missionary in Texas, had a keen interest in expanding Catholic activities in the Lone Star State.[97] Because of this connection, Bishop Claude Marie Dubuis asked the Sisters of Namur to come to Texas to establish schools. In 1873 the order established Sacred Heart Academy in Waco. From there the Sisters of Namur branched out to Corsicana in 1874, set up St. Xavier Academy in Denison in 1876, St. Joseph Academy in Sherman in 1877, and finally turned their attention to Fort Worth in 1885, where they first taught at St. Ignatius School (next to St. Patrick's Cathedral). After twenty-five years, the school required more space and the sisters began looking for land in the South Side.[98]

In 1909 the sisters of Saint Mary of Namur purchased approximately twenty-three acres of the original Shaw Dairy for $55,000 to establish Our Lady of Victory School as their local base. Architect Marshall R. Sanguinet designed the school and dedicated the cornerstone on August 5, 1909. On September 12, 1910, Our Lady of Victory School opened its doors with eight sisters eager to begin teaching their charges. One year later the school received accreditation to confer degrees to members of the order.[99]

Initially thirty-one boarders and forty-one day students attended classes in the five-story, 64,000 square-foot Gothic structure housing a library, an auditorium with stage, a cathedral-like chapel, four classrooms, four music rooms, study halls, and recreation rooms. The building also boasted offices, receiving parlors, dining rooms, dormitories, an Otis elevator, a steam laundry, electricity, and, in wintertime, vapor heat. An adjacent artesian well provided all the school's water. Tuition began at two dollars a month for day students while boarders paid $100 for a five-month session. The first group of boarders came from many different places—Quanah, Ranger, Mineral Wells, Dallas, and Galveston, Texas, Oklahoma, Arkansas, and Mexico.[100] The electric rail line on Hemphill Street made the school accessible to the day students.[101]

Boys could attend from the first through eighth grades until the early 1950s but could not board. Boys usually attended Laneri for their junior high and high school years.[102] The last graduating class at Our Lady of Victory was in May 1961. After 1961 girls from Our Lady of Victory and boys from Laneri all transferred to Nolan High School, under the auspices of the Catholic diocese of Fort Worth. Our Lady of Victory still educates children from pre-kindergarten to eighth grade; the enrollment as of April 1998 at Our Lady of Victory School was 228 students. The sisters also teach catechism classes on a regular basis at the parish churches of Immaculate Heart, San Mateo, and Guadalupe.

Chapter 6

COMMUNITY LIFE AND ORGANIZATIONS

Whether from church, school, sports, military service, or politics, Mexicanos and Mexican Americans emerged at critical times to provide leadership for their community. As community-minded individuals, they reflected the importance of political unity as the fundamental ingredient for empowerment. Their lives and actions were and continue to be positive role models for people everywhere.

RELIGIOUS FESTIVALS

Churches in the barrios celebrate ecclesiastical feast days and religious and patriotic holidays in ways that provide Mexicanos with a respite from work and ceremonies that reinforce their national identity. Barrio residents eagerly look forward to planning and participating in these annual events. Traditionally observances centered on Christmas and Easter and, in more recent times, on *fiestas patrias*. Hope Ayala recalled that at San José Catholic Church during Christmas the ritual of the *posadas* (the reenactment of the Holy Family's search for lodging) is played out in the streets. The faithful go from house to house asking for a place for Mary, Joseph, and the Baby Jesús (*pidiendo alojamiento*). Participants also recite specific prayers and sing appropriate songs of the season. *Las pastorelas* are dramatic presentations in which the people interact with actors in the *costada del Niño* (the manger scene). On January 6, congregations observe the adoration of the Christ Child by the three kings (*reyes mágos*) and the *levantada del Niño,* which commemorates the Holy Family's flight to Egypt to avoid King Herod's wrath. This day is marked by the removal of Christmas decorations and manger scenes.[1]

The church celebrates the festival of the Virgin Mary during the entire month of May. Fresh flowers, especially roses, adorn the altar and the church. In Mary's honor the more devout parishioners recite the rosary daily either at home or in the chapel.[2]

Salvador and María Gonzalez remember the *jamaicas* (fairs) that were held every Saturday during the summer at San José Church.[3] The Ayalas recalled that there were also *jamaicas* at certain times in spring.[4] The church also sponsored *jamaicas* on Mexican national holidays such as *cinco de mayo* and *dieciséis de septiembre*. The special foods served at these holiday family gatherings reflected their importance—tamales, *pollo en mole*, enchiladas, and *capirotada* (a Mexican bread pudding that is made from buttered toast, layers of cheese, pecans, *pilonsillo*—cones of raw brown sugar—and orange peels), *camarón seco* (miniature dried shrimp), or *nopalitos* (cactus strips) added to scrambled eggs.[5]

Helen Soto Mercado also recalled the San José church *jamaicas*. She thought they were held in the summer on Sunday, not Saturday, evenings. Helen said that North Commerce Street in front of the church was roped off for an entire block. The yards of area homes were the sites for food and game booths. Helen reminisced that Ignacio Vásquez made a delicious *birria*—a delicacy—goat meat cooked slowly by charcoal in a covered pit (*en poso*). A twenty by twenty foot cement slab in the school playground made an excellent dance floor. To help the church raise money, bands such as Albert Galván's donated their time and played *boleros* and *polkas*. Dances always were a great opportunity for the barrio's teenagers and young adults to meet and interact while mothers chaperoned.[6]

FIESTAS PATRIAS

Each year the Mexican American community faithfully observed *las fiestas patrias* — such as *el día de la raza* (held downtown at the main recreation center). In October 1948, representing the Club Claret of San José parish, Hope Ayala was crowned *reina de la fiesta de la raza* (Queen of the People's Day Festival).[7] Other celebrations included Mexican Independence Day, *el cinco de mayo* (celebrated in *La Fundición* at Echo Lake Park; on the North side at Marine Park; and in *La Loma* at Our Lady of Guadalupe Church), and *dieciséis de septiembre* (a commemoration of the day Father Miguel Hidalgo y Costilla called for the end of Spanish rule in Mexico, today the largest of the patriotic festivals). Aurelia López Guerra, wife of North Side physician Dr. Raúl López Guerra, organized and choreographed the dances and María Luisa Trujillo Magallón recited *dieciséis de septiembre* poems. Children also were encouraged to remember their heritage by reciting poems. Trinidad Mancilla and Ramón Escojido, neighborhood elders and counselors, addressed public gatherings where they spoke proudly and affectionately of their beloved *patria* and recited patriotic poetry.[8] The following poem, which appeared in the May 1948 Fort Worth newspaper *El eco latino*, is typical of the kind of poetry recited for the crowds:

Ignacio Zaragoza

Es el recuerdo de la Patria ausente
El que alimenta la fulgente llama,
El que nos dice con amor vehemente;
Hoy es la fecha cuya luz potente,
En nuestro pecho, el patriotismo inflama.

Porque mil héroes de sin par bravia,
A defenderte sin temor marcharon,
Y luchando por ti solo Patria mía;
Desafiando la muerte en aquel día,
De laureles tu sienes coronaron.

Y ante el fragor de la metralla insana,
Y ante fuego potente del mortero,
Surgió airosa, radiante, soberana;
Nuestra augusta Bandera Mexicana,
Hoyando la cerviz del extranjero.

Era que un genio del honor sagrado,
Llevoles por la senda victoriosa,
Y Laurencez sumiso y derrotado;
Admiro la grandeza de un soldado,
Que llamábase Ignacio Zaragoza.

Hoy que Anahuac bendice tu memoria,
Recordando tu nombre omnipotente,
Es mi canto, la estrofa de tu gloria;
El recuerdo que guarda a Ti la historia,
Admirando la aureola de tu frente.

—*Trinidad Tinajero Mancilla*[9]

Ignacio Zaragoza

The memory of the absent homeland
Nourishes a resplendent flame,
And tells us with fervent love
That today is the day whose powerful light,
In our breast, love of country ignites.

Because a thousand valiant heroes
Marched without fear to defend you,
Fighting only for you, my dear country,
And defying death on that day,
Your temples are crowned with laurels.

And before the roar of wild shrapnel,
And before the powerful mortar fire,
There arose our noble Mexican flag,
Graceful, radiant and proud,
Breaking the will of the foreigner.

And a genius of sacred honor
Carried through to the victorious path
And Laurencez was submissive and broken.
I admire the grandeur of a soldier
Named Ignacio Zaragoza.

Today Anahuac blesses your memory,
Remembering your omnipotent name,
And my song, my verse to your glory
Is the record that history preserves of you,
Admiring the radiance of your presence.

—*Trinidad Tinajero Mancilla*[10]

(1994) Northside resident Joe Lazo proudly taking part in the *dieciséis de septiembre* parade near Marine Park. *Photo taken by author.*

Every semester the sisters of San José directed school plays that raised money for various school programs. On Sunday afternoon, April 28, 1940, student thespians presented ten "mini-plays" with titles such as *"Una carta"* ("A Letter"), *"Las cinco vocales"* ("The Five Vowels"), *"Los apuros de un niño"* ("The Worries of a Little Boy"), and *"La envidiosa"* ("The Jealous Girl").[11] The short plays were both serious and humorous, but most important, they promoted moral and educational values. This community theater was held in the ample basement hall of the church.[12]

Every summer the Immaculate Heart of Mary Church sponsored three or four *jamaicas* for the purpose of raising money. Parishioners pitched in to set up booths, prepare and sell *platillos mexicanos* (Mexican dishes), and sponsor dances. Large tin tubs filled with ice kept soda bottles cold. Flowers, balloons, confetti, and other items were for sale at reasonable prices. Adults and children played the entertaining *lotería mexicana* with the hope of winning one of many prizes.[13]

RITES OF PASSAGE

Families observed important rites of passage such as First Holy Communion or confirmation with both church and private celebrations. One rite of passage, the *quinceañera*[14] (celebrated at a girl's fifteenth birthday) did not become popular in Fort Worth until the late 1960s and only then because of the influence of San Antonio's Spanish-language newspaper, *La prensa*.[15] The *quinceañera* celebrates a significant passage for a young Hispanic girl—the moment in time when she becomes a woman.[16]

María Gonzalez said that *quinceañeras* originated in the rites of pre-Columbian Indians in central Mexico to prepare young maidens for marriage. The custom has since received a Spanish Catholic emphasis and today is reminiscent of a debutante ball.

Families in grief took refuge in the comfort of rituals that harkened back to earlier days in Mexico. According to María Gonzalez, funeral wakes could be

(mid-1930s) Funeral wake of six-month-old Alvina Camarena, who died of pneumonia. Relatives, parents, and godparents look down on the angel-like face of the child, who has been dressed like a favorite saint and laid on the kitchen table surrounded by fresh flowers and candles. A professional Anglo photographer from downtown Fort Worth was summoned to take the picture. *Photo courtesy of Salvador and María (Sánchez) Gonzalez.*

(1929) Funeral wake of little Daniel Padilla on the front porch of the family home at 2106 N. Calhoun (North Side). *Photo courtesy of Michael and Hope (Padilla) Ayala.*

"weird" events where families placed the deceased on a table and took photographs of the body.[17] She provided the Gonzalez family photograph of a wake for a tiny baby on a tabletop dressed in a little saint's outfit specially made for this occasion. Looking down at the tiny baby were the grieving parents, both godparents, and a few other relatives. The baby's head is adorned by a simple crown and a small cross peaks the front. White flowers and lighted candles in candlesticks surround the body. The importance of these rituals is evidenced by the families' hiring a professional photographer to document the wake. Hope and Michael Ayala also provided a similar family photograph of Daniel Padilla's wake.

SPORTS

Raúl Manríquez was born on March 24, 1918, in the West Texas town of Beargrass, where his father worked as a coal miner. He was the second of six children born to Aurelio and Monica Acuña Manríquez.[18] Originally from Tepesala, Aguascalientes, Mexico, Aurelio married Monica Acuña in San Antonio's Sacred Heart of Mary Church in October 1914. Their children are Alicia, Esperanza, Azalia, and Arturo, all born in Strawn, Texas. The family moved often in search of job opportunities. In 1931 they moved to Fort Worth to be near Monica's mother and sister. Monica's mother lived on North Grove Street with Monica's sister, who worked for Swift and Company.[19]

Although Raúl went to grammar school in Strawn, he attended Fort Worth's J. P. Elder Junior High, where he played football for the Yearlings. After a year at Trimble Tech, Raúl transferred to Northside High School where he excelled as a halfback. In 1936 the Northside Steers won the city championship and went on to the state semi-finals, ultimately losing to Amarillo. Raúl was the only Mexican American player on the Northside football squad, which made him a target for racist threats and attempts at intimidation. He once received an anonymous letter threatening to "make tamales" out of him. In the final game against Amarillo,

(c. mid-1930s) Northside High School football coaches and players confer. L to R: Fred Shook; Assistant Coach Mack Flenniken; Marion Pugh; Head Coach Herman Clark (light coat); and, halfback Raúl Manríquez. Manríquez, who played football from 1932 to 1936, gained fame as one of the fastest runners in the entire region. *Photo courtesy of Esperanza Manríquez (sister).*

Raúl's leg was broken, but no one ever knew if it was intentional. Nevertheless, the Mexicanos of Fort Worth were ecstatic about their hometown hero.

A group formed a committee called *El comité pro Manríquez* and elected a set of officers to plan a program to honor the distinguished young athlete. Ramón Escojido was president; Amador Gutiérrez, vice-president; J. Trinidad Mancilla, secretary; Santos T. Mireles, treasurer; and, Tomás Vásquez, *síndico*. In December 1936 a reception, referred to as *Recuerdo del homenaje a Raúl Manríquez*, was held at a recreation hall on Vickery, featuring Raúl Manríquez as guest of honor, the Northside football team, and the Mexican Consul from Dallas, Adolfo G. Domínguez, and his wife, Milla. An eloquent speaker from Fort Worth's Mexican community, Trinidad Mancilla, recited a tribute.

Nuestra Ofrenda

No es sentir profano de la adulación el que nos guia ni el incienso con que el sentir humano envuelve a los falsos dioses el que nos ha impulsado a organizar éste festival, es solamente el testimonio de nuestra admiración para quien con el esfuerzo própio luchando en medio de las peripécias de la vida ha logrado alcanzar el triúnfo de sus ideales.

La humanidad entéra siempre ha sabido premiar las obras buenas, ha sibido recompensar con la palma de la victoria a quienes sabiendo cumplir con los preceptos para que fué creado, cumpliendo con los mandatos divinos a costa de su exelsa y firme voluntad logró colocar muy alto el nombre de su patria y de su raza.

Ello ha logrado un jóven Mexicano, "Raul Manríquez" su nombre suena de boca en boca y nosotros haciendo eco del sentir de nuestra colónia. En ésta ocasión, queremos patentizarle con éste sencillo homenaje, el voto de nuestra admiración.

Acudíd a su función de grácia; rodemosle en ésta noche y digámosle con toda la fuerza de nuestro corazón: Raúl, tu labor es grandiosa, tu hermanos te admiran y te bendicen.

El comité pro Manríquez
Fort Worth, Texas
Diciembre 1936

Adelante juventud Mexicana los triunfos que alcanceis en el extranjero serán lauros brillantes para nuestra amada patria.

Our Offering

It is not a simple feeling of adoration that guides us or the flattery with which human judgments envelop false gods that has prompted us to organize this festival, but rather it is only the testimony of our admiration for he who, with his own strength and battling in the midst of life's difficulties, has seen the triumph of his ideals.

All of humanity has always known to reward good works, has known to reward with the hand of victory those who, complying with the obligations for which they were created and with divine mandates at the expense of their own lofty and firm will, were able to place on high the name of their country and their people.

A young Mexicano, Raúl Manríquez, has shown these abilities. His name is known by all. Reflecting the feelings of our neighborhoood, we want on this occasion to make evident, with this simple tribute, our vote of admiration.

Attend this gathering of appreciation; let us surround him this evening and tell him from the depths of our hears: Raúl, your work is magnificent, your brothers and sisters admire and bless you.

Committee for Manríquez
Fort Worth, Texas
December 1936
Go forth, Mexican youth. The triumphs you obtain abroad will be shining laurels for our beloved country.[20]

It was an unforgettable evening for Fort Worth's Mexican American community and especially for one of its greatest athletes.[21] After graduating from Northside High School, sports champion Raúl Manríquez enrolled at Texas Wesleyan College where he played football for the Rams. But before he finished college World War II broke out and he volunteered for aviation training in California. After his initial training as a bombardier on a B-17, he was commissioned a lieutenant in the Army Air Corps. Lieutenant Manríquez was sent to Europe where his crew flew nine missions over Germany, accumulating more than 4,000 hours. On the tenth mission his plane was shot down over Germany.

He managed to parachute onto a German victory garden, where he was taken prisoner by Nazi troops and sent to the Stagluft Prison Camp. This particular camp turned out to be better than other German prisoner-of-war camps; the prisoners were treated humanely and allowed to read, exercise, and play basketball. In April 1945, units of the Soviet Army liberated the camp.

With the war over, Raúl continued serving his country in the newly created United States Air Force. He flew many missions to Africa, England, Spain, Germany, Alaska, the Aleutian Islands, South America, and Japan. In 1962, after twenty years of active duty, now Major Raúl Manríquez retired from the Air Force, a decorated military hero.

He finished his bachelor's degree at Texas Wesleyan College and went on to get his Masters at North Texas State University (now the University of North Texas.). His new career teaching math and science and coaching at J. P. Elder

(c. 1945). World War II hero Raul Manríquez gained fame as an Army Air Corps B-17 bombardier. The war hero retired as a major in the 1950s. *Photo courtesy of Esperanza Manríquez.*

Junior High and later at his alma mater, Northside High School lasted twenty-two years. He also taught in the adult education department for the Fort Worth I.S.D. in the evenings. Raúl retired in 1985 when he was diagnosed with Parkinson's disease. He was inducted into the Sports Hall of Fame at Texas Wesleyan University on April 14, 1989, and in 1993 Northside High School honored him as an outstanding alumnus. Raúl Manríquez passed away on June 26, 1997. He was buried at Mount Olivet Cemetery alongside his father and mother.[22]

❖   ❖   ❖

Wesley House's fundamental concern for the community and its residents didn't manifest itself only by providing food and medical assistance. Healthful exercise programs for area youngsters began when two lots were purchased for decent playgrounds. Adjacent to the Wesley House building on the north, the staff built a recreational area for older children that doubled as a basketball court and a baseball diamond. The playground for younger children was located on the south side and included a sandbox and a set of swings. Supervised by Fort Worth's YMCA, a Hi-Y Club provided about twenty-five older boys with instruction in boxing, wrestling, and tumbling.

For older boys Wesley House also sponsored organized sports such as football, basketball, and baseball. During the fall, football practice was held at nearby M. G. Ellis Elementary School each afternoon from four to six. The team, known as the Wesley Wildcats, played their match games on Saturday mornings. Basketball practice took place on Monday and Wednesday evenings at the Panther Boys' Club on Weatherford Street. A worker took the team for practice and games in the Wesley House car. During spring and summer the boys played baseball every Saturday morning at Sycamore Park. The following passage describes some of the realities of playing baseball during the early 1930s:

> The Mexican team does not always get a fair deal with the Anglo-Americans, as the Mexican team often has to wait on an Anglo-American team, but if the Mexicans are late they have to forfeit the game to the Anglo-Americans. The Mexican boys hoped to win the championship in the Second League City Sand Lot this summer, but

Wesley House girls' baseball team enjoying the new field, ca. 1940s. *Photo courtesy of Wesley Community House.*

one day when the deaconess who had charge of the boys' activities was away on her vacation, the boys did not get to go play a game. The game was forfeited, but the Mexicans were not given another chance to play the game. However, the Mexicans had defeated the team which won the championship, but the Mexicans were not surprised because they did not win the championship. The Mexican boys had told the deaconess early in the summer that a Mexican team did not have a chance to win the championship against an Anglo-American team.[23]

The girls were also eager participants in outdoor sports; they played baseball on the playground next to the Wesley House. The Girls' Reserve Club consisted of about thirty-five active members and was sponsored by Fort Worth's YWCA. They met once a week on Thursday afternoons under the direction of Miss Melvin Morton. Members participated in a program that incorporated a variety of games, stories, songs, parties, and other ceremonies. Hiking and baseball also complemented the many activities available to North Side girls.[24]

◆   ◆   ◆

Coach and mentor to many Hispanic children and teenagers, Ciquio Vásquez found in baseball a way for youngsters to excel and be proud of themselves. Vásquez was born in Fort Worth on November 18, 1927, seventh of the eleven children born to Inés and Emilia Camacho Vásquez.[25] Inés, born in 1895, in Villa Hidalgo, San Luis Potosí, Mexico, came to Fort Worth looking for work in 1907 at the age of twelve. He began working on area farms and ranches clearing trees and stumps from fields. Later, in Fort Worth, he worked for various construction companies before settling in a job at Texas Steel Company. Inés worked for Texas Steel for ten years, then returned to the construction industry. The entire family lived in a small one-room house with a dirt floor located at 3809 May Street on the South Side. A floor, a kitchen, and other rooms were added over the years. In the late 1930s Inés sought to earn more money as a migrant worker traveling the picking (*la pizca*) circuit in the sugar beet fields of Iowa, Michigan, and Ohio.[26]

As a child, Ciquio loved to join his siblings and friends in impromptu games of baseball, played on a large empty lot on Pafford and May streets. Isidro Hernández, owner of a neighborhood grocery store, used his pickup truck to take a team of South Side boys up to the North Side for friendly games of baseball. Hernández coached the team that was referred to as *Los de La Fundición* (those of the foundry or South Side). They played games regularly at the M. G. Ellis Elementary School field. If his boys won, Hernández rewarded the team with free *raspas* made back at his store.[27]

City-wide teams such as *Los Aztecas*, Grand Prize Beer, and *los Motorolas*, were comprised of Mexican American players and stirred up a high level of interest and following in the Hispanic community. Younger boys, eager to imitate their older brothers, created their own teams, often coached by a parent or an older sibling. In the early 1950s, a team called *Los indios* consisted of fifteen- to eighteen-year-olds and was coached by Ciquio's older brother, Magdaleno ("Leno"). In the late 1950s, *Los Morelos*, also consisting of boys in their late teens, were coached by Frank Gasca and Nicolás Vásquez. Vásquez, who worked for Texas Steel, had the money to help the team acquire baseball equipment. In a time when a neighborhood recreation center did not yet exist, he filled a void by generously donating his time and financial resources to provide South Side youngsters with fun and wholesome activities.[28]

As an adult Ciquio Vásquez was still a fan of baseball, although he had not played since the late 1940s when he used to pitch for a neighborhood team.

1947 *Aztecas* baseball team playing at San Angelo. First row L to R: Frank Cagigal, Ernest Gutiérrez, Martín Flores, Raymond Gutiérrez (bat boy), Ray Martínez, Marcelino ("Chico") Urquide, and Artemio ("Temo") Cagigal (manager). Second Row: Isidro García, George ("Lefty") Hernández, Joe Borbolla, Frank Ruelas, Rolando Borbolla, Paul Mata, Tom Gonzalez, and two unidentified players. The *Aztecas* played between 1934 and 1955. *Photo courtesy of Amador and Madeliene Gutiérrez.*

According to Vásquez, he "retired" because the opposing teams loved him as a pitcher—"they used to hit the ball a lot." Years later, in the 1960s, he became actively involved in the sport as a coach. In 1964 Nick Martínez, who coached a Little League team, announced his decision to return to his hometown of San Antonio and persuaded Ciquio to take his place as coach for the Immaculate Heart of Mary baseball team. Accepting the challenge, Ciquio stepped up to the plate and did such a remarkable job coaching that his teams won city championships in the Catholic Athletic League every year for the rest of the decade.

In the late 1960s Ciquio Vásquez organized the South Side Little League seasons and teams and sought more and better facilities for baseball. His leadership led to the first baseball field in the South Side and later to more expanded facilities in the neighboring Echo Lake area. In 1978 Vásquez retired from coaching, but his efforts to provide South Side youngsters with a solid program in which to channel their energies gained citywide attention. In recent years a new baseball field was named the Ciquio Vásquez Field in his honor.

◆   ◆   ◆

When South Side kids weren't playing baseball and the weather was warm enough, they headed for the nearest available swimming hole. Katy Lake (presently the site of Town Center Mall) was a favorite spot to swim, but it became inaccessible when it was fenced to begin construction for the mall. Mexican Americans could also swim in Echo Lake, just east of *La Fundición*. An area of Sycamore Creek just beyond of Echo Lake made a great place to dive and swim. Since no one could afford swimwear, the choice was to dive either *au natural* or in one's *chones* (undies). On hot summer days the swimming hole proved too tempting to friends who had little concern for the snapping turtles, water moccasins, or brownish polluted water.[29]

NATIONAL AND MILITARY SERVICE AND WAR EFFORTS

Fort Worth Hispanics embraced America and were eager to support their country by volunteering for national service—from the 1930s Civilian Conservation Corps (CCC) to the armed services in World War II. On returning from the war some soldiers were honored as heroes, while others faced discrimination. With the realization of the importance of their service to America came an increasingly strong unwillingness to accept the status quo of discrimination. Mexican American men who fought in the war soon became inspirations to the community and took their places as community leaders.

Gilberto Cantú García, born on August 17, 1918, in Brownsville, Texas, was the eldest of seven children of Julian and Ester Cantú García.[30] The Garcías made their living growing vegetables, fruits, and livestock at their ranchito outside Brownsville. Gilberto lived with his family in the Brownsville area until 1940. In 1936 he graduated from the Marist-run St. Joseph's Academy and joined the Civilian Conservation Corps, working with it from 1937 to 1940. The CCC, one of the most effective of President Franklin D. Roosevelt's New Deal programs, hired thousands of young men between the ages of eighteen and twenty-five for work projects throughout the National Park system.[31] Gilberto was assigned to Camp Bear Canyon, California, where he joined others to make a variety of park improvements and fight forest fires.[32]

The eldest in his family, Gilberto García felt especially responsible for helping his family get through the Depression. And the CCC funds helped greatly. After leaving the CCC in 1940 he came to Fort Worth to work for his uncle, Alfredo García, part owner of American Laundry, located on the corner of South Main and Hattie streets. Gilberto had previously expressed a desire for a better future and his uncle was happy to get his nephew out of the Lower Rio Grande Valley. He lived at his uncle's home on Stella Street while managing the laundry and began attending night school at Trimble Tech.[33]

In 1940 Gilberto attended a March of Dimes[34] benefit dance at the Crystal Ballroom of the Texas Hotel, where he met the young Herlinda Balderas, who taught him how to dance "with passion." Originally from Cleburne, Herlinda worked in Fort Worth at the regional offices of Montgomery Ward. The two began a romance, interrupted by Gilberto's service during World War II. Gilberto joined the U.S. Army and was sent to California to board a troop ship headed for the Philippines. The ship's engines malfunctioned, and García and his unit were diverted to a second transport vessel that took them instead to Oahu in the Hawaiian Islands.[35]

Gilberto García arrived in Oahu in November 1941, one month before the Japanese attack on Pearl Harbor. On Sunday morning, December 7, García woke to the sound of gunfire and at first thought it was a training exercise. Once he realized that it was a full-scale attack, García began shooting at whatever flew overhead. Back in Fort Worth, Herlinda thought that Gilberto had been killed because four months after the attack she still hadn't heard from him. Finally, she received a v-mail[36] informing her that he was safe. Gilberto was stationed in Hawaii for four more years until the war with Japan ended. Arriving back in Fort Worth in September 1945, Gilberto proposed for the second time.[37] Gilberto García married Herlinda Balderas on October 7, 1945, at the First Presbyterian Church in Cleburne. The newlyweds boarded *el aguila Azteca* (the Aztec Eagle) bound for Mexico City where they spent their honeymoon.[38]

Back in Fort Worth the couple made their first home at 1431 Elmwood, and Gilberto took advantage of the G.I. Bill to go back to Trimble Tech. In

1946 some Anglo neighbors invited Gilberto and Herlinda Balderas to a Democratic Party precinct meeting. Determined to become more involved and reform the process of choosing delegates, they joined the Young Democrats, which up to that point had been an all-Anglo organization. The Garcías met Jim Wright who was then president of the Young Democrats and the person who would teach them the most about the political process. Herlinda boldly advised Wright to learn Spanish, for it would help him politically in the near future. "I hadn't thought about that, but maybe you have a point," Wright replied. In 1949 Jim Wright recognized her at a party convention held at the Will Rogers Coliseum. He singled her out stating, "You don't realize how helpful your advice was to me."[39]

The Garcías were involved in the formation of the Fort Worth chapter of the American G.I. Forum. In 1948 Dr. Hector P. García of Corpus Christi came to Fort Worth to organize a chapter of the A.G.I.F., an organization founded in response to the problems Mexican American servicemen encountered on

(mid-1960s) In Washington, D.C., at an American G.I. Forum convention. L to R: Fort Worth civic leader and A.G.I.F. State of Texas Chairman Gilbert García; Dr. Hector Perez García; Congressman Jim Wright; Cristobal Aldrete (Del Rio); and, Executive Secretary Eduardo Idar (Laredo). *Photo courtesy of Herlinda Balderas García.*

returning home. The G.I. Bill of Rights guaranteed educational, medical, housing, and other basic benefits to returning servicemen, but people of Mexican descent were being denied these benefits. In Three Rivers, Texas, the town's Anglo-owned funeral home refused to conduct a funeral service for a Mexican American serviceman, Félix Longoria, who was killed in action during World War II. This incident provoked outrage among all Mexican Americans, especially returning veterans. Dr. García and others sent congressmen and senators a flurry of telegrams and letters to express their anger at this injustice. Word reached the newly elected senator from Texas, Lyndon Baines Johnson, who informed President Truman of the situation in South Texas. Consequently, the remains of Félix Longoria were taken to Washington, D. C., and he was given a hero's burial with full military honors at Arlington National Cemetery.

Dr. García met with about a dozen community leaders at Gilberto and Herlinda García's home to organize the Fort Worth chapter of the American G.I. Forum. Jorge Rodela, Pris Domínguez, Medardo Rangel, Domingo Martínez, and Joe Frausto were among those at the meeting. Other charter members included Joe Briseño, Joe Rodríguez, Dan Díaz, and Willie Briones. Gilberto García served as president of the local chapter for five years and conducted regular informational sessions at bank meeting rooms and restaurants. Herlinda helped organize what is now known as Women of the American G. I. Forum and served as its first president.[40]

In addition to his activities with the forum, Gilberto García was involved in many other Fort Worth organizations. He served in leadership positions with the Boy Scouts of America, the Neighborhood Youth Corps, the Community Action Agency, and the Mexican American Chamber of Commerce, and received numerous honors for his dedicated public service. There is even an award named after him—the Gilberto García Amigo Award—presented to an Anglo who has made a significant contribution to the Mexican American community. His name heads the list of outstanding Mexican American citizens that includes: Guillermo A. Walls, Louis J. Zapata, Joe T. García, Dr. Raúl López Guerra, Mary Lou López, J. Pete Zepeda, Antonio Morales, Rufino Mendoza, Sr., Ruben Magallanes, Sam García, Manuel Jara, and Guillermina Morales. Gilberto García passed away from a stroke on March 2, 1993.

❖   ❖   ❖

In early 1942 Leonard Menchaca volunteered for ranger (commando) training after completing his basic training in the army. The special unit, consisting of 210 men, was assigned to take Attu—the westernmost island of the Aleutian Island chain. Their mission was to disable all enemy communications on the island and to clear a landing area for a larger marine invasion force. In May 1943, under the cover of darkness, a submarine surfaced offshore and the ranger unit disembarked in inflatable rafts. On landing, the rafts had to be deflated and sunk to avoid detection. In the process of disposing of the rafts and waiting for ropes to be thrown down the steep seaside cliffs, most of the rangers were soaked in the freezing waters of Kiska Harbor.[41] One by one they laboriously pulled themselves up the steep cliffs surrounding the inaccessible harbor. With more than 1,000 Japanese soldiers stationed on Attu, the initial fighting was intense. After nine days of holding a portion of the cliffs the ranger unit was reinforced by the invasion force of U.S. Marines. The Japanese unit was defeated after ten more days of combat. During those twenty days Leonard's boots never dried, resulting in severe frostbite that almost cost him his feet. This injury earned him an honorable discharge and affected him for the rest of his life.[42]

❖   ❖   ❖

Salvador Gonzalez, Jr., remembers a different kind of treatment after World War II. After he and some Anglo friends had been to a *jamaica* sponsored by San José Church in 1948 they went to a tavern on North Main Street, where the Anglo bartender refused to serve Salvador.[43] This was typical of the kind of treatment that so outraged Gilberto García and Dr. Hector García and caused them to form the American G.I. Forum. Organizations such as the NAACP, LULAC, and the A.G.I.F. began earnestly pressing for the repeal of Jim Crow-style ordinances and for equal opportunities in the areas of employment, housing, and education.

COMMUNITY LEADERS

Leaders sprang from a variety of environments—the military, sports, and politics. The second generation of Mexican Americans had a strong commitment to better the circumstances of all Hispanics and didn't hesitate to take responsibility for doing so.

◆   ◆   ◆

Samuel ("Sam") García overcame early tragedy, illness, and cultural alienation to become a community leader and found an organization that awards scholarships to promising Hispanic girls. He was born on September 10, 1923, in Quiroga, Mexico, a small town near Morelia, Michoacán, where his father Lúcio García was also born.[44] Thirty days after the birth of their son, Lúcio and his wife, María Calderón García, left Mexico and settled in Pittsburg, Oklahoma, where three of Lúcio's brothers—Bruno, Jesse, and Frank—worked in the coal mines.[45] Although coal mining was dirty and dangerous work, the pay was better than the García brothers had ever received in Mexico. Sam and his family lived in a two-room mining shack; his parents shopped at the company store with company tokens. Lúcio worked at the Pittsburg mines from 1923 until 1930 when he developed tuberculosis and was admitted to Eastern Oklahoma State Sanitarium at Talihina. At the time, there was no cure for tuberculosis, but doctors thought that clean mountain air and bed rest were the best remedies.[46]

Lúcio returned home but two months later came down with tuberculosis a second time and returned to the sanitarium in eastern Oklahoma. In 1933 at the age of ten, his son, Sam, also was beset with tuberculosis and entered the same sanitarium. Unfortunately, Sam's mother, María, also became ill with the same disease but refused to go to the sanitarium. Despite the fact that the doctors gave her no hope of recovery, María opted to return to Mexico. Two years later, María Calderón García died.[47]

Learning that he could not recover, Lúcio sought an operation that the doctors at the sanitarium advised him against: he lived about a year after the operation. Before his death in 1937, Lúcio asked his brother Bruno to take care of young Sam.[48] Tío Bruno had turned to sharecropping in Pittsburg after the mines had played out. From 1937 to 1943, Sam learned to drive a team of horses, cultivate, plow, and raise cotton, corn, and wheat while attending Pittsburg Elementary School. When Sam finished the fourth grade he went to work for his uncle full-time. In 1943, although not a U.S. citizen, the seventeen-year-old was drafted into the army and posted to boot camp at Camp Stoneman in Little Rock, Arkansas.[49]

Sam García then went to New York City where he received training as a medical technician. He reported to the U.S. Army hospital ship *Thistle*, which sailed for North Africa to care for the wounded. After defeating Rommel's German troops in North Africa, the American and British armies launched attacks against Europe's "soft underbelly"—Sicily and Italy. After Naples was liberated, the city's facilities were used to treat the seriously wounded. Those who were stable enough to travel were taken back on a hospital ship—either to New York City or to Charleston, South Carolina. As a medical technician aboard the *Thistle*, Sam García crossed the Atlantic Ocean twenty-two times. After the Italian campaign ended, the hospital ship sailed toward southern France as part of "Operation Overlord"—the June 1944 amphibious invasion of Normandy.[50]

Sam García's experience in the army and his contact with men from other regions of the country furthered his education. Because he came from a small community and only possessed a fourth-grade education, Sam felt that he didn't know anything about life. During his long isolation in the sanitarium and his years with Anglo soldiers, Sam gradually forgot how to speak Spanish. The army was his education: through observation Sam learned all the things he had not been taught as a child—proper personal hygiene, social skills, practical economics, as well as an appreciation for travel.[51] After earning three Bronze Stars, Sam García was honorably discharged from the U.S. Army in late 1945. One year later, he became a citizen of the United States.[52]

When he returned to Oklahoma, he discovered that Tío Bruno had bought a small tavern and was no longer farming. Sam became the manager of the establishment, while Bruno's daughter, Aletha, made and sold sandwiches to customers. The business did well, allowing Sam to purchase a brand-new, blue Chevy pickup for $1,000. Later Sam opened his own tavern in McAlester and called it the Veteran's Bar. Although the establishment generated a good cash flow, Sam had not yet learned how to manage and hold on to that cash and in 1954 he went out of business and moved to Fort Worth.[53]

In 1960 Sam García responded to an advertisement by a home improvement company looking for a salesman. Builders' Sales and Service manager D. W. Cope placed Sam on commission selling roofs, storm doors, and windows. Sam did so well selling home improvement packages that Cope made him a partner within three years—Sam was the salesman while D. W. took care of the administration. Within five years Sam and D. W. formed Service Construction Company (on South Jones Street), which lasted for seventeen years. The partnership was dissolved in 1982, and Sam began doing business on his own as Approved Builders.[54]

The political climate of the early 1960s inspired people to community activism. In 1961, with the encouragement of Louis Zapata, Sam joined the Pan American Golf Association, eventually becoming vice-president and president. He became a member of the American G.I. Forum, IMAGE de Fort Worth, and LULAC in 1962. These organizations reintroduced Sam to his Mexican roots.

In March 1985, Sam and his second wife, María,[55] established the Hispanic Debutante Association of Fort Worth to help reverse the high dropout rate of Hispanic students and to raise scholarship money for local college-bound girls. Sam and María García have always believed that Hispanic females deserve education as much as males. "Marry a rich man" was the unfortunate advice that young women got from parents for generations. Without a proper college-level education, Hispanic women were more vulnerable to life's unpredictability, and the Garcías hoped to impart to Mexican American girls the need and the value of a college education. Through active fundraising, their nonprofit organization has enabled many Hispanic students to attend the college or university of their choice. The highlight of the organization is its annual ball (usually held in early April) where up to twelve Hispanic girls are presented as debutantes.[56]

Sam García's commitment to a myriad of community organizations earned him the honor of being names City of Fort Worth's Volunteer of the Year in 1989. From his humble birth deep in the heartland of Mexico to his bout with tuberculosis in Pittsburg to his coming of age in the U.S. Army during World War II, Sam García successfully synthesized all his experiences to create a better life for himself, his family, and for those individuals he has met through his service to his community.

◆ ◆ ◆

Born in Eastland, Texas, on September 19, 1922, Manuel Jara worked so effectively to eliminate racial discrimination that a Fort Worth elementary school was named after him. His father, Alfonso Jara, was born around 1900 in Durango, Mexico, and his mother, María Sánchez, was born in 1902 in Chihuahua. Alfonso Jara left Mexico because of the Revolution and headed for El Paso, where he found work as a *vaquero*, mason, carpenter, and railroad worker. Alfonso and María met in El Paso and married there. His job at the Texas & Pacific Railroad ultimately brought Alfonso and his young family to Fort Worth in 1931.[57]

The Jaras lived in *El Papalote* for a short time before moving to a rented house on Cherry Street in *La Corte*. Manuel, age nine, began his schooling at Peter Smith Elementary, moved on to Jennings Middle School, and finally to Trimble Tech, where he studied printing. Manuel Jara began his career as a printer for the Fort Worth Paper Company.[58]

On April 28, 1943, Manuel Jara married Jacinta Rocha in a civil ceremony in Fort Worth. Jacinta, born in Cisco, Texas, in 1920, was the daughter of Arnulfo and Elena Benavides Rocha.[59] After the death of Arnulfo, Sr., the family split up when the majority of the siblings decided to go to California.[60] In 1940 Jacinta, her mother, and sister, Helen, came to Fort Worth looking for work. They lived on Belknap Street in *La Corte* for three years, until mutual friends introduced Jacinta to Manuel Jara. After Jacinta and Manuel married they lived in an apartment before renting a house on Belknap for about three years.[61]

The Jaras had two children, both of whom became educators: María Elena ("Mary") Wright, served as principal of J. P. Elder Middle School, and Jo Linda Martínez),a teacher at William James Middle School. The year of Jo Linda's birth the family moved to a home on the 1200 block of North Houston Street. This North Side neighborhood, west of North Main Street, had been off limits to Mexicanos before World War II. Mexican Americans' service in the war was the catalyst that initiated changes in patterns of discrimination in housing, education, and jobs, leading to a gradual relaxation of hostile attitudes towards Mexicanos.[62]

Manuel Jara worked for the J. E. Snelson Printing Company for about six years before acquiring his own shop in 1960—Butler-Jara Printing Company—in partnership with friend Clyde Butler. Shortly thereafter Jara secured a loan that enabled him to buy his partner's interest and become the sole proprietor. The Jara Printing Company operated out of a rented building until Manuel bought his own property at 701 Pennsylvania Avenue. The business flourished until 1984, when it was sold to Ben Flerman.[63]

Manuel Jara became increasingly involved with his community. At All Saints Catholic Church, his parish, Jara encouraged people to attend services and get involved with church-sponsored activities. He became one of the sponsors of the Club Claret, later the Catholic Youth Organization. Jara became a member, then president, and then district chairman of the A.G.I.F. He also belonged to the Southside Lions Club.[64]

In the early 1960s, in an effort to change attitudes and foster goodwill between races, Manuel and Jacinta Jara helped organize the Fort Worth chapter of the International Good Neighbor Council (IGNC). Typical of his Mexican American generation, Manuel never chose radical activism to gain civil rights for Hispanics but instead took a rational and moderate approach. Rather than

(c. 1978) International Good Neighbor Council convention. L to R: Civic leader Manuel Jara, Speaker of the House Jim Wright, and Harold Valderas (first Fort Worth Mexican American municipal court judge). *Photo courtesy of Jacinta Jara.*

being confrontational, he believed in "talking it out" and building bridges of understanding with other people.[65]

On October 4, 1985, at the annual meeting of the International Good Neighbor Council in Dallas, Manuel Jara suffered a fatal heart attack. Because of Jara's lifelong activism and dedication, friends such as Sam García and Harold and Marisa Valderas petitioned to have a school named in his honor. On November 13, 1987, the North Side community witnessed the dedication of the Manuel Jara Elementary School at 2100 Lincoln Avenue.[66]

Chapter 7

ARTS
AND CULTURE

As the early Mexicano residents struggled to find a balance between the security of their old way of life and learning the customs of their new county, new traditions were formed. Cuisine adapted to more easily available American ingredients, and business practices slowly evolved to incorporate an American approach. *Fiestas patrias, jamaicas,* and *quinceañeras,* traditionally celebrations of Mexican heritage, gradually changed as aspects of the new culture were added. More interaction with Anglos sped up the process, especially after World War II. The fluid interchange of customs created an energy that found new expression in music and art reflecting both cultures and heritages. Despite the obstacles of poverty and discrimination, the Hispanic community of Fort Worth gave rise to notable musicians, artists, and even a movie star.

MUSIC, A MIRROR OF THE SOUL

Wherever people go, their music always goes with them. Fort Worth's barrios swelled with music from the diverse regions of Mexico and Texas. *Rancheras,* polkas, *mariachi, boleros, danzones, cumbias,* and *Tejano* all found their way into the homes, dance halls, and ballrooms of Cowtown. The music served to reassure and reconnect Mexicanos with their culture, regardless of what trials and challenges they faced. Fort Worth's Mexicanos contributed significantly to the legacy of *Tejano* music, but American musical styles such as country and western, rock `n roll, rhythm and blues, swing, and big band also influenced the music of the latino communities. Names like Margarito García, Nicho Sáenz, the Jara brothers, Claudio C. Mata, Al Cortez, Johnny Gonzalez, Gabe Salinas, Johnny Ayala,

Joe Lerma, Santos Aguilar, Ernest Vázquez, Carlos and Leo Sáenz, and Fernando Landeros are just a few of those who added to the rich musical tradition in Fort Worth and North Texas.

◆　◆　◆

Claudio Cortéz Mata became a legend on the South Side. Born on July 7, 1898, in Matehuala, San Luis Potosí, Mexico, Mata had one sister, Dionicia. Together they attended a *primaria* (elementary school) where they received their basic education. As a young man Claudio worked as both a barber and a tailor; it was not unusual for him to make his own clothes. He was also attracted to music, first learning the clarinet and eventually mastering other instruments as well—piano, violin, guitar, drums, and mandolin. Claudio was such a promising musician that his local instructor urged him to go to Mexico City to study at the conservatory, but his family couldn't afford to send him.[1]

Mata came to Fort Worth in 1916 and found work as a laborer for a construction company building the bridge across Lake Worth. By 1918 he had secured a permanent job with Texas Steel on the South Side. He worked for the mill for forty-two years until his retirement in 1960 at the age of sixty-two. During these years, Mata lived with his family at 3333 South Main Street.[2]

In October 1926, Claudio married Margarita Ruelas, who was born in 1897 in Urécuaro, Michoacán, Mexico. In 1911, when Margarita was a mere fourteen years old, she married José María Vega and subsequently had four children: Sara, Anastacio, José (nicknamed Joe), and Aurora.[3] Vega died, and when Claudio married Margarita, he adopted all four of her children.[4]

In the 1920s Mata headed a musical group called Claudio Mata and His Mexican Charro Orchestra. The group practiced twice a week in the evenings at Mata's South Side home and performed at special dances, *fiestas patrias*, and civic programs, including meetings of the Good Neighbor Council and the Pan American Round Table. By the mid-1930s Mata and his orchestra had become so popular that an Anglo-owned radio station, KFJZ, hired them to perform weekly on a live thirty-minute program.[5] The orchestra played many popular romantic pieces as well as *boleros*, *danzones*, and *rancheras* until the early 1950s, when the group broke up. Some of the band members included Pedro and Gilberto

(c. 1940s) Claudio C. Mata and His Mexican Charro Orchestra. Mata gave music lessons at his South Side home and played with his orchestra on festive occasions. *Photo courtesy of Aurora Vega Mata Burciaga.*

("Beto") Trujillo from *El TP*, Francisco Mosqueda, Ventura Hernández, José Vásquez, Gertrudis ("Tule") Aguilar, Florentino Rodríguez, and Rafael Jasso. Dressed in a colorful and typical dress from Mexico, Mata's daughter, Aurora Vega Mata, often accompanied the orchestra on piano and vocals.[6]

Claudio Mata gave music lessons to anyone, young or old, who wished to learn to play an instrument.[7] He taught music theory as well. Three times a week after work, Claudio also gave Spanish lessons to the neighborhood children who needed improvement.

Mata was occasionally inspired to compose music as well and wrote a piece entitled, "The New Freedom March," dedicated to the memory of President John Fitzgerald Kennedy. Claudio was an ardent admirer of JFK and was deeply affected by Kennedy's assassination. Claudio C. Mata passed away a year later on December 16, 1964.[8]

◆   ◆   ◆

Juan Eutimio Ayala was born on October 17, 1942, in Fort Worth's North Side, the fourteenth child of Eutimio and María Ortiz Ayala. Raised in a family in which his brother Michael played the trumpet and another brother, Stanley, played the violin, Johnny had a natural flair for music. In high school Johnny and several of his Trimble Tech friends bought some instruments, learned to play them, and in 1960 formed Johnny and the Gamblers, the first modern Mexican-American band in Fort Worth. From 1960 to 1963 the band consisted of Henry de la Paz (lead electric guitar and vocalist), Juan Moreno (electric guitar), Johnny Ayala (bass), Héctor Valdez (saxophone), Héctor Cortez (saxophone), and Raymond Cortez (drums).[9] Johnny kept busy promoting the band and searching for weekend bookings. Johnny and the Gamblers played at CYO (Catholic Youth Organization) dances, at church-sponsored *jamaicas*, and at *fiestas patrias*.[10] Like many other bands across America they were deeply influenced by the new electrified rock 'n' roll sounds of such rock idols as Bill Haley and the Comets, Elvis Presley, and Richie Valens.

In 1963 the band changed its name to Johnny Ayala and the Starlighters. Conforming more to the image of a modern *Tejano* musical group, the Starlighters included Joe Lerma (vocalist), Johnny Ayala (bass), Frank ("*Panchillo*") Ramírez (electric guitar), Felipe Ramírez (guitar/bass), Ruben Pérez (drums), Frank Morales (keyboards), and Santos Aguilar (songwriter, saxophone).[11] Ayala's two bands recorded the following songs on the Hispanic record label *El zarape*: "*Ojito verde*" and "*Ofrenda a mi madre*," 1961; "*Los amores de la güera*," 1962; "*La paranda*," "*Marisa*," "*Con esta copa*" ("With This Wine Glass"), "*La mamá de Tarzan*" ("Tarzan's Mother"), "*Mi postera*," and "*Aunque tengo otros amores*" ("Even Though I Have Other Loves"), 1963.[12] A few of these songs are included in the album produced by *El zarape* entitled *Los mejores de Tejas*, volumes one and two, which also featured songs by Little Joe, Alfonso Ramos, Shorty and the Corvettes, and Sixto Sánchez.

The band booked engagements on the weekends across North and West Texas. It was often a grueling schedule: In order to play in West Texas on a weekend, Ayala would pick up band members on Friday in the pre-dawn hours, drive to their gig, play the entire weekend, and drive back in time to drop them off at their day jobs on Monday morning. With so many bookings coming in, it was inevitable that there would be an occasional mistake in scheduling. Lerma recalled going to an engagement in Mathis, Texas, where they found the ballroom empty. Everyone was outside listening but not entering the ballroom because *era la cuaresma* (it was Lent), and dancing wasn't allowed.

One appearance was fraught with problems. The band traveled to Phoenix, Arizona, for what was supposed to be a two-week engagement; upon arrival they found that they were a week early. As they had no money coming in during that week, they ran up a tab at a local restaurant. When they were finally able to play the audience didn't like the singer they hired to replace lead vocalist Joe Lerma, who was in Vietnam. On the way back to Texas, the used car they had purchased before leaving Fort Worth broke down beyond repair, and they had to scrape up enough money to buy another car to get home.

Ayala recalled, "We had some good times, and we had some bad times!" In 1967, the band broke up and Johnny Ayala began working in community programs.[13]

◆ ◆ ◆

Joe Lerma came from a family of musicians, farmers, and ranchers originally from León, Guanajuato. His grandfather enjoyed playing the guitar, going from village to village giving performances for extra money. Lerma's father, Juan, migrated in search of work to the coal mining town of Malakoff, about sixty miles southeast of Dallas. Many Mexicanos, like Lerma, who came here to work in the coal mines, eventually settled in Fort Worth. Joe's mother, Consuelo Soto, met and married Juan Lerma in Malakoff. Her family originally came from the neighboring northern Mexico towns of Villa Aldama and Bustamante in the state of Nuevo León.[14]

Joe Lerma was born in Fort Worth on April 27, 1944. Initially attracted to music as a way to meet girls, he began assisting the musical group *El conjunto flamingo* as a band boy, and in 1960, when the lead singer took leave to be with his expectant wife, Joe Lerma's singing career was launched.[15] The following year Lerma accepted an invitation to be the lead vocalist for Johnny Ayala and the Gamblers. In the fall of 1961 Lerma left the Gamblers to form his own band known as the Latin Souls. Band members included Joe Castillo, "Cha Cha" Jiménez, Wally Almendariz, Johnny Lerma (Joe's brother), and Lonnie Aguilar (Joe's cousin).

In 1967, Joe Lerma was drafted and sent to Vietnam. He spent the next year in a Vietnamese jungle halfway around the world, far from the *Tejano* music scene.

On returning to Fort Worth in 1969 he organized a new band, calling it Mixed Company because three of the members were Anglo and five were Mexican Americans. Lerma worked days at Texas Steel, rehearsed with the band in the evenings, and played on weekends. Band members included Bill Miller, Ron Soche, John Stuller, Carlos Vela (guitar), Juan López (bass), Charlie Rodríguez (keyboard and saxophone), Sara Price (vocalist), and Joe Lerma (lead vocalist). A year later Lerma renamed the band *Alma '70* and began recording in Austin with promoter Dave Gutiérrez and his Paisano label. The band was now composed of Johnny Lerma (drums), Domingo Raya (saxophone), Raúl Rodríguez (saxophone), John López (guitar), Richard Longoria (bass), and Joe Lerma (lead vocalist). *Alma '70* performed from 1970 to 1976 and produced one album, *Los dos*, on the Paisano label in 1974.[16]

Joe Lerma knew everyone involved in the Fort Worth music scene from the 1950s through the 1970s. He recalled one of Fort Worth's earliest music and dance promoters, Vicente Pulido, who brought artists such as Vicente Fernández and *El negro reyna* to perform at the North Side's Marine Theater. These singing sensations were just a few of the stars that gave memorable performances there. Another early promoter, Gabe Salinas, brought Mexican and Mexican American artists to the Casino at Lake Worth and the Guys and Dolls Ballroom. Lerma remembered Andrés Mantecón, who was one of the first Hispanic deejays in Fort Worth to buy time on an Anglo-owned radio station and play the Mexican music popular with the local community.

One of the band's managers, "El Sport," arranged for a tour that included Oklahoma, Kansas, Colorado, and New Mexico. The manager paid for all the gas, food, and lodging but never gave the band members any money, assuring them that he would divide the proceeds at the end of the tour. The band stopped for the night at the small mountain town of La Junta in southeastern Colorado on the way to an engagement in Denver and during the night El Sport, along with all of their earnings, disappeared. The stunned band members were reduced to asking the owner of a local saloon if they could play there in return for meals. The band broke up in 1976, and Lerma concentrated on his job at the Fort Worth State School, where he became the director of vocational programming in 1980.[17]

◆ ◆ ◆

Tejano recording artist "Paula" was born Paulina (later Pauline) Willis on March 17, 1946, at Marlin, Texas, to Ernest and Eulalia Arévalo Willis. Ernest and Eulalia overcame serious family objections to their marriage and prevailed over Ernest's father's intolerance for dark-skinned people. Ernesto ("Ernest") Willis was born in Marlin, Texas, son of blue-eyed sharecropper José Willis, half Anglo and half Mexican. Eulalia Arévalo, was also born in Marlin. Her father, Epifanio Arévalo, originally from Morelia, Michoacán, passed down a dark, Indian-like complexion to his daughter. He raised cattle, horses, and pigs and was a man of means. Because of their color José Willis despised not only Epifanio Arévalo but also Eulalia. He treated her with great disdain, even to the extent of playing mean tricks like putting a dead animal under her window.[18]

A small-town Romeo-and-Juliet-like drama unfolded as both fathers forbade their children to see each other, but Ernest and Eulalia ignored their parents' edicts. Willis subsequently disowned and disinherited his son for marrying the dark-complected woman, and when Pauline (the second of five children) was born, her grandfather pronounced "*que ella era hija de un negro*" ("that she was the daughter of a black man"). This family experience taught Pauline that discrimination was not exclusively inter-racial.[19]

Ernest Willis was a devout Baptist (he was superintendent of Sunday schools), a good family man, and headed a strict, conservative household.[20] For example, the children couldn't date before they reached a certain age. When Pauline was a sophomore in college she still had to be chaperoned on dates by one or more of her siblings. "When you took a Willis girl out on a date, you took the whole family."[21]

In World War II Ernest joined the Marines and served in the Pacific Theater. His battalion was overrun by Japanese troops on Guadalcanal. He was seriously wounded and spent nine months recuperating in a Shanghai hospital. Although he was a disabled veteran eligible for a government pension, he never received any benefits, nor did he ever request any. He never complained about his wounds, even though they clearly affected the quality of his life. "I served my country. I'm a Marine," Pauline recalled him telling her. It wasn't until the end of his life that he received a Purple Heart and an appreciative letter from President Ronald Reagan.[22]

Pauline grew up in Knox City, Texas, and at the age of eleven began singing at the services and revivals at the *Primera Iglesia Bautista* in the neighboring town of O'Brien.[23] The Willis family's social life centered on the church—they spent all day Sunday as well as Wednesday evenings there. Pauline began singing as part of her church life.

> The way I saw myself was . . . hey, they want someone to sing, and I love to sing to the Lord, because I love the Lord. I mean, that was my whole life. Christ was so real in my life. I never thought that, oh, I have a beautiful voice, or this or that . . . . I was going to do something for the Lord. Talking about talent . . . if He gives you a talent, and if you use it He'll give you twice that, and if you hide it you lose it.[24]

From 1965 to 1969 Pauline attended Howard Payne College in Brownwood, a conservative Baptist school that met with her father's approval. At the time there were only about ten Hispanic students at the school and, even though they were all Baptists, there was still discrimination. Pauline's dorm mother, Mrs. Becker, for example, had a rule forbidding dating between Anglos and Mexicanos; if an Anglo was caught dating a Hispanic the dorm mother immediately wrote a letter to the parents. Mrs. Becker didn't quite know what to do with Pauline—Willis was, after all, an Anglo surname.

> I think the fact that I had been discriminated against all my life made me tough. I would date *los bolillos*[25] *adrede* (on purpose), and I'd pass under her nose so she could see me, and I'd give her the I-dare-you-say-something-to-me look! So all those years I really didn't care for them, but I was using them.[26]

She began singing in an all-female quartet in her freshman year. In her sophomore year she joined a trio, graduating to a duo the next year, and was given solos as a senior. Her groups performed at special functions and revivals throughout the year. Pauline even recorded a hymn on a 45-rpm record in a small Brownwood studio.[27]

Pauline's roommate at Howard Payne, María Elena Vela, married a Fort Worth man, Donald Moore. Donald was a graduate student at the Southwestern Baptist Theological Seminary, and María Elena worked for the Baptist Radio and Television Commission, which produced the Spanish radio program, *"La hora bautista"* ("The Baptist Hour"). The Anglo seminary choir sang all the songs for the program in Spanish, but their pronunciation was not very good. After hearing this "butchered Spanish" Pauline asked her friend María Elena to ask her boss, JoAnn Shelton, if Pauline's group could sing instead. Shelton denied the request, giving the reason that neither María Elena nor Pauline had any voice training. "It was a slap in the face! Here I was, so dedicated to God, pouring my soul into the music that I was singing to God, and it was like a slap in the face! I thought, 'When did God require that we have voice training to sing to Him?'"

Pauline's popular music career began in 1964 when her cousin, Faye Gómez (Barrera), introduced her to the leader of a new musical group called Little Joe and the Latinaires, playing at the Guys and Dolls Ballroom in South Fort Worth.[28] The huge and wildly popular dance hall had seen the likes of Harry James, Alfonso Ramos,[29] and other famous bands. At first Pauline hesitated because good Baptists are not supposed to go to dance halls, but Faye insisted. When Little Joe found out that she could sing, he said, "We've been looking for a female vocalist."

"Sure, I'd love to sing," replied Pauline, thinking that it was just polite conversation. After all, Little Joe had never heard Pauline sing, and she had never heard of his band.

"We're going to be recording in Dallas. Can you come?"

"Sure," Pauline answered, playing along as if the musician was really serious.

"I'll call you tomorrow. I'll tell you where we'll be in Dallas."

True to his word the next day Little Joe called Pauline at the home of her friend and cousin, Lucy Peña.[30] She began rehearsing songs, especially *rancheras*, with the band. Pauline chose the stage name Paula to disguise herself and evade her Baptist family's disapproval. In September 1964 they recorded *"Querido amigo"* ("Dear Friend"). Paula wasn't sure that anything would really come of this experience until she saw the album, *On Tour*, with her picture on the back cover.[31] These initial recordings were rather primitive and crude—first the music was recorded and later Paula's voice was added. The result was loud instrumentation with barely audible vocals. Regardless of recording quality, *Querido amigo* launched the *Tejano* musical style, inspiring bands like Alfonso Ramos, Sunny and the Sunliners,[32] and *Little Joe y la familia* to fuse traditional *rancheras* with an electrified rock 'n' roll sound.

Paula sang with Little Joe and his band from September 1964 to October 1966. The band consisted of three saxophones, two trumpets, an electric guitar (Little Joe), an electric bass (Raúl Reyes), drums (Cino Moreno), and a keyboard (Luis Pesina).[33] It was a modern big-band sound that made Little Joe popular with Mexicanos all over the state. Paula soon began making more money singing

(1964) Fort Worth singer Paula about the time she began singing with Little Joe and the Latinaires (now *Little Joe y la familia*). *Photo courtesy of Pauline Willis Estrada.*

on weekends than she did the entire week as a bilingual secretary for Texas Refinery and was able to quit her regular job.[34] Rehearsals were Monday to Friday, and the band booked engagements on the weekends all over Texas. Although Paula's parents were proud of her new career and heard her music on the radio, they never attended any of her live performances.[35]

Paula soon established a relationship with Dallas-based Luther and Vivian de la Garza, avid promoters of Mexican-American music throughout Texas. With Luther's brother-in-law, Johnny Gonzalez, they also operated large dance facilities such as the High Ho in Grand Prairie, the Camelot in Arlington, and *El zarape* in Dallas.[36] Vivian de la Garza convinced Paula to leave Little Joe's band and let Vivian manage her career. Acting as Paula's agent, Vivian booked tours that took the young singer all over the American Southwest, from Texas to California. From 1966 to 1967 Paula sang at dance halls in San Francisco, San José, Fresno, Los Angeles, San Diego, Las Vegas,[37] Phoenix, Tucson, and Las Cruces, New Mexico. She sang with well-known stars such as Mexico's José Alfredo Jiménez and was about to make a six-week tour of major cities in South America. But Paula's fiancé, Sam Estrada, objected to this extended tour. Pauline Willis married Sam Estrada on January 21, 1967, and began a family that included Debbie, Sharon, Karen, Sammy, and Samantha; her singing career came to an end.[38]

Samuel Estrada, born in Anson, Texas, in 1939, was one of four children raised by Manuel and Hermínia Nieto Estrada. Sam's father Manuel, a labor contractor, worked in nearby Stamford.[39] Sam Estrada joined the U.S. Air Force and received training as an aircraft mechanic. After the service he moved to Fort Worth and worked for Bell Helicopter and General Dynamics.[40]

From 1968 to 1991 Pauline also worked for General Dynamics as a senior program estimator, but the position ended with defense cuts at the end of the Cold War. She also held a position with Texas Christian University's Center for Instructional Services and taught in the university's Intensive English program.[41]

Pauline's past as a singer might well have gone unnoticed were it not for a series of unrelated events that brought her name and whereabouts to the attention of Ramón Hernández, Little Joe's publicist and authority on *Tejano* music and latino stars.[42] Hernández was delighted to rediscover Little Joe's former female vocalist and invited Paula to the February 27, 1997, Hispanic American Entertainment Hall of Fame Awards held at San Antonio's Mercado. Little Joe and other *Tejano* singers and musicians honored her as the "First Lady of *Tejano* Music." On July 15, 1997, Pauline presented a plaque inducting the musical group *Los relámpagos del Norte*[43] (Lightning of the North) into the Latino Hall of Fame at the annual *Pura Vida* awards in San Antonio.[44]

◆   ◆   ◆

Fernando Landeros, Sr.,[45] was born in Torreón, Coahuila, Mexico, on June 9, 1949. Fernando's mother, Francisca Landeros, was also from Torreón; he never knew his father. Fernando lived in Torreón until the age of sixteen when he moved to Monterrey, Nuevo León, in search of a better living as a master mason. While working for a government construction company, Landeros helped build schools in the remote areas of the state of Nuevo León in 1965. He became skilled at working with brick, stone, concrete, cement and clay roof tile, plaster, marble, and washed stone slabs. His *fachadas especiales* (special surface techniques) using broken glass and *conchas* on plaster walls were especially notable.[46]

In Monterrey Fernando met Gabriel Várgas, a fellow masonry worker who played the accordion with his group *Los fantásticos de Monterrey*. There were five instruments in *Los fantásticos*: an accordion, a *bajosexto* (twelve-string guitar, the instrument that accompanies the accordion), an electric bass, the *batería* (drums), and a saxophone. Vargas invited Fernando to rehearsals and engagements and introduced Fernando to music and musical instruments.[47]

The mid-1960s was the era of *cumbias norteñas* (the northern *cumbias*)[48] and polkas, which are of German-Swiss origin. According to Landeros, the Germans popularized both the polka and the accordion in Mexico during World War II. The polka had been popular in South-Central Texas since the mid-nineteenth century because of the extensive German community in the New Braunfels and Hill Country areas. Tony de la Rosa of Corpus Christi further popularized the polka with the Mexican-American population throughout South Texas. This musical sound quickly spread to northern Mexico as well. *Las polkas, las cumbias,* and *las rancheras* (ranch songs) together comprise the popular songs of northern Mexico and southern Texas.[49]

When Landeros turned seventeen, he quit his masonry job and voluntarily joined the Mexican army, hoping eventually to join the air force. He went to Mexico City for paratrooper training that lasted six months. After graduation Fernando applied to enter the military academy. However, it proved difficult for a *norteño* to get ahead in the south-central region of the country because of the fierce rivalry and jealousy between Mexicanos of different regions. The frequent fighting between men of different regions and states was evidence of these rivalries.[50] One of these fights involved Fernando, who severely injured his opponent; that ended his military career.

Landeros wandered around Mexico and the United States for several years, working in a variety of capacities—cook, auto mechanic, shoveling coal on a train, and as a *"coyote,"* helping Mexicanos enter the United States without papers. He ended up in Fort Worth, began working for Lone Star Gas Company, met and married Alejandra, and soon fathered Fernando Landeros, II.

At this point in Fernando's life "music entered his veins." Gabriel Díaz, *compadre de bautizo* (godfather) to little Fernando, an accordion player who had his own *conjunto,* and the other musicians who surrounded him inspired Fernando to learn to play the accordion.[51] Landeros asked Díaz if he would sell one of his five instruments, but Díaz, surprisingly, refused, perhaps fearing that selling an accordion to Fernando would inspire him to start his own *conjunto.* Nevertheless, Landeros bought an accordion in a pawnshop. He tried to teach himself but soon found the instrument more complicated than he had thought.

In those days Landeros loved to listen to Sherman's Mexican radio station *Stereo Mexicano* and *La fabulosa*, KESS, broadcasting from Dallas. One of the *conjuntos* that impressed him was *Los relámpagos del Norte*, a Monterrey band that had captured the number one spot on the radio at various times and dominated the air waves.

Fernando left Lone Star Gas Company when Carlos and Bobby Vásquez, owners of Vásquez Brothers Concrete Company, offered him a job. One of their projects was at Texas Christian University. Landeros was invaluable as the only person who knew how to install the maroon-colored washed stone along the steps in front of the Rickel Building. In the evenings Fernando played and drank with the Vásquez brothers, who had their own musical instruments and played around town. They even allowed Fernando to sing in one of their performances. Nevertheless, the ever-restless Fernando felt it was time to do something else, to change the setting (*cambiar ambiente*) of his life.[52]

In 1970 Landeros moved his family to Dallas and began working for the city of University Park, driving a municipal trash truck. He continued learning to play the accordion, making slow but steady progress. Fernando worked as a trash truck driver until 1972, when again he felt the need for change.

While still working for University Park, Landeros found a side job finishing slabs for a concrete contractor who paid eight dollars an hour. He worked under contract and soon had his own loyal crew of workers. When the side job began bringing in four to five hundred dollars per week Landeros realized that he needed more help. Thus began his sideline career as a *coyote*—someone who smuggles *mojados* (wetbacks) across the U.S. border for a price. Fernando smuggled his brother, Mario, through the border at Laredo, hiding him under the seat of the car as Fernando's toddler son slept soundly above.[53]

With a crew of three dependable workers plus his brother, Mario, Landeros was now earning $1,000 per week. He and his friends developed the habit of going to the park near his house in South Dallas to drink, sing, play instruments, and shoot the breeze. One day a *mojado* in dirty clothes approached them saying he had just arrived on the freight train from Laredo. Introducing himself as Pablo Granados, he begged them for a bite to eat, as he had not eaten in several days. Landeros took Pablo home, fed and clothed him, and made him one of his crew.

The next day after work Landeros took Granados to one of the Mexican *cantinas* where a *conjunto*, *Los regionales*, played *cumbias* and *rancheras*. Between songs Pablo Granados asked them if he could sing. On the stage he sang beautifully and played the accordion, delivering a virtuoso performance. Granados subsequently took turns playing the bass guitar, the *bajosexto*, and the *batería*—playing each instrument to perfection. The leader of the *conjunto* begged Pablo to join their group, and Landeros realized that his new friend and worker—the fellow who lived with his family and who helped him on the garbage truck—was no ordinary musician. It turned out that Pablo Granados had played with the most respected group in all northern Mexico, *Los gorriones del topo chico de Monterrey*. Their relationship meant that Fernando could play with the *conjunto*, singing and accompanying them on *el güiro* (the hand-held, round, wooden, ribbed instrument rubbed by a short wooden stick).[54]

Landeros continued driving the garbage truck, contracting cement jobs, and earning a good deal of money. Sometimes he made so much money he didn't know what to do with it—he bought rounds of drinks for anyone and everyone at the *cantinas* and on one occasion bought a .38 pistol, which he kept behind the seat in his truck. Fernando liked to frequent Gina, a neighborhood *cantina*, located on Peek and Bryan streets in South Dallas, and he was popular with the owner and the patrons alike because of his generosity.

However, an incident in the *cantina* resulted in Landeros shooting a man and going to jail for several days. His wife and friends bailed him out, and the outcome of his trial was a five-year probated sentence. The circumstances of his probation proved to be difficult, and the Landeros family moved to Mineral Wells.

In Mineral Wells, his wife's hometown, Landeros secured employment with Acme Brick Company for $1.60 per hour sweeping and disposing of brick fragments. Although this was a low pay rate their financial situation wasn't too bad—rent at the company housing was a mere $1.25 per week. They had to pay only the gas bill, as the company paid the water and electricity. The foreman set up an incentive program for bundling bricks—whoever packaged more than fifteen bundles per day would receive bonus pay. Soon Fernando was packaging sixty bundles per day, earning him recognition as the best bundler in the company, a distinction he kept for the next two years. He was now earning sixty dollars per day. The company also rewarded its exceptional employee with two miniature gold Acme bricks.[55]

But music was never far from his mind. Landeros took courses with a correspondence school to be a radio disc jockey (*para ser locutor*). He contacted Roberto del Villar, a deejay who had a radio program in Waxahachie and asked for help getting started in the business. Del Villar liked Fernando's voice and gave him a shift every Saturday from 10:00 A.M. to 2:00 P.M. In the evenings Landeros saw his friend and musical hero, Pablo Granados, who now played with *Los rebeldes del Norte*, and Granados soon began teaching Fernando to play the accordion.

Landeros was a man of restless ambition. He contacted the management of an Anglo-owned western-music radio station in Mineral Wells to buy one hour of air time a week to play Mexican music. They agreed to sixty dollars for one hour. Negotiations complete, Landeros contacted area Hispanic-owned businesses and offered to promote their businesses, for a fee of fifteen dollars, during his hour-long Mexican music program. Landeros played *polkas, rancheras,* and *cumbias,* and his program was a great success. Best of all, he pocketed two hundred dollars after paying his expenses.

Landeros continued to take advantage of new opportunities. He and Juan ("Johnny"), a friend from Mineral Wells, rented a local ballroom for a night of

(1993) *Sangre norteña* band members Fernando Landeros, Sr., Fernando Landeros, Jr. (standing with accordion), and Santos Landeros (sitting with guitar). *Photo courtesy of Fernando Landeros, Sr.*

Mexican music and dancing. They soon expanded the idea and hired *conjuntos* such as *Los monteros de Torreón* to play every weekend at Johnny's Frontier Club (named after his partner).

By this time Landeros' brother and mother lived with him in Mineral Wells. He settled into a busy routine: working for Acme during the week, deejaying in Waxahachie on Saturdays, visiting his musical pals in Dallas, doing his own program on Mineral Well's country-and-western station, and helping run Johnny's Frontier Club Friday and Saturday nights. Yet he still had the drive to pursue other challenges and stepped up his activities bringing people across the border.

After several harrowing brushes with border guards, Fernando was finally caught. He was transported to the Webb County Jail in Laredo and called attorney Eustorgio ("*Tojo*") Pérez, whose office was near the Webb County courthouse and jail. At the hearing the judge assessed Landeros a $10,000 fine and released him after he paid the sum (the attorney never got fully paid). So ended Landeros' moonlighting career as a *coyote*.[56]

When Fernando returned to Mineral Wells he found that the drummer for *Los monteros de Torreón* had left the group. The band unanimously nominated him to be the replacement drummer, and Landeros' dream of a career as a musician suddenly came true. He played the drums regularly for the next four years and continued to practice the accordion. In 1973 after *Los monteros* disbanded, he formed his own *conjunto* and called it *Los alegres de Bennett* (after Bennett, Texas, the tiny community next door to Mineral Wells where he actually lived). The group lasted about a year. Alejandra and Fernando divorced in 1978, and he moved to Fort Worth's North Side barrio where he has lived ever since. He has remarried; he and his second wife, Dolores, have two sons—Fernando, III, and Santos.

The series of *conjuntos* that Landeros was associated with over the next years were:

(1) *Los gallitos del Norte*, 1973-1975.

Bass: Gregorio ("Gollito") Gonzalez

Drums: Fernando Landeros, Sr.

Accordion: José Luis [last name unknown]

Bajosexto: Crescencio ("Chencho") (José Luis' brother)

(2) *Los Pachangueros*, 1975 (Landeros played bass guitar)

(3) *Los caminantes de Joe Hinojosa*, 1975-1977

    Dick Pacheco, *bajosexto*

    José ("Joe") Hinojosa, *güiro*

    Johnny Ayala (stand-in on drums)

    Fernando Landeros, Sr., vocalist

    Johnny Gonzalez, Sr., accordion

    Johnny Gonzalez, Jr., bass guitar

(4) *Ambición*, 1977-1980

    Victor Barrón, bass guitar

    Luis Zárate, accordion

    Fernando Landeros, Sr., drums

    José Castillo, *bajosexto*

(5) *Los forasteros de Saltillo* (The Outsiders), 1980-1992

    Juan Hernández, bass guitar

    Juan Aguirre, drums

    Fernando Landeros, III, *güiro*

    Fernando Landeros, Sr., accordion

    Cristino Cásio, *bajosexto*

(6) *Sangre norteña*, 1992 to present

    Anselmo Martínez, base guitar

    Santos Landeros, drums

    José Figueroa, *bajosexto*, vocalist

    Fernando, III, accordion, drums, keyboard

    Fernando, Sr., accordion, vocalist

Sangre norteña recorded its first album in 1992. Among the *cumbias, rancheras,* one *bolero*, one *Guapango*, and one *polka* in the album is a song composed by Landeros entitled *Mi suegra*, a humorous "tribute" to his mother-in-law.[57]

ART AND FILM

Juan Menchaca had a natural talent for art. In 1926 when he was a senior at Technical High School, Juan entered an art contest and won first prize for his painting of a howling coyote on a snow-covered hill. His prize was a canary.[58]

An Anglo doctor was impressed with Juan's talent and bought the winning painting for ten dollars. Juan was convinced that he had a talent worth developing and approached an art school in Fort Worth. The school administrator evaluated his work and was not encouraging, but he did suggest that Juan apply to the Denver Art Museum school. Juan left Fort Worth and studied art at the Denver institute for several years.[59]

After finishing his studies in art Juan returned to Fort Worth and married Felicia, whose family name is unknown. He was commissioned to paint windows for San José Catholic Church because of his simple yet elegant Gothic style. The project was designed to raise money for the church: For a fee a person could sponsor a window and dedicate it to a loved one. Menchaca also executed a painting of the founder of the Claretian order, Antonio María Claret, which hung in the church for almost thirty years.[60] After a few months visiting family and friends, Juan and his new bride returned to Denver, where they had decided to make their home. He worked for the Denver Museum of Art and some of his paintings found their way to museums in New Mexico and Wyoming and to the National Cowboy and Western Heritage Museum in Oklahoma City.[61]

◆   ◆   ◆

Movie star Pilar del Rey, was born Pilar Bouzas and raised in Fort Worth's North Side neighborhood. The family moved to Los Angeles, California, where Pilar was "discovered" and acted in numerous television programs, commercials, and motion pictures, including *Giant*, starring Rock Hudson, Elizabeth Taylor, and James Dean, *The Naked Jungle*, and *And Now Miguel*.[62]

Pilar's father, Aurelio ("Earl") Bouzas, was born on August 1, 1902, in Pontevedra, Galicia, Spain. His father was an engineer by profession, and the rest of his family was educated as well. Earl left Spain in 1924 to join his brothers in the United States. On a whim he came to Fort Worth with a friend and immediately got a job at the Worth Hotel. The city suited him; he settled down and in 1927 met and married Juanita Barrera.[63]

Earl and Juanita Bouzas lived at 909 Henderson Avenue near downtown and began a family. The first two children died, but in 1934 Pilar was born, followed by Arthur (named after Juanita's brother) in 1935. In the late 1930s the Bouzas moved from the downtown area to the North Side to be near Juanita's family. Pilar was baptized at the old San José Catholic Church and attended M. G. Ellis Elementary School from the first through the fifth grades. Dancing was her passion and she began tap lessons at Angel Morris' dance school. She even performed several times at the Isis Theater on North Main Street. This was the era when minorities were relegated to the balcony section, the only place where her family could watch their talented daughter.[64]

(1957) Ft. Worth-born Pilar del Rey (Pilar Bouzas) graces the front page in an article on her role in the movie *Giant*, starring Rock Hudson, Elizabeth Taylor, and James Dean. *Photo courtesy of Pete Zepeda.*

Fort Worth Pres

Weather: Fair and hot through tomorrow; high both days in upper 90s.

VOL. 36, NO. 246   FORT WORTH, TEXAS, TUESDAY, JULY 16, 1957   32

Dope Ki

Seized a

Ram, Sh

Officers deliberately crashed their car into a fleeing auto today to capture two narcotics suspects—one reputed to be the dope kingpin of the Fort Worth-Dallas area.

The suspects were fleeing in a hail of bullets when the auto rammed them from behind.

Nabbed were George Houk Mann, 28, of 3644 Willing, and Bobby Jack Masters, 23, of 1448 E. Richmond.

A few minutes earlier, a disguised federal narcotics agent had bought $300 worth of heroin from Masters.

The purchase was made in the 1400 block E. Richmond shortly before 1 a. m.

Unknown to the seller, two cars filled with officers lurked in the shadows.

Tries to Escape

When Masters entered Mann's 1955 Oldsmobile in the middle of the block, the officers closed in.

One car with two federal agents drove in from the east. City Narcotics Officer K. O. Glass and two federal

agents pulled in from the west.

Mann—described by Glass as the biggest dope pusher in this part of the state—tried to escape.

Douses Light

He doused his lights, put his car in reverse and screeched backward. The officers in front opened fire.

With bullets whizzing past them, Glass and his companions rammed their auto into the backing vehicle.

Both cars were nearly demolished. No one was hurt.

Long Record

Mann told officers he served a federal prison term. He has a long arrest record here, and kept company with such unsavory thugs as sex peddler Tommy Brewster and Sue Collins, a prostitute who killed a man.

Pilar Del Rey . . . city's Latin starlet

Mexican Mother in 'Giant' Was
FW Girl . . . She's Visiting Here

By MACK WILLIAMS
Press Staff Writer

Thousands who saw the movie "Giant" shed a tear for Pilar Del Rey.

In Hollywood's story of the vast West Texas ranches, she was the careworn mother of Sal Mineo, the Mexican boy who came home from the war in a coffin.

steno and dreaming of fame when a sharp-eyed talent scout saw her on a bus.

That led to modeling jobs, TV bits and finally—at 16—a role in Howard Duff's movie, "Illegal Entry."

A beauty with brains, Pilar learned luck won't build a career but hard work will.

"I took every role I could

her face each day the cameras rolled under the hot Marfa sun.

They put her in heavily padded clothes to muffle her 105-pound curves.

Pilar's parents, Mr. and Mrs. Earl Del Rey, and her 21-year-old brother Arthur are with her. When they end

When Pilar's Uncle Arthur died in a car accident, his wife Dela and his daughter moved to California, and the rest of the Dela's extended family decided to follow. Earl Bouzas immediately found work as a cook at a popular restaurant called the House of Murphy on La Cienega and Beverly Boulevard in Los Angeles.

Pilar's Hollywood career began after a chance encounter with an agent. Carlos Alvarado, whose brother, Don, had worked in silent movies, was stranded one day when his car broke down. Frantic about getting to an appointment, Alvarado boarded the same city bus that carried Pilar on her way to make up a class at Virgil Junior High during summer vacation. He introduced himself, apologized for staring, and handed Pilar a card saying that she had the looks to get into the movies and to contact him if she was interested. Alvarado later suggested to Pilar that she change her last name to a more marketable one. Pilar's mother rejected his first suggestion—"del Rio," after the popular actress, Dolores del Rio—because she thought it might be confused with the well-known actress. Earl objected to the idea of changing Pilar's last name, grumbling that Bouzas was good enough. Pilar finally settled on "del Rey" and enrolled at the Hollywood Professional School under her new stage name.[65]

Earl and Juanita Bouzas were moral, religious, and hard-working people who cared deeply about the quality of family life and the upbringing of their two children. Pilar has managed to maintain the values, morals, and Roman Catholic beliefs that her parents taught, in spite of the atmosphere of "Tinsel Town." She never married and has dedicated the last twenty years to raising the sons from her brother Arthur's failed marriage. Pilar feels that this has been part of her special calling in life.[66]

Chapter 8

CHALLENGES

The challenges of the last half of the twentieth century for Fort Worth Hispanics have been threefold—how to deal with changing immigration policies, how to become part of the city's leadership, and how to groom leaders who can boinspire the Hispanic community and seize the imaginations of Anglos. The individuals examined in this last section range from a *coyote* to the first Hispanic elected to city council and the first Hispanic elected to the Fort Worth Independent School Board—representatives of these three modern concerns.

IMMIGRATION

The life of musician Fernando Landeros also illustrates the risks Mexicanos faced in order to start a new life in America and the contradictory immigration policies that affect many lives. Fernando is a man with a restless nature, and in his younger days he was always looking for adventure. Following a brush with a military tribunal, Fernando entered the United States illegally in search of work. Subsequently he spent several years as a *coyote* and has a number of stories that demonstrate the determination and courage of the *mojados* (wetbacks). Smuggling people across the border was dangerous and difficult work and carried the threat of large fines and a jail sentence.

Fernando's adventurousness was born when he was in the Mexican army training to be a pilot. There were soldiers from many different regions of Mexico, and they often fought with each other. One soldier (also named Landeros) from the state of Durango began harassing Fernando. The tension between them built until one day they confronted each other with drawn bayonets. Urged on by a circle of jeering and cheering soldiers, Fernando stabbed the bully, pinning him to a tree with his bayonet. Military police quickly seized Fernando and whisked him off to jail.[1] He spent the next two weeks in a small dark room, furnished only with a table and chair. Prison officials gave him one loaf of bread and one glass of water a day, and he learned to sleep on the surface of the small table to avoid the rats.[2]

At the end of the two-week period, Landeros faced a military court-martial. If he were found guilty of initiating the bloody confrontation he would have faced many years in prison, but the testimony of several witnesses saved Fernando Landeros from this fate. However, in punishment for his part in the fracas, the military court offered him two choices—either join the infantry at a reduced rank or resign from the military. With his prospects for a career in the air force gone, Fernando chose to resign.[3]

Penniless, Fernando hopped freight trains and returned to Monterrey, where he resumed his previous career as a master mason, working until February 1968. On a visit to his home in Torreón he met some friends who talked about leaving to go *al norte* (to the United States) where there was plenty of work and lots of money. On one of their many *parrandas* (outings marked by drinking and carousing), they dared each other to go that very night. In spite of the fact that all were drunk and broke, the three amigos attempted to thumb a ride toward the border by way of Saltillo. After several hours passed, Landeros was finally able to flag down a large truck. His friends had passed out, so Fernando left them behind, peacefully dozing by the roadside.[4]

From Saltillo, Fernando caught a train bound for Allende, Coahuila, shoveling coal aboard the coal-car for his passage; he then caught another train from Allende to Ciudad Acuña (across from Del Rio). He had heard that the passage across the Rio Grande into the United States would be easier there than in Piedras Negras (across from Eagle Pass). Once in Ciudad Acuña, Fernando met "El Diablo," an old mason friend from Torreón who helped him secure a construction job on the Amistad Dam.[5]

Landeros worked construction until he made enough money to resume his odyssey. When he did, he found it was necessary to cross the Rio Grande on foot about twenty kilometers above Ciudad Acuña. It took Fernando three hours to descend the treacherous hills overlooking the river. The river was about three hundred feet wide and five to six feet in depth; slippery rocks on the bottom complicated the crossing. Fernando began to cross the river, supporting himself with a tree limb. Even though the current was swift and the water came up to his neck (he is six-feet tall) and at times covered his head completely, Landeros crossed successfully, finally making it safely onto American soil.[6]

Not wanting to spend the night on the banks of the river, Fernando began the long, arduous ascent of the steep hill on the Texas side, trekking along to Comstock, where he spent the night. The next day Fernando, now out of food, came upon a ranch where a Mexicano who worked as a cook and caretaker for an Anglo offered him a meal of cornbread, beans, and venison. After Landeros rested a few hours his host told him how to get to Ozona (by U.S. Interstate 10). Fernando had to leave quickly because the ranch owner, who worked for the immigration service in the Del Rio area, was due to arrive shortly.[7]

North of Comstock Fernando found himself walking in circles, completely lost, until he recalled a technique he'd learned while training with the army. He used a stick to gauge the direction the sun traveled and establish the points of the compass. Landeros continued on foot, eventually arriving at tiny Midkiff (a ghost town today), which had only about three or four buildings, the busiest of which was a small restaurant-tavern.[8]

Landeros worked as a dishwasher at the Midkiff restaurant for two days and then got a job in an oil supply field office. El Paso Natural Gas Company had a small refinery in Midkiff, and two of its supervisors offered Fernando a job keeping the grounds clean around their office and truck terminal for three dollars a day plus room and board. When he wasn't tending the grounds, Landeros assisted the mechanic who maintained the company's fleet of trucks.[9]

Fernando learned quickly and could repair anything once he had seen it done. Sometimes he took it upon himself to fix and remount flats and to repair leaking and ruptured pipes. His employers, brothers Pete and Brad Peters, appreciated how useful and resourceful he was and began to expand his duties. They asked him to drive the tractor-trailer trucks on ranch roads to extract oil from storage tanks. They also raised Fernando's pay from three to eight dollars per day.

One day two border patrol officials arrived as Landeros was loading oil onto his truck. When they asked to see his papers, Fernando's lack of English led the officials to surmise that he was in the country illegally. They arrested him, but one of his bosses came and tried to bargain with the officials. He asked what was necessary to make Fernando "legal" and even offered the officials several hundred dollars to allow their employee to stay. The officials refused, stating that they were just doing their job. Before Fernando left in the patrol car, Brad Peters told him to call as soon as he could so that Peters could wire money for his return.[10]

Landeros spent two weeks in an Ozona jail before being transported on a green border patrol bus with forty other *mojados* to the nearest border crossing at Presidio. Landeros and the others were put on a train at Ojinaga, on the Mexican side of the Rio Grande, to make the two-hundred-mile trip to Chihuahua. A few of the *mojados*, like Fernando, who were lucky enough to have some money, could purchase the seven-dollar ticket and ride in one of the passenger cars. The majority of the "wets" were herded into a cattle car where they were locked up until their arrival in Chihuahua. A border patrol officer was posted at each end of the passenger car all the way to their destination.

With some money left over Landeros boarded a bus bound for Torreón. When he arrived he immediately called Brad Peters, who asked how much money he should send. Fernando hesitated, not knowing how much to ask for. Peters eventually wired three hundred dollars and instructed Fernando to get back to Midkiff as soon as possible. Landeros boarded the next train bound for Ciudad Acuña, where he met another *mojado* who wished to make the journey with an experienced traveler. Together they set out on foot following the same route that Fernando had traveled earlier. It took three weeks to get to Midkiff; it would have taken longer if they hadn't offered a Mexicano in Rankin twenty dollars to drive them to their destination.[11]

Back in Midkiff Fernando was welcomed with great delight and celebration; his patrons even offered his companion fifty dollars for having been the instrument of Fernando's return. Everyone agreed to use their CB radios as an early-warning system to spot border patrol vehicles approaching the area.

Landeros worked for the Peters brothers until December 24, 1968, when he and his companion left for Colorado in search of something else (*necesitaba algo más, quería buscar algo más*).[12]

In preparation for his departure Fernando bought a 1959 Chevy for three hundred dollars, as well as some warm clothing. On Christmas Eve 1968, while on the way to Colorado, the pair stopped in Midland to attend a well-publicized Mexican dance at the convention center. Fernando's car stalled at an intersection. Not wanting to be late for the dance, his friend went on ahead to the convention center on foot. As he tried in vain to start the car Landeros was hit from behind by another vehicle. The driver of the other car was very angry and threatened to call the police. Fernando naturally didn't want to attract the attention of the police and headed on foot to call for a mechanic. When a police car cruised by, Landeros bolted into a nearby field, running so wildly that he slammed into a barbed-wire fence. He kept right on running until arriving out of breath at a small Mexican bar where he called a taxi that took him to Midkiff for fifty dollars.

His friend joined him in Midkiff and soon the two were off to Chicago, where the friend had heard of the tremendous job potential. The bus route to Chicago went through Fort Worth and while they waited for the bus, they met Frank Flores, a Mexicano from the South Side. Flores told them that his father, Robert Flores, could find jobs for them sanding cabinets and get them a place to live for forty dollars a week. Landeros worked for three months at a cabinet shop in Fort Worth.[13]

Landeros met another Frank Flores, also a resident of the South Side, who was a manager for Lone Star Gas Company and the saxophone player with the Jimmy Flores Band (1950s-1970s). Frank arranged for both a social security card and a job working at the gas company for Fernando. When he had been working for Lone Star for four months, he met and began dating Alejandra, a girl from Mineral Wells who was a friend of Albert Flores' daughter (Albert was Frank's *padrino de boda*—marriage godfather). They soon were married and began a family: Fernando, II, was born on November 20, 1969. His marriage to Alejandra and the birth of his son ended Fernando's immigration problems.[14]

However, discrimination seemed to stalk Fernando Landeros no matter where he went. He soon found that naturalized Mexicanos who had lived in the states for a long time resented recent arrivals from Mexico. In an eerie reprise of the situation that ended his military career, Fernando was involved in a fight in a bar in Dallas. A Chicano[15] playing pool in the bar began *"echándole madres"* (heaping insults on him). Landeros tried to defuse the situation but the bully poked him in the ribs with a cue stick, saying plainly that he didn't like *mojados,* and *se puso bravo* (he became belligerent), hitting Fernando several times with the stick.[16] Landeros stormed out of the cantina, grabbed a pistol hidden behind the seat of his pickup truck, and concealed it behind his belt, under his sport coat. Back inside the cantina the Chicano continued *cocoriando* (provoking) and spat in his face. Fernando drew his gun and shot the man in the left shoulder.[17]

He was apprehended just one block from his house on Victor and Carroll streets. The police found and confiscated the gun and arrested Landeros. Alejandra called an attorney and paid the fifteen-hundred-dollar bail.

Landeros resumed working while waiting for trial: he received a five-year probated sentence. During the probation period, Fernando's probation officers often taunted and harassed him. Thus, he found the conditions of his probation intolerable and in 1972 Landeros and his family moved to Mineral Wells. He still was required to report once a month to his probation officer in Fort Worth.[18]

Increasingly, Anglo businesses were requiring more cheap labor, and Landeros began to "import" *mojados,* transporting them to Dallas, Fort Worth, or Mineral Wells depending upon where they were needed. Orders for *mojados* poured in, and Fernando kept making runs to the border at Laredo. Landeros always went to the area around the cantinas near the international bridge on the Nuevo Laredo side to gather people who wanted transportation *al norte.* Landeros charged $120 to take them across the border. He gave careful instructions and then concealed them (usually about seven or eight individuals) inside his *troquita's* (pickup's) camper top.

By now a full-fledged *coyote,* he carefully observed the habits of the border patrol and learned that there was usually a break in their stopping vehicles on I-35 between 1:00 and 1:30 P.M. This provided a window of opportunity for him to slip by with his human cargo, bound for points north.[19]

Fernando's brother, Mario, married a woman from Torreón, but she remained in Mexico while he worked in Mineral Wells. Mario missed his new wife. He began to beg his brother to smuggle his wife in on his next border run.

This time Fernando made the border trip in an old station wagon. When he picked up his sister-in-law he gave her a jar of Vick's Vapor Rub, instructing her to put it in her mouth, in her nose, and around her eyes to give the appearance of a sick person. The "sick" person sat between other people in the back seat of the station wagon, and when immigration officials asked "What's the matter with her?" Landeros replied, "Sir, she's real sick. We're on our way now to the hospital so that a doctor can treat her immediately." The car was quickly waved through; they made it all the way to Mineral Wells without further incident.[20]

Not long after this episode Landeros was caught by the border patrol at the Roma, Texas, cemetery, a widely known and frequently used rendezvous point. Fernando explained that he was coming from Roma after visiting friends and that he happened to come across this wretched band of men whose truck experienced mechanical difficulties and who were walking, hoping to get a ride to the nearest town. The illegals corroborated the story as they were questioned, but the entire group was taken to the border patrol detention center.

All seven *mojados* were taken to smaller rooms and Fernando could hear the officials trying to extract confessions from the illegals that they had in fact paid Landeros to be transported into the U.S. In spite of the harsh interrogation all seven stuck to their story. Landeros' record was investigated along with his claim that he had a full-time job in Mineral Wells, and he was released. Landeros continued in this vein for several years, skirting the occasional arrest, until he was caught, found guilty, and assessed a $10,000 fine or prison term. He paid the fine.[21]

GROWING POLITICAL STRENGTH

Community leader and founder of the Greater Fort Worth Hispanic Chamber of Commerce, Jaime Pete Zepeda was born in 1914 to Irineo and Martina Manchaca Zepeda in the small East Texas community of Diboll, south of Lufkin. His parents met in 1910, when, at the age of twenty-three, Irineo left his home in Mexico because of the Revolution and arrived in Texas looking for work. He found it at logging mills in Diboll and Nacogdoches. It was in Nacogdoches that he met and married Martina Manchaca.[22] In 1915 Irineo brought his young family to Fort Worth, in a covered wagon pulled by mules, and rented a six-room home with another family at 2204 North Commerce Street.[23] They lived there for eleven years until they moved into a shotgun house at 2140 North Commerce in 1926.[24]

Pete Zepeda was baptized a Roman Catholic in Nacogdoches, but in Fort Worth the family joined *La trinidad*, the Mexican Methodist Church, and the Wesley Community House. Pete attended the Wesley House kindergarten and then went to M. G. Ellis Elementary School until 1927 when he transferred to the seventh grade at J. P. Elder Middle School. He stayed for one year and then dropped out to work with his father for Thurber Construction Company. Two years later he returned to finish eighth grade at J. P. Elder before moving on to Trimble Tech. A school with about one hundred eighty boys, Trimble Tech offered regular high school courses in the mornings and shop classes in the afternoons. The various shop offerings included printing, electrical, machine shop, and automotive; Pete chose to learn the printing trade. He spent two years at Trimble Tech, transferred to North Side High School, and graduated in 1935.

In the 1920s and 1930s Pete and his father worked for contractors such as the Thurber Construction Company, paving the streets of downtown Fort Worth. They also worked for the company paving streets in Stephenville and Hearne. While in Stephenville, father and son couldn't find anyone who would rent to Mexicanos, so they lived first in a horse barn and then in an empty space on the second floor of a building in the downtown commercial district; there was no heat or running water. In both situations the Zepedas had to go to a nearby service station for water.[25]

From 1935 to 1941 Pete Zepeda worked in the printing department of Globe Laboratories, a North Side enterprise that produced veterinary products for the livestock industry. He left to work in the beef boning department of Swift and Company, a job he held until 1946.

During his time at Globe Pete met and married Juanita Hernández in a private ceremony before a Dallas justice of the peace. Juanita, born in Fort Worth on August 29, 1917, was one of eight children born to Agapito and Dominga Huerta Hernández.[26]

The newlyweds lived with Pete's parents at 1319 North Commerce for six months before moving into a duplex at 2028 North Commerce. In 1941 the Zepedas bought a house in the Polytechnic (now Texas Wesleyan University) area and lived there twenty years before moving to their present North Side address at 1407 Clinton Avenue. Because he was a father and head of a large family, Zepeda was not called to serve in the armed services during World War II.[27]

From 1946 to 1947 Pete worked for Panther Oil and Grease Company as an assistant export manager. The company exported specialized oils for various kinds of machinery as well as roof coating products. From 1947 to 1950 he worked for World Wide Trading Corporation, a partnership that exported farm machinery to Venezuela and Columbia. After the company failed, Pete was hired by General Dynamics as an analyst in logistics to work with the air force to select parts for their various aircraft. At GD he joined the Office Professional Employees International Union and served as shop steward and committeeman for eighteen of the thirty-four years that he worked there. Pete retired in April 1984.

Beginning in 1949 the enterprising Zepedas engaged in other businesses to augment their family's income. Pete became the first Hispanic real estate broker in Fort Worth as well as the first casualty insurance representative and notary public. He helped people fill out their income tax forms, and he managed several rental properties on the North Side. Juanita helped Pete with these ventures and often served as a court interpreter.[28]

Pete Zepeda was involved at all levels with the Methodist church since his childhood. On the local level he served in virtually every capacity from Sunday school teacher to board president of *La trinidad*. In 1945 Pete became the first scoutmaster of Troop 150, the first Mexican American Boy Scout troop in Fort Worth. From 1960 to 1964 he was a district lay leader and from 1964 to 1971 was a lay leader with the Rio Grande Conference.[29] Zepeda was selected as the male delegate to represent the Methodist church at the 1968 meeting that combined the Methodist church with the United Brethren church to form the United Methodist church. These years of experience have served to train both Pete and Juanita Zepeda for positions of leadership within their community.

In 1971 Juanita Zepeda became the first Hispanic to announce her candidacy for an at-large position on the Fort Worth City Council. But the promise of a solid Hispanic vote was diluted by the candidacy of Joe Lazo, who threw his hat in the ring shortly after Juanita's announcement. They faced an Anglo candidate who eventually won the seat with approximately 13,000 votes. Zepeda and Lazo each garnered about 6,000 votes. Although both Hispanic candidates lost, the election was significant because almost half the voters in a predominantly Anglo city cast their votes for one or the other of the Hispanic candidates.

On December 4, 1973, Pete Zepeda helped organize what eventually became the Greater Fort Worth Hispanic Chamber of Commerce. He served as president of the organization in 1975 and has been active ever since. In 1983 a vacant seat on the Tarrant County Junior College board, traditionally held by a representative of labor, was to be offered to an Hispanic. Over a dozen people were interviewed before the board offered the seat to Pete Zepeda. Although he never sought it, Zepeda accepted the position because he deeply believed in education as the key to changing lives.[30] The Mexican community mourned Pete Zepeda's death in 2001; residents thought of him as "the godfather," in reference to his stature as a highly respected community leader.

◆   ◆   ◆

Louis J. Zapata[31] was born on October 5, 1934, to Antonio and Elena Miranda Zapata at their home on 500 Mills Street in the barrio of *La Corte*. Louis joined his brother and sisters in helping their parents manage the family grocery business. Even as a youngster, Louis was concerned for others—whenever his mother left the store to purchase supplies from area wholesalers, Louis would freely give out candy to neighborhood children who couldn't afford such a luxury. Of course, when she returned he had to face her displeasure at discovering the store's declining profits.[32]

When Louis first went to school, his parents sent him to San José School on the North Side, but he had to catch the city bus at Main and Weatherford in order to get there. He was a particularly bright child and earned promotions to the second and then to the third grade in the same year. Louis' mother was concerned about his daily commute by bus at such a young age and transferred Louis to nearby John Peter Smith Elementary School, located at Florence and Second streets. His new school didn't recognize San José's promotions and so Louis had to repeat first grade. However, he skipped a grade every year for four years—promoted from the first to the third; the third to the fifth; and the fifth to the seventh grades. For the seventh and eighth grades he attended St. Ignatius Catholic School[33] before transferring to Laneri for his freshman and sophomore years of high school. In 1951 Louis graduated from Technical High School, after completing his coursework in his junior year. The year 1951 was pivotal for Louis—he became skilled at the printing business and he fell in love.

Originally from Pittsburg, Oklahoma, Mary Frances Jiménez had come to Fort Worth to find employment. She met seventeen-year-old Louis in October at one of the Saturday night Mexican dances at the North Side Coliseum. Virtually every Saturday night during the 1950s there was a Mexican dance at either the North Side Coliseum or the Casino at Lake Worth. That particular night the Cuban "Mambo King" Pérez Prado and his orchestra played for an enthusiastic and appreciative audience. After a whirlwind courtship Mary Frances and Louis married in April 1952 at St. Patrick's Cathedral.[34]

The newlyweds made their first home at 406 Northwest 21st Street across from the Greek Orthodox Church on Ross Street. They began a family that eventually included Mary Helen Louise, Patricia Ann, and José Luis, Jr. After five months they moved to their present home at 2007 North Houston.

Right after high school Louis got a job at Snelson Printing Company on Race Street and Riverside Drive, where Manuel Jara was his direct supervisor. He later worked for Dudley-Hodgkins in Arlington and then Stafford Lowden Printing in Fort Worth. During this time he also worked a second job running offset presses at Motheral Printing as well as pursuing his freelance work. Using the platen and offset presses he set up in a twenty-by-twenty-foot shed behind his home, Louis worked as a subcontractor doing printing for General Motors and other companies but was soon hired by Bell Helicopter. In 1953 he started work with Bell in the print shop and quickly rose to the position of logistics administrator. Within a few months Zapata's leadership abilities ensured his election as shop steward of the local United Auto Workers union and in 1955 he became one of the company's four union committeemen in charge of negotiating management-labor contracts. This job required an ability to analyze figures, evaluate details, and bargain. During the thirty-eight years that Louis worked for Bell Helicopter he successfully negotiated five major contracts. He retired in 1991.[35]

In addition to his responsibilities at Bell, his freelance printing work, and his duties with the union, Zapata was a radio operator in the air force reserves. Interested in ham radio since the 1950s, he taught himself the essentials of this hobby by building his own equipment. On his weekend tours of duty Zapata flew with his air force unit all over the South, Midwest, Northeast, and even to Newfoundland.

From the late 1950s to the early 1960s Louis took night classes in electrical engineering at Arlington State College (now University of Texas at Arlington). In 1962 and 1963 he attended Texas Christian University, enrolled in fine arts and business courses. Although Zapata never earned a degree, he nevertheless accumulated ninety hours of college credit.[36]

He describes himself as a "loner, who likes to mind his own business," yet Louis Zapata's intelligence and political acumen as a union representative made him a natural for politics. Friend Pat Reece, a former city councilman, repeatedly

Louis Zapata circa 1950.
Photo courtesy of Consuelo Zapata Narvaez.

urged Louis to involve himself in city government and, in 1971, made the surprise announcement that Zapata had been appointed to the city's human relations commission. In 1973 and 1974 Zapata was chairman of the commission and introduced the affirmative action plan, which set up guidelines for hiring and promoting employees of the city. From 1975 to 1977 Louis lived in Mexico on assignment with the U.S. State Department's Agency for International Development, returning to run for city council.

While Louis was in Mexico, his political friend, Pat Reece, called to tell him that voters had approved the citywide referendum establishing single-member districts. This referendum increased the chances of non-Anglo candidates winning positions on the city council—in the past Hispanic candidates such as Juanita (Pete) Zepeda and Joe Lazo were defeated under the at-large system.[37] Pat Reece then stunned Louis by nominating him for the 1977 race for District Two.[38] A coalition of both Anglo and Hispanic supporters enthusiastically pledged to raise funds and run his campaign from a headquarters on the sixth floor of the downtown Sheraton Hotel (now the Radisson).[39]

Louis Zapata and seven other candidates—four Anglos and three Hispanics—announced their intentions to enter the race for District Two. Among the more prominent Anglos were Wade Benowski, the well-known former head of the food service division of the Fort Worth Independent School District and chief elder of the Midtown Church of Christ, and Danny Aston, the youthful vice-president of Aston Meat Company, who had strong support from younger voters. Louis' three Hispanic opponents included Pete Zepeda, José Gonzalez, a respected and astute community activist who was executive director of *Fuera de los barrios*, and Pedro Ayala. Zapata faced a formidable challenge from highly qualified and better-known candidates; his campaign was handicapped by his two-year absence from the city. In a brilliant marketing effort to overcome the lack of name recognition, he put a red, white, and green poster bearing the words "Vote Zapata" and "Viva Zapata" on every bus in the city. Puzzled citizens everywhere probably wondered "Zapata who?" but in the end the bold strategy produced the desired results.[40]

The surprising outcome of the 1977 election for District Two was a runoff between the top vote getter, Wade Benowski, and the dark-horse candidate,

Louis J. Zapata. Zapata and his campaign staff decided to concentrate their efforts and funds on the neighborhoods where a survey showed his appeal was greater, and they did a superb job of blanketing the Diamond Hill, North Side, and Washington Heights areas with calls and literature.

An exultant Louis Zapata was sworn in on April 19, 1977—the first Hispanic city councilman in the history of Fort Worth. The largest crowd of Hispanics ever to assemble at city hall included family, friends, and supporters who were there to witness the historic event.

Louis was an effective councilman and was re-elected for six more two-year terms. He holds the record for length of service on Fort Worth's city council (1977-1991). In 1991 Carlos Puente defeated the esteemed politician using the slogan "It's time for a change!"[41]

As if all these responsibilities were not enough, in 1983 the enterprising Zapata opened a funeral home in a rented mansion located at 2200 Hemphill.[42] In 1988 he bought the old Robert Hall's Clothing Store at 2301 Ephriham Avenue and with his daughter, Patricia Ann, and continued to operate the funeral home from that location until he sold the business in 1992.[43]

The former councilman now spends time working as consultant from an office located near Meacham Field. Autographed pictures of former Speaker of the House Jim Wright and Congressman Henry B. Gonzalez on his office walls join the dozens of plaques from various community organizations that express appreciation for Zapata's dedicated service on their behalf. Like his father before him, Louis Zapata has a sense of peace and fulfillment gained from his years of service to others.

◆　　◆　　◆

Community activists Rufino Mendoza, Sr., and Jr., were instrumental in ensuring that all Hispanic children receive equal educational opportunities. Charter members of the Mexican American Educational Advisory Committee (MAEAC), the Mendozas were part of a group that boldly took on the Fort Worth Independent School District—and won.

Rufino Mendoza, Sr., was born on September 9, 1927, in Pittsburg, Oklahoma, to Apolonio and Petra Rodríguez Mendoza. Originally from Irapuato,

Guanajuato, Apolonio and Petra came to the United States in the early 1920s during the influx of refugees following the Mexican Revolution. He worked in the coal mines in Michigan and Oklahoma and later was assigned to track maintenance for the Texas & Pacific Railroad in Fort Worth. The family returned to Mexico at the start of the Great Depression, but Mexico, still reeling from the aftershocks of the Revolution and the Cristero Rebellion (1926-1929), continued to be a difficult place to scratch out a living. The Mendozas returned to Fort Worth around 1935.[44]

They lived briefly on Spring Street (*El TP)* and then moved to another enclave of working-class Mexicanos off Vickery at 819 Jarvis Avenue.[45] Rufino became a driver for Westex Produce Company, delivering goods to customers in *La Loma* and North Side.

In 1945 and 1946 Rufino was a sergeant in an army infantry unit stationed in post-war Europe. After his service the G.I. Bill enabled Rufino, who had not finished high school, to attend trade school. In 1951 he took a job with the post office as one of Fort Worth's first Mexican American mail carriers.[46]

Rufino Mendoza, Sr., married Martina Franco on January 13, 1947. Martina, the daughter of farmers Reynaldo and Victoria Ozuna Franco, was born on April 14, 1930, in Karnes City, Texas. The Francos came to Fort Worth in 1937, where Reynaldo found work at both Swift and Armour.[47]

Rufino and Martina Mendoza eventually had nine children: Rufino, Jr., born in November 1947, and siblings Jorge, David, Rebecca, Ralph, Eduardo, Ricardo, Melissa, and Melinda. Rufino's commitment to community service began when Father Hoover, a priest at St. Patrick's, encouraged his involvement with "the Fishers," a service-oriented parish organization, and the St. Vincent de Paul Society, which provides assistance to the poor. In addition, on Saturdays and Sundays Rufino drove the church bus to bring children from the Rock Island barrio for catechism and Mass. Mendoza helped four parishes: St. Patrick's, All Saints, St. Bartholomew, and St. Thomas. Grateful for Rufino's faithful service, Father Hoover and Father Pat Hazel arranged a scholarship for Rufino, Jr., to attend Nolan High School. Education was a high priority for Rufino, Sr., as he knew all too well how lack of education can limit career opportunities.[48]

After work, the elder Mendoza supplemented the family income by mowing lawns in the Anglo neighborhoods of the North Side. Until the late 1960s, the area of the North Side west of North Main Street was still predominantly Anglo. Rufino developed warm relationships with customers all along Gould, Lincoln, and Park streets: Two elderly ladies, Mrs. Smith and Mrs. Nix, practically adopted him. In fact, when Mrs. Nix died, the family gave Rufino their mother's house at 1804 Harrington Street[49] in appreciation for all he had done for her and asked him to be a pallbearer at her funeral. Later, Mendoza purchased a house at 1100 Park Street from another of his favorite customers.

Rufino Mendoza, Jr., met Gloria Vásquez while both attended school at Nolan. They married in 1967 when Rufino was twenty and had just become a cadet at the Fort Worth Police Academy. When he graduated in 1969 Rufino, Jr., was the first Hispanic graduate from Fort Worth and only the third in the history of the academy. In addition to his regular job, Officer Mendoza moonlighted as

In the early 1950s, civic leader and equal-rights proponent Rufino Mendoza, Sr., was honored with the title of Grand Knight of the Knights of Columbus. *Photo courtesy of Martina Franco Mendoza.*

a security guard at Guys and Dolls Ballroom and at the Casino at Lake Worth. He also took classes at the University of Texas at Arlington.[50]

While Rufino, Jr., was a student at UTA, he met Eddy Herrera, a professor who inspired him to become more concerned about public issues affecting Hispanics. In May 1971 Herrera invited about sixty community leaders to a meeting at All Saints Catholic Church to address these issues by forming the seven-member Mexican American Educational Advisory Committee (MAEAC). Both Mendozas, father and son, were named to the committee, and Mendoza, Sr., was elected chairman. MAEAC's purpose was to aggressively advocate quality educational opportunities for Mexican Americans with the Fort Worth Independent School District. They demanded more Hispanic teachers and administrators and recognition of Mexicanos as a separate ethnic group with distinct needs.[51] In December 1971, after six futile months of urging the school board to address the committee's petitions, MAEAC filed the first class-action lawsuit against the Fort Worth Independent School District. MAEAC originally hired attorney Ron Fernández to file the lawsuit, but, as the case dragged on, the committee later retained Austin attorney Geoffrey Gay and Dallas barrister Bill Garrett. After almost ten years of legal wrangling, an agreement was finally reached in 1981 with Superintendent Carl Candoli, who was receptive to the needs of the Mexican American community. Because of the "Mendoza Lawsuit," by the mid-1990s the district employed seventy Hispanic administrators and more than two hundred teachers.[52] A second lawsuit to secure single-member district voting in school board elections was filed in November 1991. The first settlement came three years later in March 1994 and the second in October of the same year.

On Friday, May 29, 1992, while mowing his lawn, Rufino Mendoza, Sr., had a serious heart attack that left him in a coma for twenty-six days—he died on June 25, 1992. The funeral procession was miles long. Few people remembered seeing so many flowers and so many mourners at one funeral—a fitting tribute to a man who loved and cared deeply for his family and his community.[53]

◆   ◆   ◆

The first Hispanic elected to the Fort Worth Independent School District board of trustees, Carlos Puente has a long history of community activism, especially with voter registration programs. Born in Galveston on July 29, 1944, Carlos Puente was the fifth and youngest child of Genaro Badillo Puente and María Guadalupe Mendoza Puente, both from Mexico. Genaro's family fell on hard times after his father abandoned them. For a time, Genaro shined shoes in Monterrey; then the family emigrated to Webster, Texas, in search of better jobs. Genaro Puente's and Lupe Mendoza's paths crossed in Webster, where Genaro worked for a nursery and Lupe was a housekeeper for an Anglo family. The two married in Houston at Our Lady of Guadalupe Catholic Church in 1932.[54]

From the beginning of their marriage Galveston served as home base for the Puentes. Genaro worked as a stevedore on the docks, and Lupe stayed home caring for a growing family that included Genaro, Jr., María Elena ("Mary"), Avelina ("Billie"), Rebecca ("Becky"), and Carlos.

Carlos Puente attended Galveston public schools until, influenced by other boys, he dropped out in the ninth grade. For two years he worked at a TV repair shop, fixing televisions and installing antennas. He soon realized that quitting school had been a mistake and set about obtaining his G.E.D. In 1962 he enrolled for one year at the Metropolitan Business College, taking bookkeeping and other business courses. Carlos subsequently worked as a delinquent tax clerk in the collections office of the Galveston County tax collector-assessor.

Puente met María Esther Grimaldo at a social, sparking a romance that led to their marriage. María was born on November 6, 1944, in Nueva Rosita, Coahuila, one of eleven children born to Jesús C. Grimaldo and Theodora Gonzalez Grimaldo. Her father was a coal miner who became a migrant agricultural worker and brought his entire family to Texas soon after María's birth.

Carlos and María Puente's first child, Jimmy, was born in 1965. In 1966 Carlos was drafted into the Marine Corps and reported for basic training at Camp Pendleton, California. The young Marine spent thirteen months in Vietnam at the Marine base at Chu Lai, aboard the *USS Okinawa*, and at Hué, in the northern part of South Vietnam. Carlos' duties were mainly administrative—such as typing orders and processing commendations. His tour of duty ended in November 1968, and he reported to the U.S. Marine Corps Air Station at Cherry Point, North Carolina. Two months later, in January 1969, Puente was honorably discharged and returned to Galveston.[55]

(May 1991) Carlos Puente, Fort Worth City Councilman. Arriving in Fort Worth in 1971 from his native Galveston, Puente became the first Mexican American to win a seat on the Fort Worth ISD Board (1978-1984). *Photo courtesy of Carlos Puente.*

While his wife worked as a statistical typist at an accounting firm, Carlos worked for Southwestern Bell during the summers. In addition, he resumed his education by enrolling in Alvin Junior College and then transferring to Galveston College. Puente's cousin, Carlos de la Torre, who had been with him at Alvin Junior College, transferred to North Texas State University in Denton. Encouraged by his cousin's move to North Texas, Puente uprooted his family and headed for Denton where he planned to get a bachelor's degree in political science. In Denton the couple had two more children: Joseph ("Joey"), born in 1970, and Juan, 1971. A fourth child, Elisa, was born in Fort Worth in 1975.

In August of 1971, after having graduated *cum laude* with a bachelor's degree in political science, Carlos Puente accepted an internship with the city of Fort Worth planning department. He moved his family to Fort Worth, found a home at 3217 Hemphill Street, and began taking graduate courses at the University of

Texas at Arlington. In December 1973, he graduated from UTA with a Masters in Urban Affairs and began an internship with the Weatherford city manager. This position gave Puente firsthand experience in the operations of different city departments.

It did not take long for Carlos Puente to move up to other administrative challenges. He began working for the North Central Texas Council of Governments, an agency that covered an eighteen-county area. Until 1977 Puente worked as a planner for the CETA Manpower program retraining people who either had dropped out of school or were displaced.[56] The Council of Governments created a new program called the Texas Area Five Health Systems Agency and hired Puente as a health planning associate. His job was to research the number of doctors, dentists, nurses, and other health-care professionals available in the different geographic areas and to ascertain where there were shortages. The agency also gave tuition incentives to medical students in return for promising to practice in poor and disadvantaged areas. Puente worked for this agency until 1982, when President Ronald Reagan's conservative fiscal policies dismantled many of these programs.[57]

In 1982 Dr. Ralph L. Willard, president of the Texas College of Osteopathic Medicine, hired Carlos Puente to be his special assistant in charge of recruiting minorities for the medical school.[58] Puente set out to recruit Texas minority students who showed promise in spite of their Medical College Admissions Test (MCAT) scores.[59] TCOM established a special eight-week summer program to introduce seventy students to the world of osteopathic medicine. The students stayed, by special arrangement, in Texas Christian University dorms. Puente worked for Dr. Willard until 1988.[60]

While Carlos Puente attended North Texas State University (1970-71) he had become actively involved in politics during the height of the Chicano movement (1965-1975). When the family moved to Fort Worth Puente met José Gonzalez, a community organizer and Chicano activist. Both Carlos and María Puente became active in voter registration drives to help empower Fort Worth's Mexican American community. In 1972 Puente became the state vice-chairman for the *Raza Unida* party in San Antonio. Attracted to the party's *pro-familia* platform, Carlos focused all of his energies on getting out the vote. As a result, the Chicano leadership in

Texas enabled its gubernatorial candidate, Ramsey Muñiz, to garner 214,000 votes against the Democratic party opponent, Dolph Briscoe. Although Briscoe won the election, this was the high watermark for Chicano politics in the state of Texas. In the 1974 election Muñiz and the *Raza Unida* party fared worse at the polls, with only 93,000 votes. Shortly thereafter Carlos and María Puente left the party disillusioned by a succession of events that led to *Raza Unida's* downfall.[61]

In 1973, seeing a need for a representative from the Hispanic community on the Fort Worth ISD board of trustees, the Puentes concentrated their efforts on running for a seat. In 1978 Carlos Puente was elected to the District One seat, winning by a razor-thin margin over the Reverend Al Sanford.[62] This was the first election held under the new single-member district plan. Puente was re-elected to a four-year term in 1980.

Carlos Puente continued to serve the community of Fort Worth in a variety of ways: as a volunteer sponsor of the *Centro Aztlán*, a community service organization, as the director of Neighborhood Action, Inc., a part of the Community Action Agency (1976-1977), as the editor and publisher (1976-1978) of *El reporter*, a bilingual newspaper that provided local Mexican Americans information on pertinent issues and events, and as a Sunday school teacher with North Side's First Baptist Church.

Carlos Puente chose not to seek another term on the school board because he and his wife wished to dedicate more time to their family. In 1988, however, he ran for county commissioner, Precinct Four, as a Republican. Puente's defeat in this election did not diminish his desire to be a public servant. In 1991 Carlos Puente defeated Louis J. Zapata in a successful bid for the District Two seat on the Fort Worth City Council. Carlos is currently Tarrant County chapter chair of the Republican National Hispanic Assembly of Texas and continues to be involved with his community and church.[63]

APPENDIX A

LISTING OF HISPANIC INHABITANTS OF NORTH SIDE
Fort Worth City Directory, 1920

NORTH COMMERCE STREET

(E. 20TH INTERSECTS)
2000 Cisneris [sic], Octaviano
2001 Flores, Laureano
2002 Ortiz, Domingo
2003 Reyes, Mrs. Augustina
2005 Robles, Mariano
2006 Reyes, Blas
2007 Debalina [sic], Francisco
2008 Huerta, Bernardino
2009 Phillips, Frank
2010 Romero, Philip
2011 Barbosa, Manuel
2013 Sanchez, Augustino
2015 Cadjew, Mrs. Allie
2017 Barbosa, Cosme
2019 Majera, Manuel
2020 Lozano, Manuel
2022 García, Basilia
2023 Juran, Joseph
2025 Baluris, John
2028 vacant

(E. 21ST INTERSECTS)
2103 Menchaca, Francisco
2104 Duran, Anselmo
2105 Cabrero, Domingo
2106 Pavlis, Nicolas
2107 Gonzales, Francisco

2112 Zimek, Frank
2113 Marfey, Francisco
2114 Alvalis, José
2115 Hopkins, Mrs. Emma
2117 Lopez, Antonio
2122 vacant
2124 Castillo, Mrs. Bellam
2131 Wesley Methodist Episcopal
Church
2134 Kokalis, George
2135 Kaladis, John
2137 Gonzales, Florencio
2137 Cafusis, John
2138 Samanas, John, Gro[cery]
2140 Marcus & Vorgis
2141 Gutiérrez, Fco, restaurant

(E. 22ND INTERSECTS)
2200 Cisneros, Octaviano
2201 Mata, A. M. Gro[cery]
2202 Kaladis, James
2203 Martínes, Jose
2204 Metros, Gus
2205 Bernard, Jesús
2206 Farfan, Henry
2207 Cepeda, Ennis
2208 Spinas, Steve
2210 Amaro, Teofilo
2211 Leskie, Mrs. Helen
2212 Fuentez, Polito

2213 vacant
2215 De Arseben, Crus
2216 Perez, Philip
2217 Mendoza, Cecilia
2218 Czybiak, Henry
2219 Delgado, Jesus
2221 Garza, Damaro
2223 Burling S. J., trunkmaker
2228 Balkin Cold Drink Stand
2230 Balkin Cold Drink Stand
2131 Cardanas [sic], Rev. A. R.
2132 Pavlis, John
2133 Travino [sic], Jose

NORTH CALHOUN STREET

(E. 21ST INTERSECTS)
2100 Espinosa, Henry
2101 vacant
2102 Bracharach, Frank
2104 Sinek, Joseph
2106 Cihacek, J. W.
2110 Freyillo, Lino
2111 Reyes, Guadalupe
2112 Toledo, Thomas
2113 Sanchez, Alex
2114 Barber, Francisco
2115 Toledo, Tacinto
2116 Saldano [sic], Severino
2117 García, Celso
2118 Sanchez, Alexander
2119 Cruz, Mrs. Mendes
2120 Gentle, Lee
2121 Domínquez, Preceliano

2122 Romenes, Costanza
2123 Snodgrass, Mrs. Mary
2124 Castillo, Jesús
2125 García , Pablo

(E. 22ND INTERSECTS)
2200 Podilla [sic], Mrs. Maria
2201 Ayala, Pedro
2202 Gomez, Francisco
2203 Aguilar, Jesús
2204 Sendebos, Antonio
2205 Gutiérrez, Mrs. Beatrice
2206 Jimenez, Bonifacio
2207 Lopez, Jose
2210 Roche [sic], Elias
2211 vacant
2212 Guadalupe, Araiza
2213 vacant
2214 Escabido, Ramon
2216 Sordia, Victoriano
2218 Negrete, Jesus
2220 Voguida, Tomas

NORTH GROVE STREET

1302 Ramírez, Aurelio
1400 Solazara, Juan
2001 García, Heraldo
2007 Morales, Eradio
2009 Chavis, Mrs. Liberatha
2010 Alonco [sic], Augustine
2011 Gonzales, Marcelino
2012 Ramos, Jesús
2013 Hernandez, Concepcion
2015 Golcoe [sic], Macario, grocery
2017 Frausto, Guadalupe

APPENDIX B

WESLEY COMMUNITY HOUSE

DAILY SCHEDULE, 1932-1933

Monday

9:00-11:30 A.M.	Kindergarten
2:00- 4:00 P.M.	Sewing government material
2:30- 4:00	Mothers' Club
4:00- 5:00	Campfire Girls
4:00- 6:00	Manual training
4:30- 5:30	Dispense government flour
4:00- 6:00	Football practice

Tuesday

9:00-11:30 A.M.	Kindergarten
2:45- 3:00 P.M.	Young Mothers' Cooking Class
4:30- 5:30	Dispense government flour
4:00- 5:15	Girls' Cooking Class
4:00- 6:00	Football practice
7:00- 8:00	Choral hour
8:00- 9:00	Hi-Y

Wednesday

9:00-11:30 A.M.	Kindergarten
3:00- 4:00 P.M.	Parent Teacher Club
4:30- 5:30	Dispense government flour
4:00- 5:15	Girls' Sewing School
2:00- 5:00	Music lessons
4:00- 6:00	Football practice
7:00- 8:00	Basketball practice

Thursday

9:00-11:30 A.M.	Kindergarten
4:00- 5:00 P.M.	Girl Reserves

Thursday (continued)

10:00-2:00	Music lessons
4:30- 5:30	Dispense government flour
4:00- 6:00	Football practice

Friday

9:00-11:30 A.M.	Kindergarten
4:30- 5:30 P.M.	Dispense government flour
4:00- 6:00	Football practice

Saturday

9:00-11:30 A.M.	Clinic - rummage
9:00-12:00	Football games
1:00- 2:00 P.M.	Children's piano classes
2:00- 3:00	Young people's piano classes
4:30- 5:30	Dispense government flour

A P P E N D I X   C

Wesley Community Center
Report, circa 1953, on Paulita gutierrez's [sic] experience with the center[1]

Although Paulita Gutierrez was born in Texas, she lived in a Spanish-speaking community and never learned to speak English. It did not matter so much there, because no one else spoke it either. But when she married Amador and moved to Ft. Worth, she was often puzzled and stayed closely at home rather than venture far afield in the Anglo world.

At first they rented a little house on North Side, east of Main Street. Before long she heard her neighbors speak of Wesley House and of goings on there. She saw the workers employed there going about the community calling on those who had needs of one kind or another. In the early days of Wesley House many of the social agencies helpful to family welfare did not exist, and Wesley House administered relief, health services, and family counseling freely.

Next she heard about the kindergarten and learned that little children were taught English and many other things they needed. She had ideals for her children and for her home life and wanted all the help available. So she sent her little girls to the kindergarten. The teacher was kind and sympathetic, and Paulita was pleased with the care and teaching they received. Then, one by one, her girl[s] were old enough for school, and because they had learned English, the[y] made good progress. As they grew older, they joined other activities[—]sewing club, cooking club, Girl Reserves, and took piano lessons.

Meanwhile, her boys, who were younger, took their places, first in the kindergarten, then in various boys' clubs, Boy Scouts, athletic teams, playground and work shop.

About the time the youngest was half grown, they moved to a neat well-built house of their own, still not far from Wesley House, and her children, now young people, continued to come to activities. Lenore came to the Glamor Girls' Club and leaned how to dress and fix her hair attractively. Sometimes the girls entertained the boy friends, too. Later, she came to the Horizon Club and it was there Lenore met Joe. At first, they merely looked shyly at each other, but in a few months they were planning their home. The first year after her marriage, she helped the Wesley House staff in the kindergarten and proved valuable because of her knowledge of Spanish and her understanding of little folks' problems. She and Joe also came to square dancing parties and are now looking forward to enrolling Ernest in kindergarten in 1954.

Paulita's boys, too, found friends at Wesley House. It was there that Junior met Madeline, and they too established a home. They are now sponsors for a youth organization at Wesley House.

Paulita herself came to Wesley House, too; she was the most faithful member of the Mothers' Club for several year[s]. There she learned more about American ways of home making, and the experience helped her become the present efficient leader of the Woman's Society at her church. From buying the family clothing at the rummage sales, she has come to help manage them, and her cheery smile is familiar to all the customers.

She has reason to feel that through the influence of Wesley House, her home and family became stabilized, so that her husband and sons have been more successful in their business life, and their homes are made happier. At least partly because of Wesley House, her family has passed from the receiving to the giving of service.

MEDICINAL HERBS AND THEIR USES[2]

Marysol Garza believes in the natural healing properties of special herbs and carries an ample supply of most of them in her store. She explained the various uses for the following herbs:

Activol, to overcome a lethargic condition.

Ajenjible, for heart problems.

Altamisa, (not for intake) contains mysterious properties said to ward off burglars and vandals; wrap around one's waist to ensure strength for long walks; boil in water to relieve tired feet.

Anise, to overcome ill-humor; sadness; for nervous stomach.

Basíl, for kidney ailments; rheumatism; headaches; spice for foods.

Burraja, for intestinal fevers; rheumatism; high temperature; high blood pressure.

Cáscara de Nogal (pecan shell), to enrich red-blood cells.

Cuasia, for the gall bladder.

Cenizo, (used externally in baths) for depression.

Estafiate, for stomach infections; indigestion; "bloated" feeling.

Flor de Arnica, for internal bruises.

Flor de Peña, for good luck; to remove heart pressures.

Flor de Sauco, for heart problems.

Flor de Tila Roja, to ease and eliminate a nervous crisis.

Golondrina, boil and apply to skin to eliminate ulcerous conditions; warts.

Gordolobo, for chest colds.

Ipasote, for eliminating intestinal parasites; for cooking.

Manzanilla, for the elimination of intestinal gases.

Marrubio, to lower sugar levels and regulate diabetes.

Mejorana, to help in losing weight; for cooking in meats.

Mirra, (to burn) to bring good luck; good fortune.

Nervina, to overcome nervousness; insomnia; memory lapses.

Nuez Moscada (nutmeg), for nervousness; for pies.

Ojas de Boldo, for chest colds; constipation; pneumonia.

Ojo de Venado (deer's eye), to be hung on the clothing of an infant or child in order to ward off, overcome, or defeat the effects of the "evil eye."

Oregano, to end phlegm; coughing; as a spice for foods.

Palo Amargoso, for intestinal parasites; for gall bladder.

Palo Azul, for the kidneys and urinary tract.

Perejil, for losing weight; for cooking.

Piedra Alumbre, (not for internal consumption) for "sweeping" over a person, principally over the area of the heart and the mind. Prayers are recited and then the white crystal is burned. The spirit that has harmed the person is supposed to appear in the smoke.

Pimentón, to make a pesky individual go away; used in foods.

Prodigiosa, for urinary problems.

Quina Rosa, for loose gums (boil and hold in mouth then spit out).

Raíz de Angélica, for colic; menstrual cramps; organ cleansing.

Raíz de Manzo, for internal pains; gas.

Rosa de Castilla, a laxative.

Ruda, to eliminate heart palpitations; lack of menstruation.

Sacáte de Limón, a soothing tea.

Semilla de Cilantro, for gall bladder; also for cooking; pies, breads.

Té de Cena, a laxative.

Té del Mes, to counter the absence of menstruation.

Tlanchichinola, for back or leg pains; bronchial ailments.

Yerba buena, for stomach ailments; colic; diarrhea.

Yerba San Nicolás, to counter inflammation of the ovaries.

Zarzaparrilla, for urinary problems; rheumatism; a spice used to flavor pork meat.

Zazafrás, to overcome dizzyness; emotional drain; for cooking.

NOTES

INTRODUCTION

1   Stanley Ross. "Porfirio Díaz (1830-1915)." Grolier Multimedia Encyclopedia. http:// go.grolier.com/Encyclopedia Americana. (October 2, 2002).

2   Robert Patch. "Porfirio Díaz." Grolier Multimedia Encyclopedia. http://go.grolier.com:80/Grolier/Multimedia Encyclopedia. (October 2, 2002).

3   Cindy Baxman. "History of the Mexican Revolution, 1910-1920." Border Revolution. May 15, 1998. http://history.acusd.edu/gen/projects/border/page03.html. (October 2, 2002).

4   Robert A. Calvert and Arnoldo De León. *The History of Texas* (Arlington Heights, Ill: Harlan Davidson, Inc. 1990), 242.

CHAPTER ONE

1   Janet Schmelzer. "Fort Worth, Texas." The Handbook of Texas Online. The Texas State Historical Association, 1997-2002. http://www.tsha.utexas.edu/handbook/online/articles/view/FF/hdf1.html. (October 6, 2002).

2   Bud Kennedy. "Ten moments that shaped Fort Worth," *Fort Worth Star-Telegram*, June 6,1999.

3   *Abstract of the Twelfth Census of the U.S.: 1900*. Washington, D.C., Government Printing Office.

4   *Tenth Census of the U.S.: 1880*. Washington, D.C., Government Printing Office.

5   The city directories are available at the downtown Fort Worth Public Library.

6   The barrio was on the east side of the site now occupied by the Fort Worth Convention Center.

7   Gonzales finally changed jobs and worked for the Texas & Pacific Railway for a few years.

8   It is interesting to note that some of the earliest Mexicanos boarded with Anglos such as John G. Carper and Susan H. Price. If prejudice had been universal, this would never have occurred.

9   Rusk Street was renamed Commerce Street between 1907 and 1920. A 1920 Fort Worth street map by Bartholomew and Associates displays the new name, while a 1907 city map by J. E. Head & Company still referred to the thoroughfare as Rusk Street.

10   Jerry Adams. "Trade Token Tales." http://members.fortunecity.com/tokenguy/tokentales/page39.htm. (November 22, 2002).

11   Samuel ("Sammy") C. Pantoja, interview with the author, August 24, 1994, in Fort Worth.

12   Amador Gutiérrez Mercado and Madeleine Rangel Gutiérrez, interview with the author, March 30, 1994, in Fort Worth. Antonio Zapata and his wife, Elena, had their grocery on the corner of Mills and Valley. Filiberto Briones had a small grocery store and bakery at the corner of Cherry and East Bluff streets.

13   Fort Worth edged out other Texas cities in the competition to get the Armour and Swift plants because of two main considerations—the fact that Cowtown was serviced by so many railroads and that the companies were offered a bonus of $100,000 by Fort Worth citizens.

14   This information was taken from a 1913 Fort Worth City Guide reprinted through the services of the Fort Worth Writers' Project of the Works Progress Administration, document number 18429.

15   A survey of the Fort Worth city directories from 1904 to 1940, particularly in the section listing residents by street, bears this fact out. In addition, a 1934 Wesley Community House

report stated that ninety-five percent of the community was Mexican. (Fort Worth Public Library, Genealogy and Local History archives. Wesley Community House Records, Box 2, Folder 4, "Wesley Community House, Fort Worth, Texas," 1.)

[16] It would appear from the 1905-1906 city directory that the first Mexicanos in North Fort Worth lived at 2012 North Grove and at 2207 North Calhoun.

[17] Michael and Hope Ayala, interview with the author, January 26, 1998, in Fort Worth. This neighborhood was immediately north of where M. G. Ellis Elementary School stood—now a parking lot. When it rained pedestrians were forced to go around the creek via North Main Street. This tributary of Marine Creek no longer exists today. Street improvements and large-diameter underground concrete pipe silenced the *pujidos* (groans) forever.

[18] The Ayalas could not remember the names of the García boys.

[19] Ayala interview, January 26, 1998.

[20] Benito Soto Mercado, interview with the author, March 30, 1994, in Fort Worth.

[21] *La Yarda* literally translated means "the Yard." It was located about one mile east of Meacham Field.

[22] Mercado interview, March 30, 1994.

[23] Oliver Knight, *Fort Worth: Outpost on the Trinity* (Fort Worth: TCU Press, 1990), 95.

[24] The following Mexicanos lived at these Ellis Avenue addresses: Campos Rodríguez, 2600; E. S. Guardado, 2602; Valente Ochoa, 2604; Gasinto Aguilera, 2606; and Stephen Losano, 2608.

[25] The original Texas & Pacific roundhouse was located about where Commerce Street intersects with Interstate 30.

[26] Robert Pulido, Sr., interview with the author, February 18, 1998, in Fort Worth. Tony and Juanita Rodríguez are the parents of Carol, who became the wife of Robert Pulido, Sr.

[27] Knight, *Fort Worth*, 198.

[28] Entries for all five individuals, except one, noted that each resided near the plant. David Rodríguez was listed as boarding with Hezekiah Culwell, who lived in the Brooklyn Heights area of Fort Worth.

[29] Fort Worth Federal Writers Project of the Works Progress Administration, document number 7853, based on a news article from the *Fort Worth Record*, March 22, 1914.

[30] *Fort Worth Record*, March 24, 1914.

[31] Fort Worth Federal Writers Project of the Works Progress Administration, documents number 7856 and 7857, taken from the *Fort Worth Record*, March 29, 1914.

[32] A prominent factor that greatly influenced the Anglo-American perception of Hispanics was rooted in the historical context of *la leyenda negra*—the black or nefarious legend. Spain had acquired a contemptible reputation throughout Europe ever since Ferdinand and Isabela established the Inquisition to unite their fledgling country under one religion—Roman Catholicism. As a result of royal decree, persons of the Hebrew or Islamic faiths had three choices—convert to Catholicism, leave Spain, or do nothing and face certain torture and death. Although the crimes against humanity associated with the Inquisition gave seed to the "black legend," it was the repeated cruelties of the New World conquest and the European religious wars that nurtured and gave it full bloom.

CHAPTER TWO

[1] The name Riley Gonzales appeared for the first time in the *Fort Worth City Directory, 1883-1884*.

[2] Information on birthdays and places of birth obtained from the 1900 United States Census of Tarrant County.

[3] *Fort Worth City Directory, 1916*.

[4] Fort Worth Public Library, Genealogy and Local History Section. *Early Fort Worth Newspaper Index*.

[5] The refinery was located on Keller Pike, one mile north of East 28th Street.

[6] Dominga ("Minnie") Martínez Gutiérrez, interview with the author, June 27, 1994, in Fort

Worth. Gregorio Pérez, married to Secundino's sister, Augustina, already lived in Fort Worth's South Side, and he made his living working for Texas Steel Company. Later Gregorio and Augustina left Fort Worth for a better job working for the McCormick farm equipment company in Chicago.

[7]   Gutiérrez interview, June 27, 1994.

[8]   Salvador C. and María S. Gonzalez, interview with the author, March 26, 1994, in Fort Worth.

[9]   Ibid.

[10]   Ibid.

[11]   Ibid.

[12]   Some sources show his name as Juan, some as Raúl.

[13]   Gonzalez interview, March 26, 1994.

[14]   Ibid.

[15]   Salvador and María eventually had four children, Salvador, III, Ramón, Anna María, and Estela.

[16]   Gonzalez interview, March 26, 1994.

[17]   Ibid.

[18]   Ibid.

[19]   Ibid.

[20]   Each of their four children had four or more daughters, resulting in Salvador's and María's nineteen grandchildren and twenty-five great-grandchildren.

[21]   Gonzalez interview, March 26, 1994.

[22]   Mary Martínez Garza and Yvonne ("Kiki") Martínez Cisneros, interview with the author, January 29, 1998, in Fort Worth. According to family members, Martínez was not the original family surname. Although their father, Pete, had, at one time, told them, they couldn't remember the name. The daughter of Juan and Julia Ocampo, Elena Ocampo Martínez was a distant relative of Mexican political figure, Melchor Ocampo.

[23]   The family home at 1419 North Calhoun Street is still owned by the children of Pete and Elena Martínez. One of Pete's grandchildren lives there as of this writing.

[24]   Mike Martínez married Virginia Dowel, the daughter of a police chief, who, although originally against the marriage, came to appreciate and love his *latino* son-in-law. Virginia had connections with show business—she danced with Billy Rose's musical productions in Fort Worth at Casa Mañana and at his Diamond Horseshoe nightclub in New York City; her sister, Mary, was "Stuttering Sam," another of Billy Rose's performers, and her cousin was Ginger Rogers. Mike became the first Mexicano to be a member of the Colonial Country Club and bought a house directly across the street from the club.

[25]   Garza and Cisneros interview, January 29, 1998.

[26]   Ibid.

[27]   Michael and Hope Ayala, interview with the author, March 25, 1994, in Fort Worth. Eutimio and María Ayala had fourteen children: Estanislao ("Stanley"), owner, Don Ayala's Mexican Restaurant and Cantina, Acton, Texas; Isabel A. Gonzalez; María Anna Contreras; Carmen A. Felipe; a son who requested anonymity; Michael Ortiz, married to Esperanza ("Hope") Padilla,; María Rosa Herrera; Luis Gilberto ("Louis"), married Délia Pérez and is the owner of Ayala Barbershop, 1537 N. Main; María Dolores Méndes; Francisco Jesús, married Sara Martínez; Socorro A., married to Rodolfo Herrera, Zósimo's nephew; Juanita A. Ruelas; María Teresa Miranda; and Juan ("Johnny") Eutimio, who is married to Dora Pérez and who organized the 1960s band Johnny Ayala and the Starlighters. Eutimio's job at Swift & Company was curing hams and beef.

[28]   Michael and Hope Ayala, interview with the author, February 16, 1998, in Fort Worth. Mama Regina's five children were Rosalío, Román, Fermín, Ruperta (Marcelino Padilla), and María (Amaro Herrera). Margarito R. Padilla passed away May 20, 1970.

[29]   Fannie Cancino Móntez, interview with the author, February 20, 1998, in Fort Worth. Macario's parents were Antonio Loredo and Luisa Castillo; Angela's parents were Severiano Tobías and Teresa Pérez. Lina ("Linita") died in infancy of diphtheria in Mexico.

[30] Móntez interview, February 20, 1998. Angela naively thought that merely by coming to the border she would find her son.

[31] Catalina's diet included fresh vegetables and fruits, oatmeal, Cream of Wheat, and beans with cilantro (coriander).

[32] Although Refugio is often a man's name, Telésforo Cancino's mother was given that name. Román Rodríguez Cancino was brother to Fernando Cansino, who had a dance studio in San Antonio and was the father of Margarita Cansino, also known as Rita Hayworth. Román chose to spell his surname with a "c," whereas Fernando spelled it with an "s." Fannie Cancino Móntez worked for thirty-nine years at Monnig's Department Store as a visual merchandizing assistant.

[33] Móntez interview, February 20, 1998. The couple had eight children: Epifania ("Fannie"), Refugio ("Ruth"), Paulo ("Paul"), María Leticia ("Leticia"), Feliciano ("Felix"), Catalina ("Cathy"), Francisco ("Frank"), and Luis. An African American doctor delivered Fannie not long after her parents had arrived in Mexia.

[34] Catalina's mother, Angela, had somehow found Francisco and they were living in Fort Worth.

[35] Móntez interview, February 20, 1998.

[36] Yahualica is located about fifty miles northeast of Guadalajara.

[37] Román and Helen Soto Mercado, interview with the author, June 15, 1994, in Fort Worth. Román and Atilana's nine children were: María (Federico Ramos), Antonia (Juan Medrano), Cayetana, married to Anselmo ("Sam") Castillo, Guadalupe (Febe López), Benito (Elisa Castro), Román (Helen Flores), Antonio (Margaret Arteaga), and Josefina (Tony Vásquez). The first two were born in Yahualica, the rest were born in Fort Worth.

[38] Samuel ("Sammy") C. Pantoja, interview with the author, August 24, 1994, in Fort Worth.

[39] Ibid.

[40] Benito Cardona, III, interview with the author, February 4, 1998, in Fort Worth. Ester Cardona married Pasqual Ruiz, a well-to-do cattle rancher and landowner who lived near Monterrey, Nuevo Leon, Mexico. Their children: Vito Ruiz, of Laredo; Pasqual, who became a pilot; Guillermo; Ricardo; and Augusto. Raquel Cardona married Santos Mireles, a Baptist preacher. Aida Cardona married Jonas Sepulveda, formerly of Laredo, who came to Fort Worth in late 1922, lived on the North Side, and worked for Swift & Company for almost twenty-six years (1922-1948).

[41] Jonas Sepulveda, interview with the author, August 13, 1994, in Grand Prairie. *Panadería la india* (The Female Indian Bakery) was popularly referred to by locals as *"la panadería de los franceses"* (the bakery of the French).

[42] Cardona interview, February 4, 1998.

[43] Vito Ruiz, telephone interview with the author, January 2003. Eager to acquire colonies abroad, Napoleon III used the pretext of Mexico's inability to pay back loans to send a French army of occupation in 1862. He persuaded an unemployed Hapsburg, Maximiliano, to be the "Emperor of Mexico." The French finally succeeded in capturing Mexico City and drove out Benito Juárez and his government. As a government-in-exile, Juárez took refuge in the northern state of Chihuahua, waiting while French resolve and support weakened. By 1867 Napoleon recalled his troops from Mexico, leaving Maximiliano with little support. Maximiliano's army finally surrendered in Querétaro, and he was executed in a place called *El cerro de las campanas* (the Hill of the Bells).

[44] Cardona interview, February 4, 1998.

[45] Benito Cardona, Sr., was also known as *"El Colorado"* ("red") and *"El Güero"* ("blondie").

[46] Cardona interview, February 4, 1998.

[47] Ibid.

[48] A Baptist preacher, Mireles was pastor of *La primera iglesia bautista* (First Baptist Church), located on the northwest corner of Central Avenue and North Jones Street.

[49] Only two brothers survived. Rafael and Manuel Martínez relocated to Tampa, Florida, and continued to make a living hand-rolling cigars.

[50] The "Little Mexico" neighborhood in Dallas was located about ten blocks from Dealey Plaza, around Fairmont Street.

[51] Moises Cardona, also known as "Mo" or "Moche," married Beverly Hellman and had four children—John, David, Mary Jane, and Philip. Benito ("Bennie") Cardona married Gloria Martínez on May 12, 1953, and the couple had four children: Glenda, Bennie, Gloria Jean, and Martín.

[52] Cardona interview, February 4, 1998.

[53] Ibid.

[54] Ibid.

CHAPTER THREE

[1] Fort Worth Federal Writers Project of the Works Progress Administration, document number 11935, based on an article in the *Fort Worth Press*, December 2, 1925.

[2] Many North Side Mexican residents referred to Calhoun as *"la Calajún."*

[3] The Texas & Pacific Roundhouse was originally located about seven blocks west of the original stockyards, about where Main and Vickery intersect today.

[4] *Fort Worth City Directory, 1902-1903*.

[5] Marcelin was listed in the 1892-1893 city directory as a "tailor, dyer, scourer, repairer."

[6] Martín Aguilar owned a chile stand and lived at 900 Houston Street; Antonio Estrada, shown in previous directories as having his own restaurant, was listed here as a chile dealer who resided at 109 E. 9th Street; Rosalio Hernández had a chile stand on the north side of East 12th between Calhoun and Rusk streets; Alejandro Losoya was a chile peddler who resided on the north side of East 12th between Calhoun and Rusk streets (same location as Rosalío Hernández); and Louis Rodríguez, listed as a chile dealer, boarded with Antonio Valencia at 907 Calhoun.

[7] Listing Cortéz along with other barbershops in the city is interesting in that he was not segregated in the city directory as were African American barbers whose establishments were listed separately under "Barber Shops, Colored." Presumably, the surname would alert a potential customer that this particular barber was Hispanic and not Anglo.

[8] *Fort Worth City Directory, 1888-1889*.

[9] The names of Juan Gonzales and Mrs. Ramón D. Gonzales appear in the 1892-1893 city directory as operating a restaurant on the north side of East 12th between Rusk and Calhoun streets.

[10] Two other individuals, Antonio Villanueva and Manuel Visana, also had chile stands at 115 East 13th and 1401 Jennings Avenue, respectively. Along with Severio López, the three were listed in the 1901-1902 city directory under the heading "Restaurants."

[11] This address is next door to where Antonio Estrada started his lunch stand at 303 Main Street (see Figure 3-1).

[12] *Fort Worth City Directory, 1904-1905* and *Fort Worth City Directory, 1905-1906*, respectively.

[13] *Fort Worth City Directory, 1888-1889*.

[14] In the 1899-1900 city directory, Antonio Estrada was listed merely as a Mexican laborer. The following year (1901-1902) only Mollie (Mrs. Tony) Estrada, residing at 2007 Terry, was listed. Afterwards (1902-1903), no Estradas made the city directory.

[15] The city directory of 1892-1893 shows both Jesús Leal and Joseph Leal working and living with Joseph A. Leal at 311 W. 1st St.

[16] Fort Worth Federal Writers Project of the Works Progress Administration, document numbers 8717-8719, based on an article in the *Fort Worth Record*, March 18, 1917.

[17] Mario T. García. *Desert Immigrants: The Mexicans of El Paso, 1880-1920* (New Haven: Yale University Press, 1981).

[18] Fort Worth Federal Writers Project of the Works Progress Administration, document number 12723, based on an article in the *Fort Worth Star-Telegram*, August 2, 1919.

[19] Fort Worth Federal Writers Project of the Works Progress Administration, documents number 14020 and 14021, based on an article in the *Fort Worth Star Telegram*, May 10, 1921.

[20] Ramón Anguiano, interview with the author, March 30, 1994, in Fort Worth.

[21]   Fort Worth Federal Writers Project of the Works Progress Administration, documents number 4849 and 4851, based on an article in the *Fort Worth Press*, April 22, 1924.

[22]   *Fort Worth City Directory, 1927* and *Fort Worth City Directory, 1926*, respectively.

[23]   Fort Worth Federal Writers Project of the Works Progress Administration, documents number 14022 and 14023, from an article in the *Fort Worth Star Telegram*, March 22, 1923.

[24]   Oliver Knight, *Fort Worth: Outpost on the Trinity* (Fort Worth: TCU Press, 1990), 169.

[25]   University of Texas at Arlington Library, Special Collections Division. Collection 335, George W. Armstrong Papers, Vol. I, 3.

[26]   Alfredo ("Freddy") Castillo, interview with the author, June 25, 1994, in Fort Worth.

[27]   Armstrong Papers, Vol. I, 182.

[28]   Armstrong Papers, Vol. I, 22.

[29]   Arnoldo De León. *Ethnicity in the Sunbelt: A History of Mexican Americans in Houston* (Houston: Mexican American Studies Program, University of Houston, 1989), 54.

[30]   Mario Trujillo, interview with the author, March 30, 1994, in Fort Worth.

[31]   David Montejano, *Anglos and Mexicans in the Making of Texas, 1836-1896* (Austin: University of Texas Press, 1987), 241.

[32]   Knight, *Fort Worth*, 95, 123, 129.

[33]   Ibid., 203

[34]   The "New Deal" was a program (1933-1939) of public works projects initiated by President Franklin Delano Roosevelt (1882-1945) to alleviate some the economic distress brought about by the Great Depression. The programs ranged from bridge building to a Federal Theater Arts program.

[35]   Knight, *Fort Worth*, 207.

[36]   Benito Soto Mercado, interview with the author, March 30, 1994, Fort Worth.

[37]   R. Reynolds McKay, "Texas Mexican Repatriation during the Great Depression" (Ph.D. Dissertation, University of Oklahoma at Norman, 1982), 325-326.

[38]   Piñeda served from 1886 to 1898. He enlisted when he was fourteen years of age.

[39]   Piñeda choose South Texas because Spanish was widely spoken, a consideration for a Spaniard.

[40]   John J. Kane, interview with the author, July 12, 1994, Fort Worth. (John J. Kane married Eva Piñeda.)

[42]   Ibid.

[42]   Joe Holton, interview with the author, March 7, 1994, in Fort Worth.

[43]   Ibid.

[44]   Knight, *Fort Worth*, 209-210, 251.

[45]   Holton interview, March 7, 1994.

[46]   Kane interview, July 12, 1994.

[47]   The couple eventually had three children: Patricia Rae, who made her home in Waxahachie; John Lawrence, who lives outside Houston in Richmond; and Thomas Francis, who resides in Arlington.

[48]   *Noche Buena* is Christmas Eve, a time when tamales of all kinds are traditionally served.

[49]   Kane interview, July 12, 1994.

[50]   Holton interview, March 7, 1994.

[51]   Ibid.

[52]   Ibid.

[53]   Gregorio Esparza, Jr., interview with the author, March 17, 1994, in Fort Worth.

[54]   In Spanish-speaking societies, a mother's maiden name (in this case, García) has been traditionally added on after the father's last name (Tafolla). Joe's real surname, therefore, is Tafolla. There were undoubtedly several reasons why he might have chosen to use his mother's maiden name as the family surname – perhaps it was easier to recognize and pronounce.

[55] Hope García Lancarte and Mary García Christian, interview with the author, March 2, 1994, in Fort Worth.

[56] Ibid.

[57] Ibid.

[58] Ibid.

[59] Ibid.

[60] Ibid.

[61] Ibid.

[62] A shotgun house measured about twelve feet wide by thirty-six feet deep. There were three rooms in a row with openings for doors in exactly the same place. Supposedly one could fire a shotgun into the house from the front door and the buckshot would go right through the three rooms and out the back. The first room was usually a combination living room-bedroom; the second was a bedroom; and the third was a combination kitchen-dining room. The outhouse would be located at the rear of the backyard, usually near the alley.

[63] Mr. and Mrs. Frank Cagigal, interview with the author, March 30, 1994, in Fort Worth.

[64] Part of the reason for leaving Spain was the lingering after-effect of the Carlist Wars. Orencio's father had been killed in that bloody conflict, and the son's desire for vengeance prompted his sister ("Paca") to take him away to Cuba.

[65] Elisa Acuña was born on June 13, 1893, in the community of La Rosita, Nuevo León, Mexico. The Acuña children included: Tomás, a successful merchant; Monica, a seamstress in San Antonio; Cleofitas, a traveling salesman who worked from his automobile; Elisa, who married Orencio; Pablo, the "black sheep" of the family; and Ramona. La Rosita, Nuevo León, is near the northern Mexico industrial city of Monterrey.

[66] Orencio built a two-story house at 2028 North Commerce Street that still stands to this day. He built other houses, as well as provided remodeling and repair services. He even did plumbing work.

[67] Cagigal interview, March 30, 1994.

[68] Ibid.

[69] Amador G. and Madeliene R. Gutiérrez, interview with the author, March 25, 1994, in Fort Worth.

[70] During the 1920s Rafael and Isidra Valle operated a restaurant in the downtown area at 1312-B Calhoun and lived at 705 West 1st Street.

[71] Gutiérrez interview, March 25, 1994.

[72] Sara Garza Barajas Gallegos, interview with the author, July 2, 1998, in Fort Worth.

[73] Rosa bore eight children. Two died in infancy. With the exception of Alejandro, Sr., all were born in Mexico.

[74] Sara Gallegos interview, July 2, 1998.

[75] Ibid.

[76] Ibid.

[77] Ibid.

[78] Alejandro Gallegos, Sr., interview with the author, February 18, 1994, in Fort Worth.

[79] Ibid.

[80] There was a rooming house between the Marine theater and Los Alamos restaurant.

[81] *Flautas* consist of shredded chicken meat rolled up into a corn tortilla and fried in a pan.

[82] Sara Gallegos interview, July 2, 1998.

[83] Ibid.

[84] Robert Pulido, Sr., interview with the author, February 18, 1998, in Fort Worth. Dolores Pulido's wife's name was María Nárez.

[85] Pulido interview, February 18, 1998.

[86] Dolores and María Pulido had a total of nine children— five boys and four girls.

[87] Argyle is about twenty-five miles north of Fort Worth.

[88] *El Papalote* was located immediately southeast of the present-day I-30 and I-35 interchange.

[89] Pulido interview, February 18, 1998.

[90] Philip Pulido owns Don Felipe's Restaurant, at 4216 West Vickery Boulevard in Fort Worth. Shannon ("Chano") Pulido had already passed away.

[91] Mary Pulido married Edward Gámez, whose maternal grandfather, a Cuéllar, began the El Chico Restaurant chain. Rodolfo ("Rudy") Pulido married Angie Medina, whose father worked for Swift & Company. Robert Pulido, Sr., married Carol Rodríguez, the daughter of a T & P worker.

[92] Pulido interview, February 18, 1998.

[93] Around 1963, the Pulido homestead at 2921 Spring Street was sold to the Underwood Typewriter Company and razed some years later. After 1963 Pedro and Dionicia Pulido moved to Benbrook.

[94] Spring Street was called that because of the creek that originated from a spring in the Botanic Gardens and made its way toward the Clear Fork of the Trinity River.

[95] Each little round of cheese measured roughly one-and-one-half inches thick and about three inches in diameter. Mexican *asadero* cheese is a soft, white cheese used as a topping for *chalupas* or for melting in a tortilla (a quesadilla).

[96] Pulido interview, February 18, 1998.

[97] Robert Pulido, Sr., attended Brooklyn Heights Elementary School, Stripling Junior High, and Arlington Heights High School. At Arlington Heights there were only three Mexicanos— Robert and his two older brothers.

[98] Pulido interview, February 18, 1998.

[99] Employees were allowed only thirty minutes for lunch, between twelve and twelve-thirty.

[100] Pulido interview, February 18, 1998.

[101] Robert and Carol Pulido's children are Robert, Jr., Angie, and Melissa.

[102] Pulido interview, February 18, 1998.

[103] Ibid.

[104] Ibid.

[105] The Texas & Pacific Railroad was bought out by the Union Pacific Railroad in the mid-1960s.

[106] Dionicia still fixes breakfast, a hearty meal that is brought warm to the tortilla factory daily for the family to enjoy. *Papas con huevo, frijoles refritos, tamales de puerco,* and *tortillas de maís* constitute breakfast.

[107] The tortilla factory is located at 7601 Benbrook Parkway; the tamale factory at 4924 Old Benbrook Road.

[108] Pulido interview, February 18, 1998.

[109] Leonard Menchaca, interview with the author, February 19, 1998, in Fort Worth.

[110] The "Katy" referred to the Missouri, Kansas and Texas Railway.

[111] The Menchaca's children were Juan, María, Antonia, Cecilia who all died in infancy; Vicenta, Leonardo ("Leonard"), Santos (died at seven), María, Manuel (died at nineteen), and Tomasita (passed away).

[112] Menchaca interview, February 19, 1998.

[113] This area is now the Rockwood Golf Course.

[114] This man was no relation to North Side resident Bennie Cardona.

[115] Menchaca interview, February 19, 1998.

[116] Ibid.

[117] Ibid.

[118] Ibid.

[119] García had a grocery store on North Jones Street.

[120] Menchaca interview, February 19, 1998.

[121] Ibid.

[122] Ramona Alvarez was born in 1924 at Mason City, Iowa. Her parents worked in the sugar beet fields in Iowa and Minnesota.

[123] Menchaca interview, February 19, 1998.

[124] Louis Ayala, interview with the author, September 9, 1994, in Fort Worth.

[125] Minerva and José Jesús Domínguez, Jr., interview with the author, March 26, 1994, in North Richland Hills.

[126] José Jesús probably married María Concepción sometime around 1918. María Concepción Gonzalez was born in 1896 in Torreón, Coahuila, Mexico. Her father, Eduardo Gonzalez, a revolutionary and follower of Pancho Villa, was blown up on a munitions train by *federales* (circa 1921). Eduardo's wife, Macaria Barbosa Gonzalez, brought her two daughters, María and Virginia, along with her mother, to El Paso where they found jobs as domestics working for Anglos employed by the Texas & Pacific Railroad. Moving with these Anglos, they arrived in Fort Worth around 1914.

[127] Prisciliano Domínguez became a well-known and talented commercial artist who designed the logo for Joe T. García's restaurant and drew many of the sketches of legendary Texas Christian University players and coaches hanging on the walls of the Daniel Meyer Coliseum on the TCU campus. Pris passed away December 1, 1990.

[128] Domínguez interview, March 26, 1994.

[129] Ibid.

[130] The oldest of Florencio's and Felicitas' eight children, Eulogio, is still living as of this writing at age ninety-three. The other children are Isaac (female), Rodolfo, Rafael, Paz, Samuel, Alberto (still living, age eighty), and Socorro.

[131] This was the enterprising Joe T. Garcia.

[132] Rudy Rodríguez, interview with the author, February 2, 1998, in Fort Worth.

[133] Ibid.

[134] Lino's first wife (name unknown) died in Mexico when Juanita was a very young child.

[135] Rodríguez interview, February 2, 1998.

[136] Rudy is currently married to his second wife, Cindy Childers. He has a daughter, Tina Louise, by his previous marriage and two children by his second wife—Shelby Renée and Nicolas Rudolph. Ernesto is married to Socorro Reyes and they have two children. Ester married Gino Paris and they also have two children. Alice, now deceased, was married to Tommy Roland and they had two sons. Raúl married Gloria Pacheco. Charles married Leticia.

[137] Rodríguez interview, February 2, 1998.

[138] Joe T. Garcia had already moved his grocery and restaurant business one block away to the corner of North Commerce and Northwest 22nd streets. According to his daughters, Hope Garcia Lancarte and Mary Garcia Christian, in the early 1930s Joe T. sold his original grocery store to Antonio "El Arabe," who kept it for a few years before selling it to Rodolfo Rodríguez toward the end of the decade.

[139] Rodríguez interview, February 2, 1998.

[140] Rudy Rodríguez attended San José School for one year. He then transferred to M. G. Ellis Elementary, finishing at Circle Park Elementary (now Manuel Jara Elementary) when M. G. Ellis closed. J. P. Elder Junior High and Technical High School rounded out Rudy's formal education. Rudy took evening classes at Texas Christian University, earning a business degree in 1980.

[141] This was located across the street from the present El Rancho Grande restaurant.

[142] Rodríguez interview, February 2, 1998.

[143] The company created tamales filled with beef, pork, or chicken. Bean tamales are made exclusively for export to France.

[144] Most of the foods shipped within the United States are destined for states east of Interstate Highway 35. Sales in the western part of the country are spotty. Because of the high cost of truck freight, only Colorado, New Mexico, the Phoenix area, and Southern California have become profitable markets.

[145] Their employees tend to be loyal—many workers have been with the company for more than ten years (a few can claim thirty years of employment). The Rodriguezes host a Christmas dinner for employees and their families as well as a fully catered Mother's Day party. Each worker receives a turkey for Thanksgiving and a large ham for Christmas.

[146] Salvador C. Gonzalez, Jr., interview with the author, March 26,1994, in Fort Worth.

[147] Francisca had two children, Gloria and Samuel. She married Samuel Picazo, a retired minister in the United Methodist Church. Pedro Martínez also had two children, Sabino, who lives in Colorado, and Vangie Martínez Artiaga of Fort Worth. A diabetic, Pedro died one month after his father on December 19, 1984.

[148] *Leche quemada* is literally translated as "burnt milk." It is a tan colored candy made with sugar and milk.

[149] The Martínezes first lived at 1510 E. Bluff (1928-1931), then at 1515 E. Weatherford (1932-1935).

[150] Amalia Martínez Romero, interview with the author, January 30, 1998, in Fort Worth.

[151] Consuela Zapata Narvaéz, interview with the author, July 18, 1995, in Fort Worth. Jesús Zapata passed away in 1993. Josefina died in 1925, aged two. Carmen Zapata died in January 1984.

[152] The *pan dulce* sold in the store came from Gregorio Esparza, Sr.'s, bakery on the North Side.

[153] Louis J. Zapata, interview with the author, February 26, 1998, in Fort Worth.

[154] Narvaéz interview, July 18, 1995.

[155] Petra Zavala is the mother of Richard Zavala, Sr., and grandmother of Richard Zavala, Jr., who is the present director of the Parks and Community Services department of the City of Fort Worth.

[156] Zapata interview, February 26, 1998.

CHAPTER FOUR

[1] Lou Caro Whitten, interview with the author, March 30, 1994, in Fort Worth.

[2] Besides Caro's Restaurant on Bluebonnet Circle close to TCU, there are only two other known places that serve "puffed" chips with guacamole: Caro's Restaurant in Rio Grande City and Rosita's Restaurant in Laredo.

[3] Whitten interview, March 30, 1994.

[4] Ibid.

[5] Ibid.

[6] *Picadillo* is a dish made from either ground beef or pork. Half-inch cubes of potatoes may be included. *Guisos* or *guisados* are spicy stews with small cubes of either beef or pork. Cut-up pieces of potato, carrots, and onions are usually included. *Calabacita* is a stew that usually contains small cubes of pork meat cooked with cut squash and corn. *Cabrito en sangre* is a traditional northern Mexican and border area dish. The meat from a milk-fed kid goat is cooked in its own blood, which results in a dark sauce. *Cabrito asado* is a kid goat cooked slowly over mesquite charcoal. Any border city like Nuevo Laredo, Tamaulipas, will have restaurants that specialize in serving *cabrito asado*. Passing by the windows of these restaurants, little Anglo children have been known to stare at the cooking goats and remark, "Look Mom, they're cooking dogs!" *Frijoles refritos* are refried beans; *frijoles borrachos* (drunken beans) are whole pinto beans cooked slowly in water with beer added usually in the last hour of cooking.

[7] Whitten interview, March 30, 1994.

[8] These dates are approximate.

[9] Lou Caro Whitten estimated the population of Río Grande City during 1930s to be about 1,500.

[10] Whitten interview, March 30, 1994.

[11] Ibid.

[12] Four of the lots were for parking.

[13] John Day Whitten was born in Oregon and raised in California. During World War II he served his country fighting in Europe with the 82nd Airborne unit, which made parachute jumps over Italy, France, and Germany.

14 Whitten interview, March 30, 1994.

15 Ibid.

16 Ibid.

17 Ibid.

18 "*Las casas coloradas*," located either on the 3700 or 3800 block of Hemphill Street across from the plant, were company-owned housing for the employees of Texas Steel Company. These "red houses" were older than the "yellow houses," the second housing project the company built for employees.

19 Dominga ("Minnie") Martínez Gutiérrez, interview with the author, June 27, 1994, in Fort Worth.

20 José's father, Juan Gutiérrez, worked in the stockyards. José worked as a cook for the Worth Hotel and later as a chef for Colonial and Rivercrest country clubs.

21 The couple had two children, Gloria (Pablo Ramón) and Gilberto.

22 Pilar Bouzas, interview with the author, June 27, 1994, in North Hollywood, California.

23 Ibid.

24 Ibid.

25 Ibid.

26 Ibid.

27 Michael and Hope Ayala, interview with the author, February 16, 1998, in Fort Worth. Hope's great grandmother, "Mama" Regina Mascorro Rodríguez, was the one who began the tradition of family reunions. Mama Regina died in 1939 at the age of 89.

28 Ayala interview, February 16, 1998.

29 Ibid.

30 Ibid.

31 Ibid.

32 Ibid.

33 Martínez was fluent in both Spanish and English.

34 Mary Martínez Garza and Yvonne ("Kiki") Martínez Cisneros, interview with the author, January 29, 1998, in Fort Worth.

35 A brochure written October 1, 1970, by Margaret W. Harrison, entitled "The Story of Oakwood Cemetery," provided by Yvonne ("Kiki") Martínez Cisneros, describes the markers of some of the more distinguished occupants. Among the descriptions was the one of Pete Martínez's grave, which included passages like: "No visitor to the cemetery will wish to miss the Martínez monument, which is also near the Calvary section. This is a low, but rather wide, headstone of gray granite. There is a bronze plaque, [which] slips aside and reveals a picture of the deceased, Pete Martínez, a distinguished looking man, having the air of a Spanish grandee or nobleman . . . . Beneath the children's names are these beautiful words from their father: `Farewell my wife and children dear, I am not dead but sleeping here, and after me no sorrow take But love each other for my sake.'"

36 The building currently housing *Los Vaqueros* was built in 1915 originally to be a packinghouse. Construction ceased when it became evident that the railroad did not intend to create a spur to service this area. Known as the D. Hart Building, it has been used over the years by both Armour and Swift as a cold-storage facility, as a feed store, and as a warehouse. In more recent years it was bought by a Mr. Braziel, who sold used restaurant equipment. A Mr. Weaver bought the Hart Building from Braziel and sold it to John and Kiki Cisneros. It has sentimental value to them since Pete Martínez used to frequent this building when he was still working.

37 Garza and Cisneros interview, January 29, 1998.

38 Fort Worth Public Library, Genealogy and Local History archives. Wesley Community House Records, Box 1, Folder 1, Katherine Ashburn, "History of the Fort Worth Wesley House," circa 1934. 14.

[39] Mary Lou López, interview with the author, July 27, 1995, Fort Worth.

[40] Fort Worth Public Library, Genealogy and Local History archives. Wesley Community House Records, Box 1, Folder 1, "1937 Report of Jennie C. Congleton—Head Resident." 1.

[41] Dr. Raúl López Guerra, Jr., interview with the author, July 29, 1994, in Corpus Christi, Texas.

[42] The Nest Ranch

[43] *Membrillo* is a tart, gritty fruit, resembling an apple, found in Mexico and used to make a jelly-like candy with a unique flavor.

[44] Basilisa López Guerra, interview with the author, August 14, 1995, in Corpus Christi. (N.B., Although Basilisa lives in Guadalajara, Jalisco, she happened to be visiting one of her daughters in Corpus Christi and consented to an interview.)

[45] Raúl's surviving siblings are Alfredo, Francisco, Juan, Clara, Romualda, Basilisa, Genoveva, and Clementina.

[46] Basilisa López Guerra interview, August 14, 1995.

[47] Elementary school and high school

[48] Raúl López Guerra, Jr., interview, July 29, 1994.

[49] Ibid.

[50] Richard A. García, *Rise of the Mexican American Middle Class: San Antonio, 1929-1941* (College Station: Texas A&M University Press, 1991), 35.

[51] Raúl López Guerra, Jr., interview, July 29, 1994.

[52] Aurelia's father, Antonio Avila Delgado, was a second-generation medical doctor who also owned a pharmacy, an ice-making plant, a soft-drink bottling operation, as well as a cotton plantation in Durango, close to the border near Zacatecas. He received his degree from the medical school in Guadalajara in 1853.

[53] Only ten of the fourteen Avila children survived.

[54] Originally from Monterrey, Nuevo León, Aurelia Várgas Treviño was a selfless, hard-working, and family-oriented woman.

[55] Basilisa López Guerra interview, August 14, 1995.

[56] A *zarzuela* is a type of operetta that first appeared in nineteenth-century Spain.

[57] Basilisa López Guerra interview, August 14, 1995.

[58] Ostos married Aurelia's sister Adela ("*La China*").

[59] Basilisa López Guerra interview, August 14, 1995.

[60] Ibid.

[61] Ibid.

[62] Ibid.

[63] Ibid.

[64] Raúl López Guerra, Jr., interview, July 29, 1994.

[65] In addition to Hispanics, other North Side immigrants came from Eastern Europe—Greece, Poland, Czechoslovakia, Hungary, and Romania.

[66] Basilisa López Guerra interview, August 14, 1995.

[67] Raúl López Guerra, Jr., interview, July 29, 1994.

[68] Basilisa López Guerra interview, August 14, 1995.

[69] Raúl López Guerra, Jr., interview, July 29, 1994.

[70] Ibid.

[71] His son fondly recalled that "*mi papá era Mexicano hasta las cachas*" (literally, "my father was a Mexican up to his cheeks.") A better translation would be "my father was Mexican through and through."

[72] Dr. Raúl López Guerra, Jr. recalled that his father frequently stated that "*estoy más agusto acá*," meaning that he felt much more comfortable in his native Mexico than in the U.S.

[73] Raúl López Guerra, Jr., interview, July 29, 1994.

[74]   Basilisa López Guerra interview, August 14, 1995.

[75]   More difficult to translate, *papas a huevo* essentially means "potatoes once again, one has no choice."

[76]   Benito Soto Mercado, interview with the author, March 30, 1994, in Fort Worth.

[77]   Minnie Gutiérrez told the story of a local horse that was gashed by a bull's horns. The resulting wound turned ugly and began to attract flies. The owner immediately brought his bottle of volcanic oil and applied it to the horse's wound—the wound healed quickly and the horse recovered. The ingredients in volcanic oil include chlorothymol, pure gum turpentine, flaxseed oil, camphor oil, sassafrassy, and pine oil.

[78]   Gutiérrez interview, June 27, 1994.

[79]   Pure lard with mint leaves applied to the temples alleviated headaches.

[80]   Gutiérrez interview, June 27, 1994.

[81]   Román and Helen Soto Mercado, interview with the author, June 15, 1994, in Fort Worth.

[82]   Marysol Garza, interview with the author, June 24, 1994, in Fort Worth.

[83]   Ibid.

[84]   Ibid.

[85]   Ibid.

[86]   Ibid.

[87]   Ibid.

[88]   Ibid.

[89]   Ibid.

[90]   Ibid.

[91]   Ibid.

CHAPTER FIVE

[1]   Arnoldo De León. *Mexican Americans in Texas: A Brief History* (Arlington Heights, Ill: Harlan Davidson, Inc., 1993), 84.

[2]   All Saints Catholic Church, *Our Celebration: All Saints Catholic Church, Fort Worth, Texas* (South Hackensack, NJ: Custombook, Inc., 1977), 20.

[3]   North Houston was then known as Lake Avenue. The original church faced east on North Houston Avenue (1903-1952). A new brick-veneer structure facing Northwest 20th Street (same corner) was dedicated in December of 1952.

[4]   *Our Celebration*, 21.

[5]   The location of the first San José mission (1909-1919) remains a mystery. The first baptism at the mission was of Atanasio Guerra, son of Leandro Guerra and Delfina Contreras on April 24, 1909; the first marriage celebrated was between Silverio Estrada and María del Socorro Soza on April 24, 1909. Some of the mission's early pastors were the Reverend C. Gagliardoni, O.F.M. (1909-1913); the Reverend Y. Pohlen, O.F.M. (1913-1914); the Reverend F. Marti, C.M. (1914- 1916); and the Reverend R. Atanes, C.M. (ca. 1916- 1919).

[6]   Fort Worth, Sanborn Fire Insurance Map. 1911, Vol. 2

[7]   A native of Catalonia, in northeastern Spain, Antonio María Claret founded the Claretian order on July 16, 1849. Formally named the Sons of the Immaculate Heart of the Blessed Virgin Mary, the order became more familiarly known as the Claretians. The initials that followed the printed name of any Claretian priest identified him with his order—C.M.F., *Cordis Mariae Filius* (Latin for Son of the Heart of Mary). Several North Side residents joked that C.M.F. meant "*cóme más frijoles*" (eats more beans). The Claretians quickly branched out into the foreign mission fields of Europe, Africa, and Latin America before arriving in the United States at the turn of the twentieth century. Claretian missionaries came to the attention of church officials in South Texas and in Southern California: In 1902 Bishop A. Forest invited them to stay at San Antonio's San Fernando Cathedral; in 1906 at St. John the Evangelist Church in San

Marcos; in 1908 they were entrusted with administering the historic San Gabriel Mission just east of Los Angeles; and in 1910 they were placed in charge of Los Angeles' preeminent Catholic church, *Nuestra Señora la Reina de los Angeles de la Porciuncula*. In addition, Claretian missionaries arrived in China in 1933, the Philippines in 1947, Japan in 1951, and India in the 1960s.

8   *Our Celebration*, 8-9.

9   Ibid., 6-7.

10   San José's Claretian pastors included Eugenio Herrán (1926-1930); Sebastián Ripero (1930-1932); Bonifacio Mayer (1932-1937); Ignacio de Asumendi (1937-1939); Jaime Tort (1939); Miguel Castillón (1939-1940); Bonifacio Mayer (1941-1942); Antimo Nebreda (1942-1945); Celestino de la Iglesia (1945-1948); Aloysius Dot (1948-1954); and Richard Treviño (1954-1955). In 1955 San José ceased to exist, merging with its former mother church, All Saints.

11   *Our Celebration*, 10.

12   Michael and Hope Ayala, interview with the author, February 16, 1998, in Fort Worth.

13   Ibid.

14   Román and Helen Soto Mercado, interview with the author, June 15, 1994, in Fort Worth.

15   A *promesa* meant making a promise to visit a holy site if the *Virgen* would comply with a special request.

16   Ibid.

17   Jim Jones, "Nun of the Barrios: After 60 years, Sister Lawrencia still loves her students," *Fort Worth Star Telegram*, October 14, 1984.

18   Ayala interview, February 16, 1998.

19   No stranger to Mexicanos, Neville Penrose was involved in the oil business in Mexico.

20   Helen Flores Mercado, interview with the author, June 15, 1994, in Fort Worth.

21   As a point of comparison with salaries in other industries, according to Benito Soto Mercado the packinghouses paid the best—weekly wages in the late 1930s were between $7.50 and $15.00, depending on the department. In 1947 a person who washed dishes received 25¢ per hour ($10.00 per week based on 40 hours); in 1955 a person doing upholstery work was paid 75¢ an hour ($30.00 per week based on 40 hours).

22   St. Ignatius was next door to St. Patrick's Cathedral. St. Mary's was at Magnolia Avenue and St. Louis Street. St. Alice is now Holy Family Catholic School, 6146 Pershing Street.

23   Fort Worth Public Library, Genealogy and Local History archives. Wesley Community House Records, Box 2, Folder 4, *Our Golden Jubilee: Women's Missionary Society, 1880-1928*. 53.

24   A social movement and series of programs advocated by Christians from the 1870s to 1940s to apply principles of the Gospel to industrialized society—better pay and working conditions, an equitable distribution of wealth, and eradication of child labor, among other issues. The New Deal incorporated some of the Social Gospel Movement's programs.

25   Fort Worth Public Library, Genealogy and Local History archives. Wesley Community House Records, Box 2, Folder 3, Document beginning "For more than a quarter century . . . ." 2.

26   Fort Worth Public Library, Genealogy and Local History archives. Wesley Community House Records, Box 1, Folder 1, Katherine Ashburn, *History of the Fort Worth Wesley House, circa 1934*. 2 .

27   *Our Golden Jubilee*, 53-54. Eugenia Smith remained head resident until 1922. Subsequent head residents were Connie Fagan, Rena Murphy, Sue Mitchell (1928), Katherine Arnold (1934-37), Jennie Congleton (1937-early 1940s), Iva Conner (1951), and Ruth Fuessler (1956-57).

28   Ibid., 1.

29   Ashburn, 2.

30   Ibid.

31   Fort Worth Public Library, Genealogy and Local History archives. Wesley Community House Records, Box 2, Folder 3, Document beginning "The Wesley House was begun . . . ." [no page cited]

32   Ashburn, 3. This "corner" refers to the southeast corner of Northwest 22nd and North Commerce streets, across NW 22nd Street from the present-day site of Joe T. García's

Restaurant. The building still stands but was sold to the Pan American Golf Association in the 1960s.

33 Fort Worth Public Library, Genealogy and Local History archives. Wesley Community House Records, Box 2, Folder 3, Document beginning "The used clothing which is sent in . . . ." [no page cited]

34 Fort Worth Public Library, Genealogy and Local History archives. Wesley Community House Records, Box 2, Folder 1, "Wesley Community House," 1934. 2.

35 Ibid., 2.

36 Ibid., 4.

37 Ibid., 2, 9.

38 Ibid., 12-13.

39 Ibid., 12.

40 Ibid., 2.

41 Ibid., 8-9.

42 Ashburn, 11.

43 Ibid., 13.

44 Fort Worth Public Library, Genealogy and Local History archives. Wesley Community House Records, Box 2, Folder 1, *Report of Katie Herndon—Club Director.* [no page cited]

45 "The used clothing which is sent in . . . ." [no page cited]

46 "Wesley Community House," 2.

47 Fort Worth Public Library, Genealogy and Local History archives. Wesley Community House Records, Box 1, Folder 1, "Annual Report: January 1, 1933—December 31, 1933." 1-2.

48 Ashburn, 16-17.

49 Fort Worth Public Library, Genealogy and Local History archives. Wesley Community House Records, Box 2, Folder 1, "Narrative 1955-1956." 2,

50 Fort Worth Public Library, Genealogy and Local History archives. Wesley Community House Records, Box 2, Folder 1, "Annual Narrative for 1959-1960." 1-2.

51 Fort Worth Public Library, Genealogy and Local History archives. Wesley Community House Records, Box 2, Folder 1, "Annual Narrative for 1953-1954." 2. (These particular comments came from María García, a staff member and wife of the pastor.)

52 Mary Lou López, interview with the author, July 27, 1995, in Fort Worth.

53 Fort Worth Public Library, Genealogy and Local History archives. Wesley Community House Records, Box 2, Folder 1, "1937 Report of Jennie C. Congleton—Head Resident." 1.

54 "Wesley Community House," 1.

55 Ibid.

56 Ashburn, 7-8.

57 Fort Worth Public Library, Genealogy and Local History archives. Wesley Community House Records, Box 2, Folder 1, "Annual Report, July 1953."

58 Ibid., 11-12.

59 Fort Worth Public Library, Genealogy and Local History archives. Wesley Community House Records, Box 1, Folder 1, author unknown, "Ca. 1941 report on the Wesley Community House." 1.

60 Ashburn, 8, 11.

61 Fort Worth Public Library, Genealogy and Local History archives. Wesley Community House Records, Box 1, Folder 4, "Wesley House Activities Not Curtailed in Summer" [page not cited].

62 Fort Worth Public Library, Genealogy and Local History archives. Wesley Community House Records, Box 2, Folder 3, Document beginning ". . . faith in Jesus Christ . . . ." [page not cited]

63 Elisa Castillo Nájera, interview with the author, July 20, 1995 in Fort Worth.

64 William Alexander Walls, a Presbyterian minister as well, named his son after himself. The Spanish equivalent for William is Guillermo.

65 Nájera interview, July 20, 1995.

66 *Primera Iglesia Presbiteriana Mexicana.* Typewritten manuscript, "A Résumé of the Spring Reunion of Texas-Mexican Presbytery, April 23-27, 1930." 2.

67 Aside from Pastor Walls, charter members included Enrique R. Ramírez, María V. de Ramírez, Luis R. Navarro, Josefa Campos, Julia Pantoja (Sammy Pantoja's grandmother), José Pantoja, Manuela S. Pantoja, Raquel Walls (pastor's wife), Juan Frías (elder), Francisco Vega (deacon), Ramona de Vega, Teofila Vega, Beatriz Vega, German Vega, Leonardo Vega, Librado Vega, Benito Vega, Josías Balderas (elder and father of Emma B. Gaitán and Herlinda B. García), Longina de Gonzalez, José García, Tomasita de García, and Victor A. Cano.

68 "A Résumé of the Spring Reunion," 2.

69 Ibid., 2.

70 Ibid.

71 Elisa Castillo Martínez, interview with the author, July 27, 1995, in Fort Worth.

72 Mexican Presbyterian Center. Printed document, "Décimo Aniversario del Centro Presbiteriano Mexicano," ca. 1936. 2.

73 Nájera interview, July 20, 1995.

74 Ibid.

75 Martínez interview, July 27, 1995.

76 Ibid.

77 In the late 1930s Eleanor Roosevelt often visited Fort Worth because her son, Elliot, and his wife, Ruth (née Googins), lived at a ranch in Benbrook.

78 Martínez interview, July 27, 1995.

79 Although the facility still serves the same neighborhood at 960 West Bluff Street, the name was changed to Gethsemane Presbyterian Church.

80 Nájera interview, July 20, 1995.

81 Ibid.

82 *Our Celebration,* 13.

83 *Ibid.,* 13-14.

84 Ibid.

85 Dominga ("Minnie") Martínez Gutiérrez, interview with the author, June 27, 1994, in Fort Worth.

86 Cecilia Reyes, interview with the author, June 14, 1994, in Fort Worth.

87 Ibid.

88 Robert Pulido, Sr., interview with the author, February 18, 1998, in Fort Worth.

89 *Our Celebration,* 14-15.

90 Ibid.

91 By the early 1950s there were approximately seven hundred Mexicanos living in the area of *La Loma.* Compare this figure with the 1930s when, according to former resident Madeliene Rangel Gutiérrez, there were about five to seven families living there.

92 *Our Celebration,* 15.

93 Ibid.

94 The bishop saved the church money by using the same architectural plans a church in Dallas.

95 *Our Celebration,* 15, 17.

96 Bishop Timon had been the Prefect-Apostolic of the Republic of Texas. Assisting Timon in the missionary work in the Republic was Father Odin, who became the first Roman Catholic bishop of Texas. Bishop Dubuis succeeded Bishop Odin, as the second Roman Catholic bishop of Texas.

97 Sister Margaret Miller, SSMN, interview with the author, April 24, 1998, in Fort Worth.

98 Ibid.

99 Ibid.

[100] At the time, the campus was at the end of the electric rail line.

[101] Located by St. Mary's parish, Laneri was named after a local family.

[102] Miller interview, April 24, 1998.

CHAPTER SIX

[1] Michael and Hope Ayala, interview with the author, January 26, 1998, in Fort Worth.

[2] Ibid.

[3] Salvador C., Jr., and María S. Gonzalez, interview with the author, March 26, 1994, in Fort Worth.

[4] Michael and Hope Ayala, interview with the author, March 28, 1994, in Fort Worth.

[5] Ibid.

[6] Román and Helen Soto Mercado, interview with the author, June 15, 1994, in Fort Worth.

[7] Ayala interview, March 28, 1994. There were no judges in this contest. Beginning one month before the festival a group of young ladies competed for the honor of being crowned queen by raising funds that benefited San José Church. Each penny raised counted as one vote and the candidate with the most votes won.

[8] Ayala interview, March 28, 1994.

[9] *"Rincón Poético," El eco latino*, May 1948,   2

[10] Translation by Peggy W. Watson, Ph.D., associate professor of Spanish, Department of Spanish and Latin American Studies, TCU.

[11] Ayala interview, January 26, 1998. Adults 25¢, children 15¢, and students of San José 10¢

[12] Ayala interview, January 26, 1998.

[13] Cecilia Reyes, interview with the author, June 14, 1994, in Fort Worth.

[14] A *quinceañera* is an event publicly celebrating a young lady's fifteenth birthday.

[15] Since there were no Spanish-language newspapers in Fort Worth until the late 1940s and early 1950s, Mexicanos relied on San Antonio's *La prensa*, which could be purchased at some neighborhood stores.

[16] Gonzalez interview, March 26, 1994.

[17] Ibid.

[18] Esperanza Manríquez, telephone interview with the author, July 19, 2001, in Fort Worth. Aurelio Manríquez was born on October 20, 1886. Monica Acuna was born on May 4, 1894 in Monterrey, Nuevo León, Mexico.

[19] Manríquez interview, July 19, 2001. Alicia died at the age of eight or nine in 1928 in Strawn, Texas. As of July 19, 2001, Esperanza lived in Fort Worth. Azalia Manríquez Duran passed away in 1971. As of July 19, 2001, Arturo lived in Fort Worth. He retired after working many years with Swift & Company.

[20] Translation by Peggy W. Watson, Ph.D.

[21] Manríquez telephone interview, July 19, 2001.

[22] Aurelio Manríquez died in Fort Worth on February 12, 1955. He had abandoned his family in the early 1930s and returned to Mexico. Sudden illness in 1952 brought him back to Fort Worth where his daughters could take care of him. Monica Acuña Manríquez died on June 1, 1943.

[23] Fort Worth Public Library, Genealogy and Local History archives. Wesley Community House Records, Box 1, Folder 1, Katherine Ashburn, "History of the Fort Worth Wesley House," circa 1934. 10.

[24] Ibid., 13.

[25] Ciquio and Josie Vásquez, interview with the author, July 13, 1995, in Fort Worth. The eleven children were Concha (Gómez), deceased; Vicenta (Elizondo); Trinidad (Rodríguez); Tiburcio; Magdaleno; Anselma (Puente); Ciquio; Antonio; Pablo; Pasqual; and Ernesto.

[26] Vásquez interview, July 13, 1995.

27 Ibid.

28 Ibid.

29 Ibid.

30 The seven children were Gilberto, Angelica (Garza), Roberto, Julian, Alfredo, Guadalupe ("Lupe,") who lives in Fort Worth and is retired from the navy, and Eulogia (Abrego).

31 To combat the effects of the Great Depression, young men hired by the CCC were given lodging, clothing, food, and paid $30 per month. They could keep eight dollars, but the balance had to be sent back to support their families.

32 Herlinda Balderas García, interview with the author, July 19, 1995, in Fort Worth.

33 Ibid.

34 The March of Dimes gained widespread support during this era due in part to President Franklin Delano Roosevelt, who himself was a victim of poliomyelitis (infantile paralysis).

35 García interview, July 19, 1995.

36 V-mail ("Victory mail") was a system of pre-printed correspondence forms whose contents were transferred to microfilm to save shipping space during the war. One wrote a letter in the limited space of the v-mail form and sent it to the post office where it was microfilmed and shipped in a mail sack. The system reduced the size of mail loads considerably—to carry 150,000 one-page letters required 37 mailbags; with v-mail, it required only one sack to ship the same number. At the sites where the microfilm was developed, the letters were reproduced at about a quarter of the size of the original and delivered to the addressee. The mail was sometimes weeks or even months old and for security reasons was often censored. "V-Mail." Learn More about It. National Postal Museum. http://www.si.edu/postal/learnmore/vmail.html (December 4, 2002).

37 García interview, July 19, 1995. He had originally proposed before reporting for basic training, but Herlinda was not quite ready.

38 Ibid.

39 Ibid.

40 Ibid.

41 A special unit of mountain climbers had already scaled the cliffs and had dropped ropes down to the rest of the Rangers.

42 Leonard Menchaca, interview with the author, February 19, 1998, in Fort Worth.

43 Gonzalez interview, March 26, 1994.

44 Sam García, interview with the author, June 30, 1998, in Fort Worth. Lucio's father, Jorge, died in Quiroga, while his mother, Valeria (born in 1864) died in 1932 and was buried in Pittsburg, Oklahoma.

45 Bruno's wife was Catarina; they had one daughter, Aletha, who was four years older than Sam. Bruno played the trumpet; Jesse García played the fiddle and the bass. Bruno was buried in Pittsburg; Jesse died in the late 1930s and was also buried in Pittsburg. Frank García returned to Mexico in the early 1930s.

46 García interview, June 30, 1998. Lucio had to spend at least sixteen hours a day resting in bed.

47 Ibid.

48 Ibid.

49 García interview, June 30, 1998.

50 Ibid.

51 Because there were so few Mexicanos in Pittsburg and at the sanitarium, he soon forgot how to speak Spanish.

52 García interview, June 30, 1998.

53 Ibid.

54 Ibid.

55 Born on April 4, 1930, María married Sam in 1966; she passed away December 11, 1996.

56 García interview, June 30, 1998.

[57] Jacinta R. Jara, interview with the author, August 15, 1994, in Fort Worth. Alfonso and María Jara had eight children: Vicente, Manuel, José, Adela, Roberto, Gonzalo (the first born in Fort Worth), Alfonso, and Juan ("Johnny").

[58] Ibid.

[59] The Rochas had nine children: Inés, Jacinta, Arnulfo, Jr., Elena ("Helen"), Guadalupe ("Lupe"), Oscar, Olga, Lidia, and Ramón.

[60] With the exception of Jacinta and Helen, the rest of the family settled in either San José or San Francisco.

[61] Jara interview, August 15, 1994.

[62] Ibid.

[63] Ibid.

[64] Ibid.

[65] Ibid.

[66] Ibid.

CHAPTER SEVEN

[1] Aurora Vega Mata Burciaga, interview with the author, July 12, 1994, in Fort Worth.

[2] Ibid.

[3] Sara passed away in 1967. Joe Vega worked as a pharmacist and is now retired. Aurora Vega Mata married Ramón ("Raymond") Medellín Burciaga on July 31, 1947.

[4] Burciaga interview, July 12, 1994.

[5] This same radio station (KFJZ) has had Spanish-speaking programming for the last ten years.

[6] Burciaga interview, July 12, 1994.

[7] Some of Mata's music students included Margaret Dolores Hernández, Cecilia and Betty Reyes, and Aurora Vega Mata.

[8] Burciaga interview, July 12, 1994.

[9] Johnny Ayala, interview with the author, August 9, 1994, in Fort Worth. Héctor and Raymond Cortez were brothers.

[10] Johnny Ayala interview, August 9, 1994.

[11] "Panchillo" Ramírez and Felipe Ramírez were the brother and uncle of Augustín Ramírez of Austin, a well-known *Tejano* musician. A talented and versatile songwriter, Santos Aguilar also played saxophone for The Starlighters. His father, Tule Aguilar, taught music, and his brother, Ralph Aguilar, played drums for *Ernest Vázquez y el conjunto flamingo*. Santos Aguilar's wife is first cousin of Paulino Bernal (Kingsville, Texas), widely acclaimed to be the greatest Mexicano accordion player of all time.

[12] *El zarape* Records was owned and managed by Johnny Gonzalez of Dallas. According to Joe Lerma it was Gonzalez, the "starmaker," who managed the career of Little Joe, propelling him and his band into the limelight. Gonzalez also managed other *Tejano* bands throughout the state, including that of Shorty (Guadalupe Ortiz) and the Corvettes, based in Austin.

[13] Johnny Ayala interview, August 9, 1994.

[14] Joe Lerma, interview with the author, August 9, 1994, in Fort Worth.

[15] *Ernest Vázquez y el conjunto flamingo* was formed in 1960 and consisted of the following musicians: Raymond Muñoz (accordion); Ernest Vázquez (*bajosexto*); Joe Lerma (lead vocals); Ralph Aguilar, brother of Santos (drums); and Andrew Muñoz, Raymond's brother (bass).

[16] Lerma interview, August 9, 1994.

[17] Ibid.

[18] Pauline Willis Estrada, interview with the author, July 20, 1994, in Fort Worth. Ernest and Eulalia Willis had five children: Dora, Paulina, Ernest, Jr. (deceased), Emily, and Dorothy.

[19] Estrada interview, July 20, 1994.

[20] Willis worked hard, adapted well to various work environments, and was a good provider. In Marlin he owned a small grocery store; in Waco he was a chef at a hotel. In Knox City he was a ranch foreman, and in Fort Worth he worked for Texas Steel Company.

[21] Estrada interview, July 20, 1994.

[22] Ibid.

[23] Knox City and the neighboring town of O'Brien are located about seventy miles north of Abilene. The Willis family moved there from Waco in 1955 and lived there for four years, finally moving to Fort Worth in 1959.

[24] Estrada interview, July 20, 1994.

[25] *Bolillo* literally means a roll of white bread (such as a French roll). Mexicanos have long used the word as a nickname for white Anglos.

[26] Estrada interview, July 20, 1994.

[27] Ibid. She couldn't remember the name of the hymn.

[28] It wasn't until the 1970s that the band became known as *Little Joe y la familia*. Little Joe's full name is José María De León Hernández.

[29] Headquartered in Round Rock, near Austin, Alfonso Ramos and his band were important figures in the genesis of the *Tejano* musical style.

[30] Estrada interview, July 20, 1994.

[31] A picture of Little Joe and his band, taken at Calderon's Ballroom in Phoenix, Arizona, is featured on the *On Tour* album cover.

[32] Sunny Ozuna and his band are headquartered in San Antonio. They have been playing since the early 1960s and continue to perform. They played at the 1994 *cinco de mayo* fiesta held at Marine Park on the North Side.

[33] Little Joe's band didn't add an accordion until much later, in the late 1970s or early 1980s.

[34] Paula typically made at least $75 per night.

[35] Estrada interview, July 20, 1994.

[36] Johnny Gonzalez married Irene de la Garza, Luther's sister. He was Little Joe's best friend and, in the 1960s, his agent.

[37] Paula sang mostly American songs in a lounge at the Golden Nugget Casino in Las Vegas.

[38] Estrada interview, July 20, 1994.

[39] Stamford is about sixteen miles north of Anson. Anson is approximately twenty-one miles northwest of Abilene.

[40] Sam Estrada, interview with the author, July 20, 1994, in Fort Worth.

[41] Ibid.

[42] Ramón Hernández, who, at last report, lives in San Antonio, has amassed thousands of files on latino stars in the entertainment business—music, radio, television, and movies. His ambition is to establish a latino hall of fame for Hispanic stars in all fields of entertainment. Hernández also possesses one of the largest collections of classic long-playing, thirty-three-rpm records featuring a staggering variety of latino bands.

[43] Two of the more famous musicians associated with *Los relámpagos del Norte* were Cornelio Reyna (died January 1997) and Ramón Ayala.

[44] Estrada interview, July 20, 1994.

[45] Fernando Landeros, Sr., interview with the author, July 19, 1994, in Fort Worth. Fernando Landeros, Sr., has a son by his first marriage named Fernando, II, and a son by his second marriage named Fernando, III.

[46] Landeros interview, July 19, 1994.

[47] Ibid.

[48] The genesis of the *cumbia* can be traced to the popular music of Colombia in South America. It is a style that blends African rhythms with indigenous instruments.

[49] Landeros interview, July 19, 1994.

[50] Ibid.

[51] Gabriel Díaz's conjunto, *Los caporales* (The Ranch Foremen) consisted of an electric bass guitar, a *bajosexto*, *la batería* (drums), and his accordion. Gabriel's son eventually had his own *conjunto*, known as *Steve Diáz y sensación*.

[52] Landeros interview, July 19, 1994.

[53] Ibid.

[54] Ibid.

[55] Ibid.

[56] Ibid.

[57] Ibid.

[58] Leonard Menchaca, interview with the author, February 19, 1998, in Fort Worth. Juan presented the canary as a gift to his mother. Unfortunately, she did not get to appreciate the gift for long: Much to Mrs. Menchaca's chagrin her cat ate the canary and, for a time, that cat lived in fear of its life.

[59] Menchaca interview, February 19, 1998.

[60] When San José was merged into All Saints Catholic Church, the painting was given to Juan's brother, Leonard.

[61] Menchaca interview, February 19, 1998.

[62] Pilar Bouzas, interview with the author, June 27, 1994, in North Hollywood, California.

[63] Ibid.

[64] Ibid.

[65] Ibid.

[66] Ibid.

CHAPTER EIGHT

[1] Fernando Landeros, Sr., interview with the author, July 19, 1994, in Fort Worth.

[2] Ibid.

[3] Ibid.

[4] Ibid.

[5] Built to control flooding of the Rio Grande and for recreation, Amistad Dam is located a few miles north of Del Rio.

[6] Landeros interview, July 19, 1994.

[7] Ibid.

[8] Ibid.

[9] Ibid.

[10] Ibid.

[11] Ibid.

[12] Translation: he needed something more, he wanted to look for something more.

[13] Landeros interview, July 19, 1994.

[14] Ibid.

[15] Landeros used this term to apply to a longtime resident of the United States as opposed to one who has arrived in more recent times.

[16] Landeros interview, July 19, 1994.

[17] Ibid.

[18] Ibid. Landeros said that detectives came to his house or workplace once a week to harass him; occasionally they would put him in jail overnight.

[19] Landeros interview, July 19, 1994.

20   Ibid.

21   Ibid.

22   J. Pete Zepeda, interview with the author, March 3, 1998, in Fort Worth. Already a widow, Martina Manchaca had been married to a Frenchman named Carrier. They had six children by the time Carrier died. At least half of these children died in the influenza pandemic of 1918.

23   Irineo and Martina had five children: Lucy Gonzalez, Pete, John, and Lydia Vázquez. The family's second child (between Lucy and Pete) died of influenza in infancy in 1918. Their first home in Fort Worth at 2204 North Commerce Street does not exist anymore. It is the present site of the outdoor patio and swimming pool area at Joe T. García's North Side restaurant.

24   J. Pete Zepeda, interview with the author, March 8, 1994, in Fort Worth..

25   Ibid.

26   Ibid. Agapito Hernández was born in Roma, Texas, in 1873. He came to Fort Worth to live on the 3600 block of Stuart Drive and worked for Texas Steel Company. Pete's father passed away on February 29, 1960. Dominga Huerta Hernández was born in 1884 in a village near Morelia, Michoacán. She passed away on August 20, 1938.

27   Pete and Juanita Zepeda raised five children. Ronald Lee graduated from Texas Wesleyan University with an accounting degree. Gilbert Ray graduated from TWU with a microbiology degree with hopes of going to medical school. He applied to fifteen schools at a time when few Mexican Americans were accepted. David George graduated from TWU with a music degree and became an opera singer in Germany. Their adopted children, Ramón ("Raymond") and Connie both attended TWU.

28   Zepeda interview, March 3, 1998.

29   The structure of the United Methodist Church is divided into the following levels in ascending order: local, district, conference, jurisdictional, and general conference. The Rio Grande Conference of the Methodist Church is made up of about 140 churches in Texas and New Mexico.

30   Zepeda interview, March 3, 1998.

31   Louis J. Zapata, interview with the author, February 26, 1998, in Fort Worth. Although the name on the birth certificate is José Luis Zapata, he has always gone by Louis J. Zapata.

32   Zapata interview, February 26, 1998.

33   St. Ignatius School was located downtown next to St. Patrick's Cathedral.

34   Zapata interview, February 26, 1998.

35   Ibid.

36   Ibid.

37   Under the at-large system, a candidate for city council received the votes of the entire electorate, regardless where he or she lived in the city. A single-member district system, on the other hand, allowed a person to receive the votes of the particular geographically defined district that the cnadidate hopes to represent.

38   District Two includes Oakhurst and Riverside as well as the North Side, Diamond Hill, and Washington Heights sections of North Fort Worth.

39   Zapata interview, February 26, 1998. At the end of the 1977 race for District Two, Zapata was saddled with a campaign debt of $21,000. It took two years for him to pay off the entire debt by raffling off TVs, radios, and other tangible goods. Zapata has observed that most Mexicanos do not appreciate the political process and the power in unity.

40   Zapata interview, February 26, 1998.

41   Ibid.

42   This mansion on Hemphill is presently the law office of James Stanley.

43   Presently it is Alonzo Funeral Home.

44   Martina Franco Mendoza, interview with the author, July 19, 1995, in Fort Worth. Apolonio and Petra Mendoza had thirteen children altogether: Tereso ("Ted"); Rufino, Sr., deceased; Rodolfo ("Rudy"); Guadalupe ("Lupe") Esparza; Lydia Bonilla; Alicia Pedroza; Consuelo Rodríguez; Apolonio Robert Mendoza; and Luis Gilberto. Three of their children passed away.

Rufino Mendoza, Sr., was a toddler when the family returned to Mexico; they stayed about five years.

[45] Jennings Avenue seemed to be a dividing line; a small Mexican barrio was located to the west of Jennings Ave. (around Vickery and Jarvis streets) while African Americans populated the neighborhoods to the east of Jennings.

[46] Rufino Mendoza, Jr., interview with the author, July 18, 1995, in Fort Worth. Other early mail carriers included Mike Ayala and Salvador Gonzalez, Jr. Mendoza worked for the post office for thirty-one years until his retirement in 1982 at the age of fifty-five.

[47] Mendoza interview, July 19, 1995. Reynaldo and Victoria Ozuna Franco had twelve children: Beatriz, who married Mario Saenz; Lilia, who married Daniel Flores; Martina married Rufino Mendoza, Sr.; Servando; Cristina F. García; Rebecca F. Espinoza; Ramon; Dolores F. Eisenstar; Daniel; Roberto ("Bobby"); Gloria Franco; and Raquel F. Arredondo, Fort Worth.

[48] Mendoza interview, July 18, 1995. Mendoza led by example and instilled pride and self-esteem in his children: Rufino, Jr., is superintendent of Code Enforcement for the City of Fort Worth; George is principal at Kirkpatrick Middle School; David works for the railroad; Rebecca teaches at Riverside Middle School; Ralph is Deputy Chief of Police; Eddy is a sergeant in the police department; Ricardo works for the U.S. Post Office; Melissa is a schoolteacher and housewife; and Melinda is a housewife.

[49] Presently, Rufino's second son, Jorge ("George") Mendoza, lives at this residence.

[50] Mendoza interview, July 18, 1995.

[51] In 1971, only two percent of FWISD teachers were Hispanic.

[52] Mendoza interview, July 18, 1995.

[53] Ibid.

[54] Carlos Puente, interview with the author, August 9, 1994, in Fort Worth.

[55] Ibid

[56] A government program, CETA stands for Comprehensive Employment and Training Act.

[57] Puente interview, August 9, 1994.

[58] This institution is part of the University of North Texas system.

[59] MCAT is the entrance exam for medical school and is one of the determining factors used for admission.

[60] Puente interview, August 9, 1994.

[61] Among the major reasons were party infighting and Muñiz's arrest for the alleged possession of a controlled substance.

[62] This seat represents the Diamond Hill and North Side areas.

[63] Puente interview, August 9, 1994.

APPENDICES

[1] Fort Worth Public Library, Genealogy and Local History archives. Wesley Community House Records, Box 2, Folder 3, Document beginning with "Although Paulita Gutierrez . . . ."

[2] Marysol Garza, interview with the author, June 23, 1994, in Fort Worth.

BIBLIOGRAPHY

BOOKS

Blackwelder, Julia Kirk. *Women of the Depression: Caste and Culture in San Antonio, 1929-1939*. College Station: Texas A&M University, 1984.

Calvert, Robert A., and Arnoldo De León. *The History of Texas*. Arlington Heights, Ill: Harlan Davidson, Inc., 1990.

Camarillo, Albert. *Chicanos in a Changing Society: From Mexican Pueblos to American Barrios in Santa Barbara and Southern California, 1848-1930*. Cambridge: Harvard University Press, 1996.

De León, Arnoldo. *Ethnicity in the Sunbelt: A History of Mexican Americans in Houston*. Houston: Mexican American Studies Program, University of Houston, 1989.

———. *Mexican Americans in Texas: A Brief History*. Arlington Heights, Ill: Harlan Davidson, Inc., 1993.

———. *They Call Them Greasers: Anglo Attitudes Toward Mexicans in Texas, 1821-1900*. Austin: University of Texas Press, 1983.

Farber, James. *Fort Worth in the Civil War*. Belton, TX: Peter Hansborough Bell Press, 1960.

García, Mario T. *Desert Immigrants: The Mexicans of El Paso, 1880-1920*. New Haven: Yale University Press, 1981.

García, Richard A. *Rise of the Mexican American Middle Class: San Antonio, 1929-1941*. College Station: Texas A&M University Press, 1991.

Garrett, Julia Kathryn. *Fort Worth: A Frontier Triumph*. Fort Worth: Texas Christian University Press, 1972.

Green, Stanley C. *The Mexican Republic: The First Decade, 1823-1832*. Pittsburg: University of Pittsburg Press, 1987.

Griswold del Castillo, Richard. *The Los Angeles Barrio, 1850-1890: A Social History*. Berkeley: University of California Press, 1979.

Jackson, Jack. *Los Mesteños: Spanish Ranching in Texas, 1721-1821*. College Station: Texas A&M University Press, 1986.

Knight, Oliver. *Fort Worth: Outpost on the Trinity*. Fort Worth: Texas Christian University Press, 1990.

Miller, Ray. *Texas Forts: A History and Guide*. Houston: Cordovan Press, 1985.

Montejano, David. *Anglos and Mexicans in the Making of Texas,1836-1986*. Austin: University of Texas Press, 1987.

Myers, Sandra L., ed. *Force Without Fanfare: The Autobiography of K.M. Van Zandt*. Fort Worth: Texas Christian University Press, 1968.

Pate, J'Nell. *Livestock Legacy: The Fort Worth Stockyards, 1887-1987*. College Station: Texas A&M University Press, 1988.

———. *North of the River: A Brief History of North Fort Worth*. Fort Worth: Texas Christian University Press, 1994.

Romo, Ricardo. *History of a Barrio: East Los Angeles*. Austin: University of Texas Press, 1983.

Rosales, F. Arturo. *Chicano: The History of the Mexican American Civil Rights Movement*. 2nd ed. Houston: Arte Público Press, University of Houston, 1997.

Sánchez, George J. *Becoming Mexican American: Ethnicity, Culture and Identity in Chicano Los Angeles, 1900-1945*. Oxford: Oxford University Press, 1993.

Scott, James C. *Weapons of the Weak: Everyday Forms of Peasant Resistance*. New Haven: Yale University Press, 1985.

Selcer, Richard F. *Hell's Half Acre: The Life and Legend of a Red Light District.* Fort Worth: Texas Christian University Press, 1991.

Thernstrom, Stephan. *Poverty and Progress: Social Mobility in a Nineteenth Century City.* Cambridge: Harvard University Press, 1964.

Thompson, Jerry Don. *Juan Cortina and the Texas-Mexico Frontier, 1859-1877.* El Paso: Texas Western Press, 1994.

Turner, Victor., ed. *Celebration: Studies in Festivity and Ritual.* Washington, D.C.: Smithsonian Institution Press, 1982.

Worcester, Donald E. *The Spanish Mustang: From the Plains of Andalusía to the Prairies of Texas.* El Paso: Texas Western Press, 1986.

———. *The Texas Longhorn: Relic of the Past, Asset of the Future.* College Station: Texas A & M University Press, 1989.

THESES AND DISSERTATIONS

Cuéllar, Carlos E. "Doing Business Along the U.S.-Mexico Border, 1881-1939." Masters thesis, Texas A&M International University, 1990.

McKay, R. Reynolds. "Texas Mexican Repatriation During the Great Depression." Ph.D. dissertation, University of Oklahoma at Norman, 1982.

NEWSPAPERS

Early Fort Worth Newspaper Index. Fort Worth Public Library, Geneology and Local History Archives. Fort Worth.

El eco latino, May 1948.

Jones, Jim. "Nun of the Barrios: After 60 years, Sister Lawrencia still loves her students," *Fort Worth Star-Telegram*, October 14, 1984.

Kennedy, Bud. "Ten moments that shaped Fort Worth," *Fort Worth Star-Telegram*, June 6, 1999.

MISCELLANEOUS DOCUMENTS

All Saints Catholic Church. *Our Celebration: All Saints Catholic Church, Fort Worth.* South Hackensack, NJ: Custombook, Inc., 1977.

"*Décimo Aniversario del Centro Presbiteriano Mexicano.*" Printed Report, circa 1936. Fort Worth Public Library. Geneology and Local History Archives. Wesley Community House Records. Three Boxes.

Harrison, Margaret W. "The Story of Oakwood Cemetery." Printed Brochure, October 1970.

Hopkins, Kenneth. "The Early Development of the Hispanic Community in Fort Worth and Tarrant County, 1849-1949." *East Texas Historical Journal* 38, no. 2 (2000): 54-67.

Primera Iglesia Presbiteriana Mexicana. A Resumé of the Spring Reunion of Texas-Mexican Presbytry, April 23-27. Typewritten Report, 1930.

ENCYCLOPEDIAS

The New Handbook of Texas. Vol. I. "George W. Armstrong, " by Leon B. Blair. Austin: The Texas State Historical Association, 1996.

———. Vol. I. "Ripley Allen Arnold, " by Thomas W. Cutrer. Austin: The Texas State Historical Association, 1996.

———. Vol. III. "Middleton Tate Johnson, " by Donald S. Frazier. Austin: The Texas State Historical Association, 1996.

———. Vol. V. "John Peter Smith, " by Kristi Strickland. Austin: The Texas State Historical Association, 1996.

———. Vol. VI. "William Jenkins Worth, " by Arvin W. Turner. Austin: The Texas State Historical Association, 1996.

WEBSITES

"V-Mail." Learn More about It. National Postal Museum.
   http://www.si.edu/postal/learnmore/vmail.html (December 4, 2002).

Adams, Jerry. "Trade Token Tales." Theatre Comique Saloon: John T. Leer and "Rowdy" Joe
   Lowe, Fort Worth, Texas. 2001.
   http://members.fortunecity.com/tokenguy/tokentales/page39.htm. (December 17, 2002).

Baxman, Cindy. "History of the Mexican Revolution, 1910-1920." Border Revolution. May 15,
   1998. http://history.acusd.edu/gen/projects/border/page03.html. (October 2, 2002).

Patch, Robert. "Porfirio Díaz." Grolier Multimedia Encyclopedia.
   http://go.grolier.com:80/Grolier/Multimedia Encyclopedia. (Oct. 2, 2002).

Ross, Stanley. "Porfirio Díaz (1830-1915)." Grolier Multimedia Encyclopedia. http://
   go.grolier.com/Encyclopedia Americana (Oct. 2, 2002).

Schmelzer, Janet. "Fort Worth, Texas." The Handbook of Texas Online. The Texas State
   Historical Association, 1997-2002.
   http://www.tsha.utexas.edu/handbook/online/articles/view/FF/hdf1.html. (October 11, 2002).

UNPUBLISHED MATERIALS

Arlington, Texas. University of Texas at Arlington. Library Special Collection 335. George W.
   Armstrong Papers.

PUBLIC RECORDS

Fort Worth City Directories, 1877-1950

Fort Worth Federal Writers Project of the Works Progress Administration. Fort Worth Public
   Library.

Fort Worth Hispanic Chamber of Commerce: 1993-1994 Business Directory and Referral Guide. Fort
   Worth: Walker Publications, Inc., 1993.

U. S. Department of Commerce. Bureau of the Census. *Ninth Census of the United States, 1870.*

———. Bureau of the Census. *Tenth Census of the United States, 1880.*

———. Bureau of the Census. *Twelfth Census of the United States, 1900.*

INTERVIEWS

Angiano, Ramón. Interview with author, Fort Worth, Texas, March 30, 1994.

Ayala, Johnny. Interview with author, Fort Worth, August 9, 1994.

Ayala, Louis. Interview with author, Fort Worth, September 9, 1994.

Ayala, Michael and Hope Padilla Ayala. Interviews with author, Fort Worth, March 25, 1994,
   January 26, 1998, and February 16, 1998.

Bouzas, Pilar. Interview with author, North Hollywood, CA, June 27, 1994.

Burciaga, Aurora Vega Mata. Interview with author, Fort Worth, July 12, 1994.

Cagigal, Frank and Maggie Cagigal. Interview with author, Fort Worth, March 30, 1994.

Cancino, Fannie. Interview with author, Fort Worth, March 20, 1998.

Cardona, Benito, III. Interview with author, Fort Worth, February 4, 1998.

Castillo, Alfredo ("Freddie"). Interview with author, Fort Worth, June 25, 1994.

Christian, Mary García. Interview with author, Fort Worth, March 24, 1994.

Cisneros, Yvonne ("Kiki") Martínez. Interview with author, Fort Worth, January 29, 1998.

Domínguez, José Jesús and Minerva Domínguez. Interview with author, North Richland Hills,
   Texas, March 26, 1994.

Esparza, Gregorio, Jr. Interview with author, Fort Worth, March 17, 1994.

Estrada, Pauline Willis. Interview with author, Fort Worth, July 20, 1994.

Estrada, Sam. Interview with author, Fort Worth, July 20, 1994.

Gaitán, Emma Balderas. Interview with author, Fort Worth, July 12, 1995.

Gallegos, Alejandro, Sr. Interview with author, Fort Worth, February 18, 1994.

Gallegos, Sara Garza Barajas. Interview with author, Fort Worth, July 2, 1998.

García, Herlinda Balderas. Interview with author, Fort Worth, July 19, 1995.

García, Sam, Interview with author, Fort Worth, June 30, 1998.

Garza, Mary Martínez. Interview with author, Fort Worth, January 29, 1998.

Garza, Marysol. Interview with author, Fort Worth, June 23, 1994.

Gonzalez, Salvador C. and María S. Gonzalez. Interview with author, Fort Worth, March 26, 1994.

Gutiérrez, Amador G. and Madeliene R. Gutiérrez. Interview with author, Fort Worth, March 25, 1994.

Gutiérrez, Dominga ("Minnie") Martínez. Interview with author, Fort Worth, June 27, 1994.

Hernández, Margarita Burciaga. Interview with author, Fort Worth, June 21, 1994.

Hernández, Ramón. Interview with author, Temple, Texas, September 2, 1994.

Holton, Joe. Interview with author, Fort Worth, March 7, 1994.

Jara, Jacinta. Interview with author, Fort Worth, August 15, 1994.

Kane, John J. Interview with author, Fort Worth, July 12, 1994.

Lancarte, Hope García. Interview with author, Fort Worth, March 24, 1994.

Landeros, Fernando. Interview with author, Fort Worth, July 19, 1994.

Lerma, Joe, Interview with author, Fort Worth, August 9, 1994.

López Guerra, Basilisa. Interview with author, Corpus Christi, Texas, August 14, 1995.

López Guerra, Dr. Raúl, Jr. Interview with author, Corpus Christi, Texas, July 29, 1994.

López, Mary Lou. Interview with author, Fort Worth, July 27, 1995.

Manríquez, Esperanza. Telephone interview, July 19, 2001.

Martínez, Elisa Castillo. Interview with author, Fort Worth, July 27, 1995.

Menchaca, Leonard. Interview with author, Fort Worth, February 19, 1998.

Mendoza, Martina Franco. Interview with author, Fort Worth, July 19, 1995.

Mendoza, Rufino, Jr. Interview with author, Fort Worth, July 18, 1995.

Miller, Sister Margaret , SSMN, interview with author, Fort Worth, April 24, 1998.

Nájera, Elisa Castillo. Interview with author, Fort Worth, July 20, 1995.

Narvaéz, Consuelo Zapata. Interview with author, Fort Worth, July 18, 1995.

Pantoja, Sammy. Interviews with author, Fort Worth, August 24, 1994 and September 14, 1994.

Puente, Carlos. Interview with author, Fort Worth, August 9, 1994.

Pulido, Robert, Sr. Interview with author, Fort Worth, February 18, 1998.

Reyes, Cecilia. Interview with author, Fort Worth, June 14, 1994.

Richardson, Inés Becera. Interview with author, Fort Worth, July 11, 1994.

Rodríguez, Rudy. Interview with author, Fort Worth, February 2, 1998.

Romero, Amalia Martínez . Interview with author, Fort Worth, January 30, 1998.

Ruiz, Vito. Telephone interview with author, January 2003.

Sepúlveda, Jonás. Interview with author, Grand Prairie, Texas, August 13, 1994.

Soto Mercado, Benito. Interview with author, Fort Worth, March 30, 1994.

Soto Mercado, Román and Helen Soto Mercado. Interview with author, Fort Worth, June 15, 1994.

Trujillo, Jovita S. Interview with author, Fort Worth, July 12, 1995.

Trujillo, Mario. Interview with author, Fort Worth, March 30, 1994.

Valenciano, Pauline. Interview with author, Fort Worth, April 4, 1994.

Vásquez, Ciquio and Josie Vásquez. Interview with author, Fort Worth, July 13, 1995.

Whitten, Lou Caro. Interview with author, Fort Worth, March 30, 1994.

Zapata, Louis J. Interview with author, Fort Worth, February 26, 1998.

Zepeda, J. Pete. Interviews with author, Fort Worth, March 8, 1994 and June 27, 1994.

INDEX

Page numbers in italics refer to illustrations. Material in the endnotes is not indexed.

A

Activol, 205
Acuña, Elisa, 57-58, *58*
Acuña, Monica, 135
Acuña, Simón, 57
Addams, Jane, 105
Adelita, 80-81
adobe, making of, 32
Aguilar, Concepción "Concha," 118
Aguilar, Hijínio, *5*, 6, 7-9, 38
Aguilera, Joe, 93
Aguirre, Jesse, *104*
Aldrete, Cristobal, *145*
Aldrete, Eduardo, 44
Alma '70, 160
Altamisa, 205
Alvarado, Carlos, 175
Alvarez, Ramona, 70
Ambición, 172
American G.I. Forum, 145-146
Americanization, xv, 111-112, 120
Andrews Theatre, 38
Anise, 205
Arévalo, Epifanio, 161
Armstrong, George W., and sons, 44-45
arnica, 94
Arnold, Katherine, 117
Arnold, Major Ripley S., 1
aseite de volcánico, 94
assimilation. *See* Americanization
Avila, Aurelia, 88-93, *92*, 131
Avila Delgado, Antonio, 88
Ayala, Angelo, *103*
Ayala, Eutimio, 26-27, 157
Ayala family, 82-85
Ayala Grocery, 84
Ayala, Hope Padilla, 27, 82-85, 129, 130
Ayala, Jesse, *104*
Ayala, Juan Eutimio, 157-159
Ayala, Louis, 70

Ayala, María Ortiz, 26-27, 157
Ayala, Michael, 70, 84-85, 101-102
Aztecas baseball team, 141, *142*

B

bakeries, 30-34, 52-53
Balderas, Herlinda, 144-145
Balderas, Josías, 119
Bandrés, Fr. Antonio, *104*, 124
Barajas, Librado, 61
Barajas, María Infante, 61, 62
Barajas, Sara, 61
barbershops, 37-38, 59, 70
Barrera, Juanita, 81-82, 173, 175
barrios
  La Corte, 7, 8, 9-10, 29, 75-76, 81, 99, 117-123, 151, 186; *La Diecisiete*, 7-9, *8*, 14, 35, 72, 75; *La Fundición*, 15, 16, 80, 99, 123, 124, 130, 141, 143; *La Loma*, 7, 14, 30, 125-127, 130, 191; *El Papalote*, 7, 10-11, 63, 151; *El TP*, 14-15, 63, 125, 157, 191; *La Yarda*, 7, 14; North Side, 7, 11-15, 25-26, 30-33, 35, 43, 47, 49, 52-53, 58-60, 68, 70-74, 81-82, 84-87, 89-93, 99-117, 120-129, 134, 140-141, 151, 157, 160, 171-174, 184-188,191-192, 197, 199-200; South Side, 7, 15-16, 21, 44, 81, 89, 123-127, 141-143, 156-157, 181
baseball, 139, 140-143
Basíl, 205
Berber, Alice, *103*
Big Swing, xiv
Birdville, 1-2
Bolt Works, 44
Borbolla, Joe, *142*
Borbolla, Mike, *104*
Borbolla, Rolando, *142*
Bouzas, Aurelio "Earl," 10, 81-82, 173, 175
Bouzas, Juanita Barrera, 81-82, 173, 175
Bouzas, Pilar. *See* del Rey, Pilar
bracero (hired hand) program, 121

Briscoe, Dolph, 197
Burciaga, Raymond, 61
Burraja, 205
businesses, Hispanic. *See also* individual businesses, 46-48

C

Cabello, Consuelo, 52-53
Cagigal, Artemio "Temo," *58*, *142*
Cagigal, Elisa Acuña, 57-58, *58*
Cagigal, Frank, *58*, *142*
Cagigal, Orencio Doce, 57-58, *58*
Cagigal, Orencio, Jr., *58*
Cagigal, Simon, *58*
Camarena, Alvina, *133*
Los caminantes de Joe Hinojosa, 172
Campirano, M., 120
Campfire Girls, 111
Cancino, Refugio, 28
Cancino, Telésforo, 28-29
Candelária de Várgas, Romana, 67
Candoli, Carl, 193
canela, 94
Cantú García, Ester, 143
Cantú García, Julian, 143
Cardona, Benito, Jr., 30-34
Cardona, Benito, Sr., 30-31, *31*
Cardona, Bennie, III, *34*
Cardona de la Bastida, Bonifacio, 30-31
Cardona, Gloria M., *25*, 34
Cardona, Moises, *33*
Caro, Eduardo, 77-78
Caro, Felipa, 77-79
Caro, Juan Bautista, 77-79
Caro, Lou, 77-80
Caro, María "Lou" de Lourdes. *See* Caro, Lou
Caro, Modesta Cavázos, 77-79
Caro's Restaurant, 77-80
Carrico, Thomas, 100
Cáscara de Nogal, 205
casitas amarillas, 45
Casso, Alicia, 95

Castorena, Beatriz, 20-22
Cavázos, Bernardina Hinojosa, 78
Cavázos, Jacinto, 78
Cavázos, Modesta, 77-79
CCC. *See* Civilian Conservation Corps (CCC)
Cenizo, 205
Cerda, Ramona, 94-95
chain stores, 47-48
cinco de mayo, 121, 130
cinnamon stick, 94
Cisneros, John Valentine, Jr., 86
Cisneros, María, 80
Cisneros, Yvonne "Kiki," *25*, 26, 86
citizenship, 111-112, 120
City Directory. *See Fort Worth City Directory*
Civilian Conservation Corps (CCC), 143-144
Claret, Antonio María, 173
Claretians, 100-102, 105, 123-124, 125-127, 173
Clark, Herman, *135*
Claudio Mata and His Mexican Charro Orchestra, 156-157, *157*
cominos, 94
Comique Theatre, 9, 10
community leaders
  García, Gilberto Cantú, 143-146
  García, Samuel, 148-150
  Jara, Manuel, 151-153
  list of, 146
  Mendoza, Rufino, Jr. and Sr., 190-193
  Puente, Carlos, 193-197
  Zapata, Louis, 186-190
  Zepeda, Pete and Juanita, 183-186
Concepción Gonzalez, María, 71
Congleton, Jennie C., 114-115
cooking classes, 116
Cope, D. W., 149-150
Corazón de María, 102
Cortéz, Joseph, 37-38
Courtright, "Longhair" Jim, 2
Cowtown, 2
coyotes, 168, 171, 182-183
crafts, Mexican, 122
Cristero Rebellion, 29, 191
Cruz, Doña Josefa "Chefa," 10
Cuasia, 205
cumin seeds, 94
curandismo, 10, 78, 94-98

D

Danglmyar, Fr. A., 126
de la Garza, Luther, 165

de la Garza, Vivian, 165
de la Rosa, Msgr. Emeterio, 127
De León, Arnoldo, 46
De León, Contreras, 111
deer's eye, 206
del Rey, Pilar, 81-82, 173-175, *174*
Del Rio, Francisco, 88
del Villar, Roberto, 169
Delagarcía, José, *5*, 6, 7-9, 38
Delgado, Isabel M., *25*
deportation, 42, 48-49
día de la raza, 130
Díaz, Gabriel, 167
Díaz, Porfiro, xiii-xiv
dieciséis de septiembre, 130-131
diet, 93
discrimination
  after military service, 145-146, 147
  community leaders vs., 91, 151-153
  in daily life, 23-25, 68, 82, 116, 174
  deportation as, 48-49
  education and, 111, 162
  in employment, 42-44
  exceptions to, 29-30, 68
  intra-racial, 161, 181-182
  newspapers and, 16-17
  sources of, xiii, 48-49
  in sports, 135-136, 139-140
Domínguez, Adolfo G., 136
Domínguez, José Angel, 70
Domínguez, José Jesús, Sr., 61, 70-71
Domínguez, Prisciliano, 70
Dot, Fr. Aloysius S., 125-126
Dr. J. H. McLean's Volcanic Oil, 94

E

Echo Lake, 143
ecumenical relations, 113
education
  church schools, 102-105, 114-117, 126-128, 201-204
  employment and, 47, 150, 191
  language barrier, 119-120
  language barrier in, 111-112, 115
  López Guerra, Raúl, 91
  MAEAC, 190, 193
  Puente, Carlos, 193-197
el barrio de la garra (of the rag), 13
el barrio del pujido (of the groan), 13
El faro (The Light) grocery store, 70
El Papalote, 7, 10-11, 63, 151
El Sport, 160

El TP, 14-15, 63, 125, 157, 191
employment services, 43-44, 121
Enlow, Miss, 116-117
Escojido, Ramón, 131, 136
Esparza, Gregorio, Sr., 34, 52-53
Estafiate, 205
Estrada, Antonio, *6*, 36, *36*, 37, *37*, 38, 39
Estrada, Hermínia Nieto, 165
Estrada, Manuel, 165
Estrada, Samuel, 165
ethnic minorities, non-Hispanic, 10, 11, 100, 117
exorcism, 96

F

Fashion Theatre, 9
Fernández, F., 16
Fernández, Ron, 193
festivals, religous. *See* religious festivals
fiestas patrias, 130-132
Flamenco, Msgr. Eustace, 101
Flenniken, Mack, *135*
Flor de Arnica, 205
Flor de Peña, 205
Flor de Sauco, 205
Flor de Tila Roja, 205
Flores, Albert, 181
Flores, Frank, 181
Flores, Juan, 43-44
Flores, Martín, *142*
Flores, Robert, 181
football, *104*, 134-143, *135*
Los forasteros de Saltillo, 172
Fort Worth City Directory
  1885-1886, *5*
  1886-1887, *6*
  1888-1889, *36*
  1890, *37*
  1905-1906, *12*
  1920, *199-200*
  1928, *15*
  earliest immigrants in, 4-6
  North Side, 11-13, 199-200
  occupations in, 11, 16, 36-39
Fort Worth Federal Writers Project, 16
Foster, Mrs. W. L., 120
Fox, Lillie G., 105-106
Franco, Hilarión, 72
Franco, Martina, 191
Franco, Reynaldo, 191
Franco, Victoria Ozuna, 191
Frías, Juan, 119
Frías, Luisa, 120, 121

G

Gallegos, Alejandro, Sr., 59-62, *60*

Gallegos, Mike, 61-62

Gallegos, Rosa Sánchez, 59-61

Gallegos, Sara Barajas, 61

Gallegos, Vicente, 59-61

Los gallitos del Norte, 171

Galván, Albert, 130

Galván, Jesse, *104*

Gámez, Edward, 65, *65*

García, Alfredo, 144

García, Arturo, *104*

García, Bruno, 148-149

García family, 13

García, Gilberto Cantú, 143-146, *145*

García, Hector P., *145*, 145-146

García, Hope, 53-54, *56*

García, Isidro, *142*

García, Jesusa Torres. *See* Mama Sus

García, Joe T., 53-57, *54*, *55*, 68, 72, 73

García, Lúcio, 148

García, María, 53

García, María Calderón, 148

García, Paula, 59

García, Pauline, *56*

Garrett, Bill, 193

Garza, Elvira M., *25*

Garza Gutiérrez, Rafael, 95

Garza, Luther de la, 165

Garza, Manuela, 30

Garza, Mary M., *25*

Garza, Marysol, 95-98, 205-206

Garza, Vivian de la, 165

Gasca, Frank, 141

Gay, Geoffrey, 193

Gilbert, Mrs. M. S., 120

Girls Reserve Club, 140

Golondrina, 205

Gómez, Faye, 163

Gonzales, Félix, *5*, 6

Gonzales, Riley, *5*, 5, 6, *6*, 7, *12*, 19-20, 36, *36*, *37*

Gonzales, Sarah, 19

Gonzales, Thomas E., 19-20

Gonzalez, José, 196

Gonzalez, Jovita, 99-100

Gonzalez, María Sánchez, 22-25, 130, 133-134

Gonzalez, Raleigh L.. *See* Gonzales, Riley

Gonzalez, Salvador C., Jr., 21-25, *60*, 75, 130, 147

Gonzalez, Salvador C., Sr., 20-22

Gonzalez, Tom, *142*

Googins, Ruth, 51

Gordolobo, 205

Gorman, Bishop Thomas K., 127

Granados, Pablo, 168, 169

Great Depression, 26, 48-49, 117, 143-144

Grimaldo, Jesús C., 194

Grimaldo, María Esther, 194-197

Grimaldo, Theodora Gonzalez, 194

groceries, 58, 70-71, 73, 84

Guajardo, Dominga, 24

Guajardo, Eufemio, *85*

Guajardo, Fernando, 24

Guerra Sánchez, Basilisa, 87

Guerrero, C. S., 122

Gutiérrez, Amador F., 59, 117, 136, 204

Gutiérrez, Amador G., 59

Gutiérrez, Dave, 160

Gutiérrez, Ernest, *142*

Gutiérrez, José, 81, 124

Gutiérrez, Minnie Martínez, 80-81, 124

Gutiérrez, Paulita, 117, 203-204

Gutiérrez, Raymond, *142*

H

Los Hacheros del Mundo, 85

Hawkins, C. Pearre, 86

health care, 86-98, 115, 119

Helbing, H. V., 87

Hell's Half Acre, 2-3, *8*

Hernández, Agapito, 184

Hernández, Benito, 107

Hernández, Dominga Heurta, 184

Hernández, George "Lefty," *142*

Hernández, Juanita, 184-186

Hernández, Ramón, 165-166

Herrán, Fr. Eugene, 101

Herrera, Eddy, 193

Herrera, Rudy, *104*

Hispanic Chamber of Commerce, 183, 186

Hispanic Debutante Association, 150

Holton, Joe, 52

Holy Name Society, 101-102

home remedies. *See remedios caseros*

Huerta, Victoriano, 31

I

Idar, Eduardo, *145*

Iglesias, Fr. Celestino, 104

Ignacio, Zaragoza (poem), 131

illegal immigrants. *See mojados*

Immaculate Heart of Mary Catholic Church. *See Santuario del Corazón de María*

immigrant workers. *See also Fort Worth City Directory*; tenth U.S. Census, ix-x, xiv-xv, 39-46

immigration. *See also* immigrant workers, ix-x, xiv-xv, 177-183

Infante, María, 61, 62

inmates, jail, 3, *4*

interchurch relations, 113

International Good Neighbor Council, 152, *152*

Ipasote, 205

J

jails, 3, *4*

jamaicas, 130

Jara, Alfonso, 10, 151

Jara, Manuel, 151-153, *152*, 187

Jiménez, Mary Frances, 187

Jimmy Flores Band, 181

Joe T. García's, 53-57, *54*

Johnny and the Gamblers, 158

Johhny Ayala and the Starlighters, 158-159

Juárez, Benito, 30-31

K

Kane, John J., 52

Katy Lake, 143

kindergarten, 114-117, 119-120, 126, 201-204

Kirby, John H., 45

L

La Corte, 7, *8*, 9-10, 29, 75-76, 81, 99, 117-123, 151, 186

La Diecisiete, 7-9, *8*, 14, 35, 72, 75

La Fundición, 15, 16, 80, 99, 123, 124, 130, 141, 143. *See* South Side; Texas Steel Company

la lídia, 94

La Loma, 7, 14, 30, 125-127, 130, 191

La Primera Iglesia Presbiteriana Mexicana, 117-123, *118*

La Villita restaurant, 62

La Yarda, 7, 14

Lakey, W. C., 86-87

Landeros, Fernando, Sr., 166-172, 177-183

Landeros, Francisca, 166

Landeros, Mario, 168, 182-183

language barrier, xv, 111-112, 115, 119-120

Latin Souls, 159

Lawrencia, Sister, 102-104, *103*

Lazo, Joe, *132*, 185

Leal, José, *5*, 6, 9

Leal, José A., *12*

Leal, Joseph, *6*, 37, 39

Leal, Joseph A., 36, *36*, *37*, 37, 39

leg opera, 9
Lerma, Joe, 158-159, 159-160
Lerma, Juan, 159
literacy test, 39-40
Little Joe and the Latinaires, 163-165
little yellow houses, 45
Longoria, Félix, 146
López de Valdívia, Francisco, 87
López, Frank, *104*
López Guerra, Aurelia, 88-93, *92*, 131
López Guerra, Raúl, 72, 82, 87-93, *89*, *92*
López, Juan, 87
Loredo, Catalina Tobías, 27-29
Loredo, Macario, 27-28
Los Alamos restaurant, 59-62
los Santos, Juan. *See* Santos, Juan los
Los Vaqueros restaurant, 86
Luna, E., 120, 121
Lynch, Bishop Joseph P., 101, 123, 125

M

Macune, The Rev. Dennis, 107
MAEAC. *See* Mexican American Educational Advisory Committee
Mama Sus, 53-55
Manchaca, Martina, 183
Mancilla, J. Trinidad, 136-137
Mancilla, Trinidad Tinajero, 131
Manríquez, Aurelio, 135
Manríquez, Monica Acuña, 135
Manríquez, Raúl, 134-139, *135*, *138*
Mantecón, Andrés, 160
Manuel Jara Elementary School, 153
Manzanilla, 205
map, 8
Márquez, Dionicia, 63-66
Márquez, Eufemia Cruz, 63
Márquez, Mauricio, 63
Marrubio, 205
Martínez, Cándida, 32
Martínez, Dominga. *See* Martínez, Minnie
Martínez, Elena Ocampo, *25*, 25-26
Martínez, Elisa C., 120, 122
Martínez, Hermenejildo R., 22, *23*, 74-75
Martínez, Johnny, *25*
Martínez, Jo Linda, 151
Martínez, Mike, *25*

Martínez, Minnie, 80-81, 124
Martínez, Nick, 142
Martínez, Pascacio "Pete". *See* Martínez, Pete, Sr.
Martínez, Pete, Jr., *25*
Martínez, Pete, Sr., *25*, 25-26, 34, 85-86
Martínez, Ray, *142*
Martínez, Fr. Raymond, 127
Martínez, Richard, *25*
Martínez, Robert, *25*
Martínez, Sabina Vásquez, 22, 74-75
Martínez, Secundino, 20, 80-81
Martínez, Tomasa Muñoz, 20, 80-81
Martínez, Yvonne "Kiki," *25*, 26, 86
Mary, festival of, 130
Mascorro Rodríguez, Regina, 27
Mascorro Rodríguez, Ruperta, 27
Mata, Claudio Cortéz, 156-157, *157*
Mata, Paul, *142*
Matthews, Mrs. Pat, 111
Mead, Jack, 70
Medrano, Michael, *103*
Mejorana, 205
Mena, María, 121
Menchaca, Anacleto "Francisco," 66-70, *67*
Menchaca, Juan, 68, 69, 172-173
Menchaca, Leonard, 68, 69-70, 147
Mendoza, Apolonio, 190-191
Mendoza Lawsuit, 193
Mendoza, Martina Franco, 191
Mendoza, Petra Rodríguez, 190-191
Mendoza, Rufino, Jr., 190-193
Mendoza, Rufino, Sr., 190-193, *192*
Mercado, Helen Soto, 130
mercurio, 94
mestizaje, xiii
Methodist Church. *See* Wesley Community Center School; Wesley Community House
Mexican American Educational Advisory Committee, 190, 193
Mexican Presbyterian Church. *See La Primera Iglesia Presbiteriana Mexicana*
Mexican Relief Work, 42
Mexican Revolution
  and immigration, ix, 20, 27-28, 31-32
  origin of, xiii-xiv
  and prejudice, 17
Mi Casita restaurant, 86

midwives. *See parteras*
military service. *See also individual stories*, 143-153
mint tea, 94
Miranda, Antonia Elena, 75-76, 186
Mireles, Santos T., 32, 136
Mirra, 205
Mixed Company, 160
mojados, 177-183
Molina, Don Pedro, 10, 94
Molleda, Margaret, 117
Montejano, David, 48
Moore, Donald, 163
Morton, Melvin, 140
Mothers' Club, 110-111, 204
mugwort, 94
Mulholland, Mrs. H. A. "Annie," 100
Muñiz, Ramsey, 197
Muñoz, Felipa, 30
Muñoz, Tomasa, 20, 80-81
music lessons, 111
musicians
  Ayala, Juan Eutimio, 157-159
  Landeros, Fernando, Sr., 166-172
  Lerma, Joe, 159-160
  López Guerra, Aurelia, 88
  Mata, Claudio Cortéz, 156-157
  Paula, 161-166

N

names, variant spellings of, 6
Nervina, 205
New Freedom March (song), 157
North Side, 7, 11-15, 25-26, 30-33, 35, 43, 47, 49, 52-53, 58-60, 68, 70-74, 81-82, 84-87, 89-93, 99-117, 120-129, 134, 140-141, 151, 157, 160, 171-174, 184-188,191-192, 197, 199-200
Northside High School, *135*, 135-136
Noval, Fr. Miguel, 101
Nuez Moscada, 206
nutmeg, 206

O

Obregón, Alvaro, 42
Ocampo, Elena, *25*, 25-26
occupations. *See also Fort Worth City Directory*
  cattle industry, 2, 4, 26, 66-70,
  construction, 74-75, 149-150, 184
  in *La Corte*, 9-10
  in *La Diecisiete*, 7-9
  medicine, 87-93

railroad, 3, 14-15
  South Side, 15-16
  in tenth U.S. Census, *4*
Ojas de Boldo, 206
Ojo de Venado, 206
Oregano, 206
Original Mexican Eats Café, 49-52
Ortiz, María, 26-27, 157
Ostos, Enrique, 88
Our Lady of Guadalupe Mission, 125-127
Our Lady of Guadalupe School, *126*
Our Lady of Victory School, 127-128
The Outsiders, 172

P

Los Pachangueros, 172
Paddock, B. B., 48
Padilla, Daniel, *134*
Padilla family, 82-85
Padilla, Hope, 27, 82-85, 129, 130
Padilla, Marcelino, 27
Padilla, Margarito, Jr., *103*
Padilla, Margarito Rodríguez, 27
Palo Amargoso, 206
Palo Azul, 206
Panther City, 3
Pantoja, Sammy, 10, 29-30, 94
parteras, 10, 21, 78, 80, 94
passage, rites of. *See* rites of passage
pastorelas, 129
Paula, 161-166, *164*
pecan shell, 205
Peña, Lucy, 163
Perejil, 206
Pérez, Eustorgio *"Tojo,"* 171
Pérez, Gregorio, 20
Pérez Mercado, Román, 29
Pérez Soto, Atilana, 29
Peters brothers, 179-180
Piedra Alumbre, 206
pilgrimages, 102, 124
Pimentón, 206
Piñeda, Eva, 49-50, 52
Piñeda, Geronimo, 49-52, *51*
Piñeda, Lola San Miguel, 49-52, *51*
Piñeda, Ruth, 49-52, *51*
polkas, 155, 166
Porfiriato, xiii-xiv
posadas, 129
prejudice. *See* discrimination
Presbyterian Church. *See La Primera Iglesia Presbiteriana Mexicana*

Prodigiosa, 206
Puente, Carlos, 193-197, *195*
Puente, Genaro Badillo, 194
Puente, María Grimaldo, 194-197
Puente, María Guadalupe Mendoza, 194
puffed tostadas, 78, 79, 80
Pugh, Marion, *135*
Pulido, Dionicia Márquez, 63-66, *65*
Pulido, Dolores, 62
Pulido, Pedro, Sr., 62-66, *65*
Pulido, Vicente, 160
Pulido's Restaurant, 15, 62-66

Q

Quina Rosa, 206
quinceañeras, 133

R

racism. *See* discrimination
railroads, 3, 14, 14-15, 36-37
Raíz de Angélica, 206
Raíz de Manzo, 206
Raza Unida party, 196-197
Reece, Pat, 188-189
religious festivals, 129-130
remedios caseros, 53, 93-94, 205-206
Resa, Fr. Andrew, 101
restaurants
  Caro family, 77-80
  Cisneros, John and Yvonne "Kiki," 86
  early, 38
  Gallegos family, 59-62
  Joe T. García, 53-57
  Piñeda family, 49-52
  Pulido, Pedro, Sr., 62-66
  Sammy Pantoja, 10, 29-30
  Zapata family, 75-76
Rey, Pilar del, 81-82, 173-175, *174*
Reza, Anita, 102
Richardson, Inés, 50
Ripero, Fr. Sebastian, 101
rites of passage, 133-134
Robb, W. H., 39-40
Robledo family, 13
Robles, Manuel, 44
Rocha, Arnulfo, 151
Rocha, Elena Benavides, 151
Rocha, Jacinta, 151
Rocha, Raquel, 118-120, 121, 122-123
Rodríguez, Charles, 72, 74
Rodríguez, Ernesto, 72, 74
Rodríguez, Felicitas, 72

Rodríguez Festive Foods, Inc., 73-74
Rodríguez, Florencio, 71-72
Rodríguez, Helen M., *25*
Rodríguez, Juanita, 15, 102
Rodríguez, Juanita Trujillo, 71-73
Rodríguez Padilla, Margarito, 27
Rodríguez, Raúl, 72, 74
Rodríguez, Regina Mascorro, 27
Rodríguez, Rodolfo, 71-74
Rodríguez, Román, 28
Rodríguez, Rudy, 72, 73-74
Rodríguez, Ruperta Mascorro, 27
Roosevelt, Eleanor, 122
Roosevelt, Elliott, 51
Rosa de Castilla, 206
Rosa, Msgr. Emeterio de la, 127
Ruda, 206
ruedas espirituales, 97
Ruelas, Frank, *142*
Ruelas, Margarita, 156
Ruiz, Gilbert, *104*

S

Sacáte de Limón, 206
saints, vigils to, 96
Saldaña García, Juan, 53
Saldivar, Ofelia, 95
Salinas, Gabe, 160
Sammy's Restaurant, 30
San Antonio Restaurant, 38
San José Catholic Church, 91, *92*, 173
San José Catholic Mission, 100-102
San José School, 102-105, *103*, *104*
San Juan Mission, 125
San Mateo Mission, 125
San Miguel, Lola, 49-52, *51*
Sanborn maps, 5-6
Sánchez, Aurora, 22, 24
Sánchez, Juan, 22, 24
Sánchez, María, 22-25, 130, 133-134, 151
Sánchez, Rosa, 59-61
Sanford, The Rev. Al, 197
Sangre norteña, *170*, 172
Sanguinet, M. R., 127
Santos, Juan los, 107
Santuario del Corazón de María, 123-124, 132
Satnoyo, Bernardino, 60
séances, 97
Semilla de Cilantro, 206
sewing classes, 105-106, 110
Sheffield, Gordon, 52
Sheffield, Louise, 52

Shelton, JoAnn, 163

Shivers, Allan, *55*

Shook, Fred, *135*

Sisters of Saint Mary of Namur, 102-104, 124, 127-128

Smith, Eugenia, 106-107, 117

Soto, Atilana, 29

Soto, Consuelo, 159

Soto Mercado, Benny, *104*

Soto Mercado, Helen, 130

Soto Mercado, Román, 14, *104*

South Side, 7, 15-16, 21, 44, 81, 89, 123-127, 141-143, 156-157, 181

Spanish language classes, 120-121

sports, 134-143

Stewart, Jimmy, 51

street listings, 199-200

Sycamore Creek, 143

T

Tafolla García, José. *See* García, Joe T.

Tafolla, Refugio, 53

tarot cards, 97-98

Tarrant County, early history of, 1-3

Tarrant, Edward H., 1

Té de Cena, 206

té de estafiate, 94, 205

té de hierba buena, 94

Té del Mes, 206

tenth U.S. Census, 3-4, *4*

Texas Steel Company, 44-45

Texas Wesleyan University, 37

Theatre Comique. *See* Comique Theatre

Tlanchichinola, 206

Tobías, Angela, 27-28

Tobías Loredo, Catalina, 27-29

Torrente, Fr. Camillo, 101

Torres, Jesusa. *See* Mama Sus

transience, 5-6, 38

Treviño, Aurelia Várgas, 88

Treviño, Frank, *5*, 6, *6*, 7-9, 38

Trujillo, Daniel, *103*

Trujillo, Juanita, 71-73

Trujillo, Lino, 72

Trujillo Magallón, María Luisa, 131

Trujillo, Mario, 47, *103*

Trujillo, Raquel, *103*

U

Uranga, Alfred, *104*

Urquide, Marcelino "Chico," *142*

Urrútia, Aureliano, 88

V

vacation Bible school, 121

Valderas, Harold, *152*

Valdívia, Genoveva, 87

Valencia, Irma, 113-114

Valle, Rafael "Ralph" Y., 59

Várgas de Meave, Adela, 88

Várgas, Gabriel, 166

Vásquez, Bobby, 167-168

Vásquez, Carlos, 167-168

Vásquez, Ciquio, 140-143

Vásquez, Emilia Camacho, 141

Vásquez, Gloria, 192

Vásquez, Inés, 141

Vásquez, Magdaleno "Leno," 141

Vásquez, Nicolás, 141

Vásquez, Sabina, 22, 74-75

Vásquez, Tomás, 136

Vásquez Zapata, Isabel, 75

Vega, Francisco, 119

Vega, Luz, 21

Vega, Ramona, 21

Vega, Teófila, 120, 121

Vidaurri, The Rev. Eugenio, 107

Villar, Roberto del, 169

Virgin Mary, festival of, 130

voter regristration, 196-197

W

wages, 39-40, 41

wakes, *133*, 133-134, *134*

Walls, Guillermo A., 29-30, 117-123, *118*

Walls, Raquel Rocha, 118-120, 121, 122-123

Walls, William Alexander, *See* Walls, Guillermo A.

Washington Heights, 113

Wesley Community Center School, 112-113, *114*, 114-117, 203-204

Wesley Community House, 42, 86-87, 105-114, *106*, *108*, *109*, 139-140, *140*, 201-202

Whitsitt, L. M., 119

Whitten, John Day, 79-80

Whitten, Lou Caro. *See* Caro, Lou

Willard, Ralph L., 196

Willis, Ernesto, 161

Willis, Eulalia Arévalo, 161

Willis, Pauline. *See* Paula

Woman of the Revolution, 80-81

women, role of, 95

Woodard, Stanley, 56

Woodmen of the World, *85*

Works Progress Administration, 16, 33

Worth, Williams Jenkins, 1

WPA. *See* Works Progress Administration

Wright, Jim, 51, *145*, 145, *152*

Wright, María "Mary" Elena, 151

Y

Yañez, Mary, 24

Yañez, Tomás, 24

Yerba San Nicolás, 206

Yerba buena, 206

Young Mothers' Cooking Class, 116

Z

Zapata, Antonia Elena Miranda, 75-76

Zapata, Antonio Vásquez, 10, 75-76, 186

Zapata, Consuelo, 75-76

Zapata, Elena Miranda, 75-76, 186

Zapata, Jesús, 75

Zapata, Louis, 150, 186-190, *188*, 197

Zaragoza, Ignacio (poem), 131

Zarzaparrilla, 206

Zavala, Petra, 76

Zepeda, Irineo, 183

Zepeda, Jaime Pete. *See* Zepeda, Pete

Zepeda, Martina Manchaca, 183

Zepeda, Pete, 117, 183-186

Zweifel, Henry, 44